LIBRARY/NEW ENGLAND INST. OF TECHNOLOGY

3 0147 1001 8525 8

 W9-BWV-095

HF 5415.5 .S64 2002

Spector, Robert, 1947-

Anytime, anywhere

DATE DUE

DEMCO 38-297

NEW ENGLAND INSTITUTE
OF TECHNOLOGY
LIBRARY

ANYTIME, ANYWHERE

Also by Robert Spector

The Nordstrom Way:
The Inside Story of America's #1 Customer Service Company

Lessons From The Nordstrom Way:
How Companies Are Emulating the # 1 Customer Service Company

Amazon.com: Get Big Fast
Inside the Revolutionary Business Model That Changed the World

ROBERT SPECTOR

ANYTIME,

How the Best Bricks-and-Clicks Businesses

Deliver Seamless Service to Their Customers

ANYWHERE

NEW ENGLAND INSTITUTE
OF TECHNOLOGY
LIBRARY

PERSEUS
PUBLISHING

6-02

#48911889

Many of the designations used by manufacturers and sellers to distinguish their products are claimed as trademarks. Where those designations appear in this book and Perseus Publishing was aware of a trademark claim, the designations have been printed in initial capital letters.

Copyright © 2002 by Robert Spector

All rights reserved. No part of this publication may be reproduced, stored in a retrieval system, or transmitted, in any form or by any means, electronic, mechanical, photocopying, recording, or otherwise, without the prior written permission of the publisher. Printed in the United States of America.

Cataloging-in-Publication Data is available from the Library of Congress
ISBN 0–7382–0510–9

Perseus Publishing is a member of the Perseus Books Group.
Find us on the World Wide Web at http://www.perseuspublishing.com
Perseus Publishing books are available at special discounts for bulk purchases in the U.S. by corporations, institutions, and other organizations. For more information, please contact the Special Markets Department at the Perseus Books Group, 11 Cambridge Center, Cambridge, MA 02142, or call (800) 255-1514 or (617)252-5298, or e-mail j.mccrary@perseusbooks.com.

Text design by Jeffrey P. Williams
Set in 11.5-point New Caledonia by Perseus Publishing Services

First printing, December 2001

1 2 3 4 5 6 7 8 9 10—03 02 01

For Barry Provorse,

*for the pivotal role
he's played in my career,
and for being my friend*

Contents

Acknowledgments   *ix*

Introduction   1

1 Multichannel Mavens:
       A Baker's Dozen That Get It   5

2 Anytime, Anywhere, Anyhow:
       Multichannel Synchronization   45

3 The Web Channel   81

4 Customize and Personalize:
       Enriching the Web Channel Experience   121

5 The Brick-and-Mortar Channel:
       Let Me Entertain You   163

6 Seamless Customer Service   203

       Source Notes   *253*
       Index   *259*

Acknowledgments

Every book is a group effort and this one is no exception.

Thanks, as always, to my stalwart agent, Elizabeth Wales, who always answers the call.

To my editor, Nick Philipson, thanks for supporting this project and for being a joy to work with.

My heartfelt appreciation goes to Jacqueline Murphy for "getting" the concept of this book before anyone else, and making sure that Perseus would be the publisher.

The participation and cooperation of the baker's dozen companies featured in *Anytime, Anywhere* would not have been possible without the help of the following:

800-CEO-READ: Jack Covert and Sandy Balzo; Enron: Marty Sunde, Greg Piper, Bob Crane, Peggy Mahoney, Jennifer Walker, Laurie Nickel, and Suzanne R. Rhodes; FedEx: Laurie A. Tucker, Karen Rogers, Sheila T. Harrell, Cynthia L. Henson, Sally Davenport, and Steve Barber; Frederick's of Hollywood: Gary Landry and Penny Mullins (of Jacobson Communications); The Geek Squad: Robert Stephens; Lands' End: Bill Bass, Andrea Stephenson, and Tara Roth; Nordstrom: Dan Nordstrom and Shasha Richardson; Oncology Therapeutics Network: Sue Dubman, Kathy MacDonald, Louis W. Chinn, Patrick Walsh,

Peggy Lehmann, Michael Rorick, Robyn K. Sippel, Mary Seguine, and Toto Haba; Powell's Books: Michael Powell, Sheila Keane, and Darin Sennett; Recreational Equipment, Inc.: Matt Hyde, Joan Broughton, Brian Unmacht, and Jennifer Lind; San Francisco Giants: Tom McDonald, Jerry Drobny, Russ Stanley, and Juliet Hippert; Tesco: John Browett, Tim Mason, Russell Craig, and Andy Cropper; and Wells Fargo: Gailyn A. Johnson, Concetta F. Conkling, Avid Modjtabai, Wendy Grover, Michele Scott, and Carin R. Guisti.

On the home front, my thanks, love, and devotion to my wife, Marybeth, and our daughter, Fae, for getting me through my 15th book.

Robert Spector
Seattle, Washington

ANYTIME, ANYWHERE

Introduction

Turns out, it's all one business. Web site. Mail-order catalog. Telephone. Brick-and-mortar store. The customer will choose the channel. The challenge for companies is to deliver a consistent multichannel customer service experience.

And the Web? It's a channel that drops the cost of communication and increases the flow of information. It's an incredible tool that's changing the world. But it's not the business. At least not yet.

How quickly the landscape has changed.

It wasn't long ago that the pundits were writing off so-called "old economy" companies, particularly retailers, because the amazon.coms of the world were going to render them irrelevant. Why, the argument went, would anyone want to go to a brick-and-mortar store, when he could shop online in his pajamas at 2 in the morning in the comfort of his own home? In early 2000, one "new economy" business magazine, in a gushing article about Webvan, cheered the online grocer for heroically "spending $1 billion to spare shoppers the agony of ever pushing a balky shopping cart again."

Well, in the Spring of 2001, the wheels on Webvan's virtual shopping cart completely fell off, and the company filed for bankruptcy and then liquidation. Contrast Webvan's fate with one of

1

this book's featured companies, Tesco PLC, the United Kingdom's biggest brick-and-mortar grocery chain, which makes money on its Web site by employing an approach that is 180 degrees from Webvan's. Tesco fulfills customer orders right from the shelves of its stores.

The "experts" who predicted that the Web would make the real world obsolete are the nephews and nieces of the pundits who predicted the "paperless" office and the 30-hour work week.

That's because a funny thing happened on the way to the "new economy." After a slow start out of the gate, long-established companies began figuring out ways to incorporate the latest technological innovations into their own Web-related businesses and to integrate the Internet into a coordinated multichannel strategy.

More important, these companies came to the table with a host of built-in advantages: seasoned management, established brands, ongoing relationships with suppliers and customers, deep pockets, and, yes, hard assets, such as stores, warehouses, and distribution centers. Because they are established in other channels, these companies have lower customer-acquisition costs, and greater opportunities for cross-marketing, cross-promoting, and cross-selling. They know their individual customers across all channels. The best of them have extensive databases that provide the buying history of particular customers to every employee and every channel those customers choose to use, anytime, anywhere.

But what about customer service? Ironically, the Internet has made customer service more important than ever. In the old days—not that long ago, actually—shoppers stayed loyal to favorite stores for many years. No more. Today's consumer is apt to be more loyal to the *deal* than the dealer.

At the same time, customers are more demanding than ever. They want what they want when they want it. They want the companies they deal with to know them across all channels, but they demand that their privacy be protected. They want companies to be proactive, but not invasive. They want to be able to track and check the status of their order, and they want to be able to easily return unwanted items.

Consequently, companies are continually pressed to do more and more for their customers. One way to ingratiate yourself is being available to your customers anytime, anywhere, and via any channel. That means providing telephone numbers, fax numbers, and e-mail addresses—that are easily accessible—because most customers want to communicate directly with *someone*; someone who can take care of them. Is there anything more essential than communication to good customer service?

With the ascendance of the multichannel approach, it's no wonder that catalog retailers such as L.L. Bean and Coldwater Creek, and direct-mail companies such as Gateway, are opening stores, and amazon.com mails out catalogs and forms alliances with the likes of Toys 'R' Us and Borders Books. They understand that each channel represents a *touchpoint*—a unique contact with the customer.

This book has a simple premise: winning companies are the ones that provide an excellent customer service experience across all channels. We will explore the operations of a diverse group of companies in a wide variety of industries. We will see how these different companies in different industries have devised—and carried out—common strategies to provide their customers with a seamless multichannel experience.

But that is not to say that these companies have all the answers. We will examine the mistakes as well as the triumphs. All of these companies admit that their initiatives and strategies for "channel synchronization" require ongoing refinement.

"It's a job that will never be done," said Matt Hyde, senior vice president at Recreational Equipment, Inc., a retailer of authentic outdoor gear and apparel. "It's just like our physical stores. You wouldn't say that our flagship Seattle store is the pinnacle of all physical stores and we'll never get any better at it. So, how we play off our online store, our 800 number, and our physical stores is going to continue to improve and evolve."

A seamless multichannel approach to customer service requires collaboration and partnering with every part of an organization. Cynthia Henson, vice president of customer service at FedEx, put it best: "Customer service is not the department, it's the company."

ONE

Multichannel Mavens

A Baker's Dozen That Get It

Whatever you do, or dream you can do, begin it. Boldness has genius, power and magic in it.

— JOHANN WOLFGANG VON GOETHE

The cliché of the late Nineties is that old economy companies needed the success of Internet companies to prod them into action. The companies featured in this book belie that notion. With the commercial advent of the Web, they all immediately saw the importance of a multichannel approach and took bold steps to create a Web site that would complement their business.

They are an eclectic group. Their individual annual sales range from a few million dollars to hundreds of billions. Some have a handful of employees; others have tens of thousands. Some are privately held; others are publicly traded. Six are strictly business-to-consumer: **Tesco PLC**, the largest supermarket chain in the United Kingdom; **Recreational Equipment, Inc.** (REI), America's leading purveyor of outdoor apparel and equipment; **Lands' End**, the innovative mail-order apparel company; **Nordstrom, Inc.**, the 131-store chain renowned for customer service; **Frederick's of Hollywood**, the legendary lingerie retailer; and **Powell's Books**, one of America's most-admired independent booksellers. Two are strictly business-to-business: **Enron Corp.**, the revolutionary energy-trading company, and **Oncology Therapeutics Network** (OTN), a conduit of cancer medication for small medical practices. The rest are B-to-C *and* B-to-B: **FedEx**, the overnight package delivery company; **Wells Fargo & Co.**, the diversified financial services company; **800-CEO-READ**, a leading seller of business books to businesses; **The Geek Squad**, the iconoclastic Minneapolis-based computer repair firm; and the **San Francisco Giants** National League Baseball team (which caters to both fans and corporate sponsors).

Here are the players:

Lands' End

Lands' End, Inc. was founded in Chicago in 1963 by a former advertising copywriter named Gary C. Comer. An avid sailor, Comer's first catalogs consisted of sailboat hardware and equipment, and a smattering of apparel. In 1975, Lands' End mailed its first full-color catalog. Three years later, the company launched one of the first mail-order toll-free 800 numbers, which in 1980 was expanded to 24 hours a day.

Today, Lands' End, which has long been based in Dodgeville, Wisconsin, sells traditionally styled casual clothing for men, women, and children; soft luggage; and home products. *Catalog Age* ranked Lands' End as the 19th-largest general direct mail company and second-largest for apparel and home goods exclusively. Lands' End sells products through its print catalogs (269 million mailed out annually), Web site (landsend.com), 16 outlet stores in four states—Wisconsin, Minnesota, Illinois, and New York—two in the United Kingdom, and one in Japan. Customers shop directly from home or office, by phone or mail, by fax or Web.

The company has a history of testing new selling options "in small ways; not big ways," explained Bill Bass, vice president of e-commerce. "No one here came up with a strategic future. It was more, 'let's test stuff and if something works, we'll pursue it.'" In the late 1980s and early 1990s, before the creation of the browser, Lands' End used AOL, CompuServe, Prodigy, and other online services to sell overstocked goods and test sales; the company also experimented with a distribution of its catalog on CD-ROM disks.

In 1995, Lands' End modestly launched its Web site with fewer than 100 products. First month sales were $163.00.

"The philosophy at the time was 'Get it up, and see if people like it. And if they like it, we will continue to improve it,'" Bass recounted. People liked it. Online sales grew from $4 million in 1996, the first full year the site was operational, to $211 million in 2000. According to the company, 30 percent of the site's new customers had never bought from a Lands' End catalog. An even more remarkable statistic: 50 percent of people who placed products in a shopping cart on landsend.com actually purchased those products, compared with a figure of 22 percent at all consumer e-tail sites, according to the market research firm Datamonitor PLC.

On an average day, close to 300 phone lines handle between 40,000 and 50,000 calls. In the weeks prior to Christmas, over 1,100 phone lines field more than 100,000 calls daily. Lands' End processes 15 million calls and 231,000 e-mail messages annually; each e-mail receives a personal response. The company is among the best at combining cutting edge technology with old-fashioned customer service, as epitomized by its simple, unconditional, life-time, money-back guarantee, which consists of one word and a punctuation mark — GUARANTEED. PERIOD.®

Asked what it takes to be successful online, Bass answered: "brand, customer base, and existing infrastructure. Because we already had a brand, we didn't have to divert money, time, and effort into a marketing campaign. We have a proprietary [private label] product, which makes the economics work out a lot better. If you are selling direct to consumers with your own product, you are not competing on price with other retailers." Just as important, Lands' End's customer base matches that of the Internet customer. The average household income for Lands' End customers is $70,000 and 88 percent have attended college. "So, we have an educated, upper-middle income audience. If you look at computer penetration, that's exactly who was online [in the second half of the '90s]. We didn't have to divert money, time and effort, and management attention toward building a distribution infrastructure; we were already delivering direct to consumer. Everything comes out of the same warehouse, first come, first serve. Pricing and shipping is the same as we do in the catalogs."

With all those inherent advantages, "We were then able to focus on the Web site, and to think about how you build a great customer experience shopping on the Internet," said Bass. Lands' End's site is so highly thought of that the company was inducted into the Smithsonian Institution for outstanding achievements in "leading the information technology revolution to enhance and enable the relationship between company and customer."

FedEx

The FedEx story is one of the most famous in the annals of American business. In 1971, an ex-Marine named Frederick W. Smith founded Federal Express Corporation in Little Rock, Arkansas. Two years later, the company began operations, delivering 186 packages overnight to 25 U.S. cities, and with that, the modern air/ground express industry was born. In 1979, FedEx launched COSMOS®, a centralized computer system to manage vehicles, people, packages, routes, and weather scenarios on a real-time basis, and in 1981 introduced The FedEx Overnight Letter®. Today, FedEx Corp., which employs more than 175,000 people around the world, delivers nearly 5 million shipments every business day, and conducts more than 100 million electronic transactions.

As a $20-billion-a-year market leader in transportation, information, and logistics solutions, FedEx Corporation provides strategic direction for five major operating companies: FedEx Express, FedEx Ground, FedEx Freight, FedEx Custom Critical and FedEx Trade Networks. Each company operates independently, focused on its market segment, but also competes collectively under the FedEx brand worldwide. FedEx is a two-part network—an international channel of planes and trucks that move packages and a digital technology information network.

"When Fred Smith launched the company in 1973, he began investing in information technology that was built around providing the customer with something new—visibility into the movement of their shipments. The philosophy was if FedEx Express costs more, we had better deliver more value," recounted Laurie A. Tucker, senior vice president, global product marketing, who has been with the company since 1978.

Inevitably, FedEx customers wanted to know how to get their shipping information faster and how they could integrate FedEx services into their businesses.

"We knew we had to find efficiencies in productivity," said Tucker. "Paperwork on packages put an upper limit on how much business a customer could process in a given day. Thus, we conceived the idea of putting a computer on our customers' shipping dock, which was where shipments and transactions were processed. We didn't want cumbersome airbills to be an inhibitor to the amount of packages they could give us on any given night. The larger the customer, the more challenging that became."

In 1984, FedEx developed and introduced to the market a service for high-volume customers, which it called PowerShip. The free system leveraged an already established worldwide network called COSMOS, a proprietary system that tracks the status of every package moving through the FedEx distribution system. Using FedEx hardware and software, today 70 percent of all FedEx Express shipping transactions are electronically processed through automated shipping systems. "We deployed PowerShip for 15 years, providing the PCs, the software, and the servers that connected customers of all size, all over the world," said Tucker.

By the early Nineties, FedEx's technology staff "began to understand that the Internet could actually be a network that we could use to connect customers and to be able to transfer data," Tucker recalled. "We saw that not only were we able to help our customers do more business with us, we might also be able to help our customers do more business with *their* customers by using our network. We looked at how we could network those computers to make it easier for our customers to sell to each other." Unfortunately, FedEx found that the technology that was distributed to customers wasn't networkable. Like many other companies, FedEx tested CD-ROM technology, but few customers had CD-ROM drives back then. FedEx beta-tested a back-end electronic commerce software package for the Web called BusinessLink, which was designed to unify every aspect of electronic commerce. But that package also had its limitations.

In 1994, FedEx launched fedex.com, which was the first shipping Web site that enabled customers to track the status of their package. Tucker described the company's initial effort as essentially little more than "brochure-ware—a screen with a big FedEx logo at the top; a box in the middle that said 'type in your tracking number here' off the FedEx airbill. It would pop up with all the scans that the package had received. We didn't realize what we had done, but we were one of the first transactional Web sites. Once we began to receive accolades, our marketing folks jumped in. We started to dress up the site, added information, and started thinking about other applications that we could use the Internet for. We wanted to take the value propositions that we had built our business on and make them even more accessible to the customer."

The underlying premise of the FedEx site was putting value directly into the customer's control.

"We asked ourselves: 'If customers are coming in to use this Web site to track packages, what else might they want to do? What do customers do? They ship. So, how do we put shipping on the Internet?'" said Tucker. "That was easier said than done because our shipping process required that we identify the customer and be able to provide the customer with a unique tracking number. The customer needed to be able to print a bar code that we can scan when we do the pickup. These things needed to be available in a paper hard copy or through our online environment."

It took FedEx about two years to launch shipping from the site. Beginning in the summer of 1996, customers began using Fedex.com to produce the shipping label from their own printers, which was "a revolution for us," Tucker declared. "It gave the ability to use FedEx to companies who wanted to give their employees access to FedEx shipping, but didn't want to have to maintain our software on their network, or didn't feel they were large enough to qualify for one of our hardware devices. It saves us money and time, and gives us the ability to give our customers personalized service. Customers can maintain their own address book and other information on the Web site without having to reenter it. The site includes all the features that customers wanted, such as help in finding physical drop-off locations and their closing times."

Today, FedEx's core mission is to be a global provider of transportation and services. To Laurie Tucker and her colleagues, the challenge is "to find unique ways to use technology to offer customer services that never existed before. That's what's fun about the dot-com environment. Without the Internet, we couldn't do any of this stuff."

Frederick's of Hollywood

Before Victoria had a secret, there was Frederick's of Hollywood.

Frederick Mellinger, like many U.S. solders who fought in World War II, was inspired by the pinups of movie stars such as Betty Grable and Rita Hayworth, clad in seductive lingerie, that hung on the walls of his army barracks. But unlike his comrades in arms, Mellinger chose to make it his life's work to transform *every* woman into a pinup girl. The trick was designing the most flattering lingerie.

With the war over, Mellinger began designing the kind of sexy, alluring lingerie that he had seen in France in the early 1940s. In 1946, Mellinger opened his first lingerie shop, Frederick's of Fifth Avenue in Manhattan. His target market were his fellow ex-GIs, who were home from the war and who were looking for lingerie for their wives or girlfriends. A year later, deciding to add a dose of movie-star glamour to his business, Mellinger headed to Los Angeles. There, he reopened his business as Frederick's of Hollywood, where his clientele included the pinup girls who originally inspired him.

Frederick's of Hollywood became one of the most recognized brand names in the world, synonymous with sexy intimate apparel and what one might describe as "fantasy fashions," such as front-hook bras, shoulder-pad bras, and the world's first push-bra, The Rising Star; as well as padded girdles, body shapers and colorful fashion bustiers for women of all sizes. Some suggestive ensembles came with names such as "Harem Girl" and "French Maid." No wonder Frederick Mellinger's motto was "Don't dream it . . . live it."

Today, Frederick's is owned by Wilshire Capital LLC of Los Angeles, which acquired the company in June 2000. Frederick's, which has annual sales of $200 million, continues to sell the products that made it famous, as well as newer categories, including dresses, sportswear, swimwear, and even a smattering of menswear, which customers can buy in more than 200 retail stores (in 40 states), a mail order catalog, and the fredericks.com Web site (There is a 35 percent carryover between catalog and Internet shoppers). The company's more diverse merchandise reflects Frederick's move to broaden its appeal to women, who account for more sales in the stores and from the catalogs, while men are more apt to shop via the Web site. True to its roots, Frederick's is still popular among military personnel who order items for wives and girlfriends.

According to Gary K. Landry, president of fredericks.com, 90 percent of customers also shop at rival Victoria's Secret. While Frederick's prime demographic target is women 18 to 39, the females who relate to the Frederick's concept and "attitude" (a favorite word of retailers) range from 14 to 65. "We say to this community: If you are thinking about being sexy, bold, and confident as a woman, then you can get everything about feeling that way at Frederick's."

Enron Corp.

Created in 1985, the result of a merger of Houston NaturalGas and Omaha, Nebraska–based InterNorth, Enron Corp. has been described by *eCompany* magazine as "the biggest, baddest B2B e-commerce company on the planet." For six straight years, *Fortune* ranked Enron as America's number one company for innovation.

In 1995, at a time when most of its revenue was coming from the gas-pipeline business, Enron set a goal to become the world's leading energy company. At that time, gas buyers and sellers were dealing with volatile pricing and fluctuating spot markets. Seizing an opportunity, Enron created a market for long-term fixed-price natural gas. Enron's primary business is managing the price risk for North American and European clients who enter into long-term contracts for natural gas, electricity, and other energy products. In 2001, it did, indeed, become the world's leading energy company.

Capitalizing on the deregulation of natural gas in the late Eighties and the deregulation of electricity in the early Nineties, Enron single-handedly created the swaps, hedges, derivatives, and other esoteric financial instruments that make it possible to trade energy between utilities and corporations. The company recognized that it could make money by offering large, diversified pools of energy supplies to satisfy both buyers and sellers. As the intermediary, Enron would get a piece of the action both ways.

With the popularization of the Web in the 1990s, Enron saw the opportunity for doing most of its transactions online, rather than by telephone, which had long been the norm. As company chairman, president, and chief executive officer Ken Lay likes to say, Enron was Net-ready before there was an Internet. Enron sold off its own power plants and transformed itself into a logistics company that coordinates supply and demand for commodities and creates the most cost-effective way to move those commodities to their destinations. Today, Enron uses the power of the Internet to create markets by acquiring, packaging, and selling energy, and coordinating buyers and sellers. Enron, which acts as the principal in all transactions, actually buys the product and then sells it.

Through its EnronOnline division, which is the largest e-commerce site in the world in terms of dollar volume, the company trades more than 1,600 products in 13 currencies. While most trades still involve natural gas and electricity products, Enron also deals in metals, steel, crude oil, petrochemicals, forest products, coal, weather derivatives, and bandwidth. More than 40 percent of Enron's $101 billion in revenues in 2000 came from businesses less than four years old—many of them centered around the company's ability to build and run e-markets.

Enron's two shining office towers in downtown Houston are overflowing with thousands of traders making deals on a wide variety of commodities, such as gas, electricity, pulp, and paper. (Some traders can execute an amazing $1 billion in trades in a single day.) The decisions they make will determine whether Enron will make its profit. So, they gather real-time information from Enron's thousands of pipeline experts, weather forecasters, currency traders, billing personnel, researchers, and credit checkers. There's even a former shuttle astronaut whose job it is to schedule time on the satellite. Speed is critical at Enron, so much so that the company knocked down walls at its old headquarters to install stairways, which eliminated time that was "wasted" waiting for elevators.

We will look at two Enron divisions: **Enron Energy Services,** which manages energy needs for businesses large and small, and **clickpaper.com,** which services the volatile forest products market.

Enron Energy Services. EES is an energy management company that offers products and services that can lower energy costs and improve operational efficiency for commercial and industrial customers. EES also provides capital to upgrade or replace equipment, monitors energy usage, and runs and maintains facilities with in-house engineering and construction support. EES's team of analysts show clients the impact of electricity costs on their per-unit profits.

When EES was founded in 1997, the division "did not inherit a legacy that we had to change. We could build the organization from scratch," recalled vice chairman Marty Sunde. By doing so, "We focused it totally around the premise that no matter how hard you try to outsource everything, no client will be able to do that all on the first blush. All clients' businesses will change. So, if you get in there and do a good job, trust and confidence will drive more and more and more things to do together."

EES has a varied list of clients, in a wide variety of endeavors, including retail, pharmaceuticals, higher education, banking, com-mercial real estate development, consumer products, and profes-sional sports. EES installs equipment that allows these clients to operate on either electricity or natural gas. So, if the price of elec-tricity suddenly skyrockets, EES can switch the client to gas, and then sell the client's unused electricity (at a higher price) on the spot market. The company also helps clients save money by installing more efficient heating, cooling, and lighting equipment. For example, Enron installed new transformers at a client's plant, which enabled that facility to secure inexpensive power from high-voltage lines. For another client, Enron upgraded equipment and metering at the client's manufacturing and distribution facilities.

Clickpaper.Com. In July 2000, Enron launched clickpaper.com, an Internet-based transaction system where customers can take advantage of a spot market to buy and sell—in real time—pulp, paper, and wood products, without having to pay commission.

Forest products, like most commodities, are subject to volatile and unpredictable pricing, which causes hit-or-miss capacity plan-ning and roller-coaster financial results. This market was a natural opportunity for Enron, with its extensive experience in risk management and its innovative financial tools. Through Clickpaper, Enron buys and/or sells pulp, paper, and lumber, both physically and financially, across North America and Europe.

"We're offering true liquidity and price discovery to the forest products industry," says Greg Piper, president and CEO of Enron Net Works, which includes clickpaper.com. "At the click of a mouse, customers can come to Clickpaper, review hundreds of products and prices, and transact with Enron, instantaneously and commission-free."

Newsprint is a particularly capricious commodity, whose price is buffeted by the whims of the market. Because newsprint represents 15 to 20 percent of their operating budget, newspaper companies prefer prices that are guaranteed "locked in" over a set period. But publishers often find themselves buying their newsprint on the spot market, where they must negotiate prices every month. Enter click-paper.com. To bring more stability to its business, a publisher can enter into a three-year contract with the Enron division for physical delivery of newsprint that would guarantee a price for the duration of the agreement—plus Enron gives customers the option of paying in forest products rather than cash. And by leveraging its energy capabilities, Enron helps clients control energy costs by supplying them with either natural gas or electricity.

Enron Industrial Markets, the business unit that oversees the buying and selling of forest products via Clickpaper, owns some physical properties, including a couple of paper mills. But, as we will learn in Chapter 5, the company takes a radical approach to its brick-and-mortar assets.

Powell's Books

Powell's City of Books store in downtown Portland, Oregon, is a Pacific Northwest institution. Customers have had their weddings there. One passionate bibliophile requested his ashes be interred at Powell's where he spent so much of his life. (The request was politely declined.) When visiting the 68,000-square-foot City of Books—one of the world's largest bookstores—visitors are given a map with color codes and legends, in order to navigate through stacks that hold one million new and used books

Michael Powell, a native of Portland, matriculated at the University of Chicago in 1962 with the goal of earning a graduate degree in political science, and then to pursue a teaching career. But after coming upon Chicago's Maxwell Street flea market, Powell began buying bargain books, which he in turn sold on consignment to the University co-op. "I enjoyed the treasure hunt," he recalled. In 1969, Powell borrowed $3,000 from a group of University of Chicago faculty members, including author Saul Bellow, and opened a small used-paperback book shop.

Not long after that, Michael's father, Walter, a retired schoolteacher, carpenter, and painting contractor, visited from Portland. Intrigued by his son's venture, the senior Powell returned to Portland to open his own used store, Powell's Books, where he did the unusual thing of displaying paperbacks and hardbacks on the same shelves. In 1979, when his father decided to retire, Michael, then 38, returned to Portland to take over the running of the store.

Today, Powell's has seven stores in the Portland area, including its West Burnside Street flagship, which is on the site of a former car dealership. Although the company sells new books, its specialty is used, rare, and out-of-print volumes, which comprise 70 percent of Powell's stock and 50 percent of its sales volume, and is that part of the business "where you can bring your passion to bear," said Powell. Every day, Powell's highly trained staff buys over 3,000 used books, many of which can not be found anywhere else. On a visit to Powell's, Doris Kearns Goodwin, the historian and biographer, located some books on Abraham Lincoln that she had not been able to find in Cambridge, Massachusetts, where she taught at Harvard. When the Mexican author Carlos Fuentes was on a search for five obscure titles, he found two bookstores in the world that carried two of the titles. That was the best he could do, until he came to Powell's, which stocked four of those titles.

In the early 1990s, Powell's move into electronic commerce was promoted by the company's technical bookstore, which had computerized its inventory and was running an Internet Bulletin Board system where customers could place an order by accessing the database via Telnet. In May 1994 (14 months before amazon.com was launched), the company launched powells.com, which initially sold only technical books. In February 1996 the main "City of Books" location went online, with the store's entire inventory of more than one million books.

After the Web site was up, Michael Powell experienced what he described as "a critical event":

> I got a letter from a customer in England. He thought I would be interested in knowing that when he was looking for a particular out-of-print book, he was told in England that it would cost $85 and it would take 6–8 weeks to deliver. On a whim, he went to the Internet to see if he could do any better, and discovered we had the book. He ordered it on a Monday and had it in his hands on Wednesday for $44. I said to myself: "Sounds like a business to me." Then I started putting more resources behind this effort.

Much to Mike Powell's surprise, the Internet has revolutionized his rare book business. "Routinely, we sell expensive books over the Internet," he marveled. "In fact, the most expensive book we ever sold—$90,000 for a first edition of the 1814 Lewis &

Clark journal, *History of the Expedition*—the customer found out about it from the Internet."

Powells.com connects the inventory of the seven stores and two warehouses in one convenient location. The Web site gets 42,000 visitors and more than a 1,500 buyers per day, with an average order of $35. Used books account for about 70 percent of Web sales. That's a nice little business because the margin on used books runs as high as 66 percent, compared with 40 percent on new titles. This is welcome news for Powell because, industry-wide, online sales of new books have leveled off.

Powells.com also sells used college textbooks on its Web site, because "College students are highly motivated to save a buck and avoid going to the college book store. I felt it was the best target audience in the world for the Internet. We discovered that there was a huge audience," said Powell.

In 2001, *Forbes*'s *Best of the Web* issue selected Powell's as having the best site of any Internet bookseller. Not bad for a tiny operation with five programmers and one systems administrator. The magazine praised its "full panoply of information, reviews and excerpts on new titles, its author interviews and links to other literary sites." It was also noted that, "The used section is brilliantly subdivided into browsable sections and boasts a list of new arrivals by section." *Yahoo! Internet Life* rated powells.com the best source for used books on the Web.

That kind of performance is a reflection of one of Powell's online ads: "We recommend books the old-fashioned way. We read them first."

Despite the popularity of online book buying, Powell doesn't expect readers to stop visiting book stores. "You can't be so in love with bookstores you lose sight of the real goal—to get books from inactive status into readers' hands."

The Geek Squad

When he was a boy growing up in Chicago, Robert Stephens took programming classes at Great Lakes Naval Air Station, where he learned to program in COBOL, FORTRAN, Pascal, and C.

After moving to Minneapolis in the early 1990s, he worked in a day care center while fixing dryers and televisions in his spare time. A roommate helped Stephens get a night job at the Human Factors Research Lab at the University of Minnesota, where he repaired, serviced, and backed up the computers. As his reputation spread, people began hiring him to come to their homes and offices to fix their PCs. His customers liked Stephens's approach: "My theory of troubleshooting is that anything that can be assembled can be disassembled," he explained. "It's fun; like detective work." It wasn't long before Motorola, Cargill, and other major Twin-Cities corporations were seeking out his services.

Stephens attributes his early success to a very basic philosophy of customer service: "People told me, 'You know, Robert, you're great at fixing computers, but we like you because *you return our phone calls*. You don't track mud on our carpet. You talk to us and you look out for us. You're not hoarding your knowledge. You're not trying to nickel-and-dime us to death.'"

Eventually, Stephens decided to form a computer-repair company built around that customer service philosophy. His first notion was to name his new enterprise "Techno-Medic," with a logo of a runner holding a wrench in his hand. But, "Techno-Medic sounded like we fixed medical equipment. I didn't want a name that said 'Computer Repair,' because one day I want to transition to other services."

In the Spring of 1994, after playing word associations in his head, he came up with "The Geek Squad." He sketched out a logo that consisted of an oval with the word "Geek" in black script on an orange background and "Squad" in white block printing on a black background. "I wanted a graphically pure logo like STP, which is timeless, and never changes," he explained. A brilliant self-promoter, Stephens created a guerrilla marketing and advertising campaign around the Geek Squad name. His fondness for old cars led him to buy a lime green 1958 Simca Arande, which became the first "Geekmobile." He drove the distinctive car, emblazoned with the Geek Squad logo, around Minneapolis and St. Paul, and pretty soon, people began taking notice.

Today, The Geek Squad has a staff of 50 computer-repair specialists, with a physical office in Minneapolis and virtual ones in Los Angeles, San Francisco, and Chicago. Customers run the gamut from the one-person home-office business to the Rolling Stones world tour. The company has been featured on CNN and in a wide variety of publications, including *Fortune*, *Newsweek*, and *InStyle*.

The Geek Squad offers a wide range of services, for repair both on-site and at their offices in Minneapolis. The company charges flat—not hourly—rates for all services, gives customers fixed prices for the services they need over the phone, and charges only for labor and parts. "We don't sell computers. We don't do programming. We provide support: Set-ups, installs, and upgrades," said Stephens. "We can spend two hours with you going over stuff for your new computer for a $249 flat rate. We will go over anything you want. We will help you purchase a computer. We don't make a dime off of that. It keeps us clean and focused. I think to be great at something, you have to focus. Michael Jordan is a great basketball player. He is not a great baseball player." Stephens keeps the menu of services focused. "That's why I'm not going to franchise The Geek Squad because I want to control the quality. Mine is a reputation-based company, which means that anything that will hurt the reputation of the company I won't do."

Like every company featured in this book, The Geek Squad's image is the result of a specific plan. First of all, why "The Geek Squad"?

"The image of a geek is someone so dedicated to a particular field of study that, because of that focus, they allow the rest of their life to degrade—to an almost humorous effect," said Stephens. "We are so dedicated to this that we live it. After work, we all go home at night and play with our computer. How many people get off work and go home at night and play with their sledge hammer?"

"I think people actually enjoy saying the name 'The Geek Squad.' If they enjoy it, then that can be part of the marketing," said Stephens.

Stephens created a geek uniform. Inspired by *Dragnet* and *Get Smart*; *Ghostbusters* and *The Blues Brothers*, he put together an ensemble of black slacks, starched white shirt, black shoes, and white socks. The piece de resistance is a black clip-on tie. "If you give a tie to 10 different computer techs, you'll get 10 different knots. We give them a clip-on, so everyone looks the same. At a time when everyone in corporate America is dressing down, I wanted to bring back the tie." And what would a uniform be without an official-looking badge? Stephens gives every employee a die-cast badge made by the same manufacturer used by police departments. Employees are given titles such as "Special Agent" and "Inspector."

Stephens, also known as Chief Inspector and Special Agent No. 66, admitted that he had "no idea what kind of effect the uniform would have on employees as they did their job. It transforms them and allows them to play that role. I've already set up the customer with the expectation that these guys are a little odd—that's why they are good; that's why you want to use them. That allows them to be themselves, but to also play this character." As a result, "We feel like celebrities. People recognize us on the street. It makes it easier for them to wear this dorky uniform. A strong culture makes it easier for people in the group to play along."

Then there are the cars that employees drive to clients' homes and offices—the Geekmobiles, including old Fords and Simcas and new VW Beetles painted with the company logo. One of the stars of the fleet is the Geek-2, a tiny, powder-blue 1963 Renault Dauphine.

With the poetic motto "We'll Save Your Ass," The Geek Squad is, in Robert Stephens's words, "a living comic book . . . and a profitable corporation."

Wells Fargo & Co.

Wells Fargo & Co. is one of the legendary names in American business. Seizing upon opportunities sparked by the California Gold Rush of 1849, two Eastern businessmen, Henry Wells and William G. Fargo, founded their "Express and Banking House" in 1852, for the purpose of buying and transporting gold, cashing checks, selling bank drafts payable in other states and overseas (known as exchanges), accepting deposits, and making loans.

Operating out of offices in San Francisco and Sacramento, Wells Fargo was a pioneering multichannel service organization that connected the Pacific Coast with eastern and European financial capitals. During the Gold Rush, the company provided regular communications, including the first electronic transaction, by telegraph in 1864. Early on, Wells Fargo was involved in transcontinental transportation with its signature stage coach business—the Great Overland Mail stageline—that delivered mail and cash. The company formed alliances with steamships and railroad lines. In 1888, Wells Fargo established direct "Ocean-to-Ocean" service, with large networks in the Northeast and the Midwest. By the beginning of the 20th century, Wells Fargo had over 10,000 offices nationwide, plus an extensive network in Mexico, and overseas agencies from Shanghai to Berlin.

Today, Wells Fargo is the fourth-largest bank in the U.S., with $290.0 billion in annual assets and 5,400 locations across the nation. The company offers consumer and business banking services, as well as investment services and products, venture capital investment, and international trade services (through a joint venture with HSBC Bank). Wells Fargo is one of the U.S.'s largest mortgage bankers, and one of its largest insurance brokers. The firm employs more than 120,000 people.

Early on, Wells Fargo understood that the Internet is a medium that deals essentially with information, which makes it a perfect channel for financial products, which are pure information. In 1989, Wells Fargo was one of the first companies to develop an online banking strategy, offering rudimentary dial-up, text-only service through Mastercard and Prodigy. In the early Nineties, the company began a campaign that offered customers access for investments, packaged bank products, and investment products in a combined statement—*anytime, anywhere.*

During that period, Wells Fargo, like most companies, was trying to determine the future direction of online banking. "We were playing multiple games at the time; not knowing whether the winner was going to be CD-ROM or Prodigy or AOL or the Internet," recalled Gailyn A. Johnson, executive vice president for online customer services. In the mid-Nineties, Johnson managed the marketing and products for the savings and investment group, from which the online initiative was spun. "We were keeping our options open. At the same time, we were building the infrastructure, figuring out how to manage security on the Internet."

Being located near Silicon Valley, Wells Fargo was well positioned when new technology made electronic commerce feasible.

"We were working with Netscape as they were putting out the
first secured browser," Johnson told me. "In 1995, we were sitting
around the room talking with Mark Andreessen [inventor of the
Netscape Navigator] about how Netscape's browser could be
securely used in a bank environment."

Wells Fargo's first Web site and user interface were developed
in-house by four programmers. There was another small team of
technologists focusing on the network and firewall technology.
"By doing it ourselves and keeping it simple, we could more easily throw out what didn't work," said Johnson. Launched in
January 1995, with a home page featuring the familiar stagecoach
logo, the site enabled the company to collect survey data on what
customers wanted from a Wells Fargo Web site. "About 60 percent of the people said, 'If you just gave me my balance and transactions, I'd be thrilled. I would even switch banks.'" Because the
Wells Fargo team already had been building the infrastructure for
its other online channels, it took only two months to develop the
industry's first Internet banking service in May 1995—giving customers Internet access to their accounts. Refinements followed
steadily every few months. The goal was to have something new
on the Web site every week.

Security was obviously important because many customers at
that time had fears about the Internet, so Wells Fargo had to
ensure that its service was safe. "If you called us to obtain a new
password, we would ask you a number of questions to prove you
were who you said you were," Johnson recalled. "We'd ask static
data that only we would have, such as your last deposit. Some
tech-savvy customers would complain, but other customers would
say, 'Thank God you're asking those questions.'"

Wells Fargo initially built its online customer service operations not only to help customers with Internet-related issues but
also to service personal financial software programs such as
Money and Quicken. At one time, online customers were considered to be a unique customer set that required segregated
servicing for all of their products and services. Today, the bank
has integrated its online business into the entire company,
"because it's mainstream now in the minds of the customers,"
said Johnson.

Wells Fargo has more than 3.3 million online customers, and
has been described by *Worth* magazine as "the most popular"
Internet bank. Online initiatives are run out of its Internet
Services Group (ISG), which is composed of four divisions corre-
sponding to the traditional bank's structure: consumer, small business, investment, and wholesale. ISG is headed by executive vice
president Clyde Ostler, whom *Institutional Investor* named the
number two e-commerce innovator. Ostler's stance is that Wells
Fargo is "reinventing the bank around the Internet."

Ostler reports directly to president and CEO Richard
Kovacevich, who constantly reminds employees that the Internet
is another channel for providing customers with "anytime, anywhere" banking.

"With more than a decade of online trailblazing to our credit,
we're taking anytime, anywhere banking to the next stage with
added service, convenience, and advice for our customers," said
Kovacevich. "We're integrating services on the site with a single
sign-on for brokerage and banking, while working across channels
to provide a uniform customer service experience. For example,
with WellsChoice®, a customer can trade and invest online or
offline with the help of a trusted advisor. With Tax and Portfolio
Trackers, an investor can manage the tax consequences of trading

with a service so completely integrated that customers never have to reenter their data."

Wells Fargo was the first major financial services company to integrate these kinds of portfolio and tax management tools directly into its online brokerage Web site. These tools were added to wellsfargo.com in April 2001.

At Wells Fargo, the first phase of online financial services focused on getting services onto the Internet and building a consumer base. The next stage is focusing on seamless integration of online and offline services for an even broader customer base including investors, small businesses, and large corporations.

"The winners will be those who can deliver on the promise of anywhere, anytime accessibility and enhanced service, convenience, and advice," said Kovacevich.

Oncology Therapeutics Network

Oncology Therapeutics Network (OTN) is a healthcare services and distribution firm that distributes a broad range of anti-cancer medicines and related products and services to more than 2,300 office-based oncologists in the United States. The company was launched in 1990 in response to the growing shift in the administration of chemotherapy from the hospital to the outpatient setting. During this transition, OTN recognized that physician office-based oncology practices needed a full complement of services and management tools to run their business.

OTN, which is based in South San Francisco, was an early entrant into business-to-business transactions. Today, the company, which was acquired by Bristol-Myers Squibb Company in 1996, claims 50 percent of the physician-office oncology market, and does business with 95 percent of the physician office-based oncologists in the U.S. OTN has information on almost half the cancer patients in the U.S. With about $2 billion in sales, OTN is one of the largest B-to-B operations in health care. Its services include access to more than 2,800 drugs and supplies, extensive administrative support, and clinically-oriented pharmaceutical procurement and information programs.

Of OTN's $2 billion in sales, about 25 percent comes from its Web site, lynx2otn.com. That total doesn't include revenue from electronic transactions via the Lynx drug-dispensing machines that OTN installs in doctors' offices (and which will be described in greater detail in Chapter 5). In all, about 75 percent of OTN's sales transactions are handled electronically. That number is growing, according to Sue Dubman, vice president and chief information officer. But that growth also presents customer-service challenges.

"When 75 percent of your transactions are electronic, how do you listen to your customers? What's the best way to listen to your customers?" Dubman asked rhetorically. "You have to modify how you communicate with them." With competition increasing in the electronic market, where oncology products are priced like commodities, "We had to ask ourselves how we were going to add value." OTN decided it was going to add value through information processing, product availability, and outstanding customer service via its physical and electronic channels.

"In the B-to-B market, everyone focuses on the partners/suppliers," added Dubman. "But, more than anything else, we've focused on the customer side."

OTN was the first distributor to provide free, next-day delivery via Federal Express.

Tesco PLC

Headquartered in the northeast London suburb of Cheshunt, Tesco PLC is the largest food retailer in the United Kingdom and

Republic of Ireland, with 646 stores in the U.K. and 75 in Ireland. Tesco is also the world's largest online grocery retailer.

Quite an accomplishment for a company founded in 1924 by Jack Cohen, a grocer from London's East End, whose autobiography, *Pile It High and Sell It Cheap*, aptly described Tesco's deep-discount retailing strategy.

Although Tesco possessed one of Britain's most powerful brands, "you could have raised a laugh in the City [of London] by suggesting Tesco of all companies was destined to be Britain's prime contender for membership of an elite of international retailers," clucked the *Financial Times*, which went on to describe the Tesco of the early Nineties as "an organization in shock, with its prices out of kilter with its customers." But Tesco had already begun to reinvent itself into a more upscale retailer while trying not to alienate its discount-devoted customer base. Tesco listened more closely to customers, focused more on value, and made its ordering and distribution operations more efficient. By the mid-Nineties, Tesco had surpassed rival Sainsbury as the number one food retailer in Britain.

In 1994, when company executives first saw a demonstration of the Internet, "We realized that by using the technology of the Internet, you would be able to do home delivery," recalled John Browett, chief executive officer of tesco.com. "Customers have always wanted their groceries delivered. The challenge is that it's not simple to do." Under Browett's direction, Tesco first tested its online-ordering service in one store in December 1996, and slowly rolled out nationally. By the beginning of 2000 the service was available in only 100 stores; that August, it was expanded to 237 stores, covering 90 percent of the U.K. population.

Browett defends this deliberate, extended trial run as key to the success of the service:

We began with a massive advantage: our retail operation and infra-structure were already in place. But that advantage also meant we had to get things right before launch. People trust the Tesco brand. We couldn't afford to make mistakes, so we rolled out very slowly. The one thing we have always focused on is the customer experi-ence. Grocery shopping is boring, so we made it as easy as possi-ble. It's taken us several years to perfect that model and make the Web site a profitable stand-alone. Everything has to stand on its two feet. You can't have loss leaders because we're in a thin mar-gin business.

Browett said Tesco owes the success of its online operations to the company's ability to source products from its brick-and-mor-tar supermarkets, a process that reduces costs and increases effi-ciency. Rather than fill orders from a centralized warehouse like the failed Webvan, Tesco's platoon of pickers retrieve goods right from the shelves in Tesco stores. (A full description of Tesco's online fulfillment operations appears in Chapter 5.)

Tesco has found that it sometimes takes a year to gain cus-tomers' trust and convince them to buy fresh food through the Web site. People will buy soap powder but initially are reluctant to purchase fresh produce, which they like to touch and feel.

Consequently, Tesco has found it easier—and more profitable—to expand its selection of nonfood products, which, unlike gro-ceries, are sold out of warehouses or delivered through agreements with third-party wholesalers. Tesco offers a broad range of more than 20,000 nonfood product lines, including books, videos, CDs, electrical goods, home furnishings, clothing, baby products, house-hold supplies, and clothing. Tesco eventually hopes that 45 to 50 percent of its online sales will come from products other than gro-ceries, because nonfood items generate higher profit margins.

In 1997, Tesco made its initial online venture into nonfoods with a virtual financial services division—a 50/50 joint venture with Royal Bank of Scotland Group PLC—that offers a variety of products, including credit cards (Tesco has over 1 million cardholders), loans, savings accounts, and a wide range of insurance for cars, travel, pets, and vacations. These products can be accessed via telephone (either at home or in a Tesco store), fax, or the Web site, which is completely secure and open 24 hours a day. The division, which moved into the black in 1999, "has been a very successful business, because on a little bit of space, we are able to recruit tens of thousands of customers and sell them millions of products," said Browett. "Our view is that by using the Internet, we are able to access customers' expenditure in a way we couldn't dream about doing in the stores."

Tesco claims 80 to 90 percent of the U.K.'s online grocery trade, and further claims that 30 percent of its million-plus customers shop nowhere else online. Of Tesco's $15 billion in total sales in 2000, about $367.4 million were from its online operations. Tesco.com customers collectively generate weekly online sales of almost $8 million. At $145, the average online basket size is four times the in-store average. Tesco, which levies an $8 delivery charge, says the profit margin on each delivery is 7 to 8 percent.

While Tesco continues to enhance its online channel, the company is also expanding its brick-and-mortar stores on the European continent as well as in Asia. Tesco operates 34 supermarkets on the continent and is on track to open another 18 in 2001. In Asia, the company has almost 50 stores in Malaysia, Thailand, Taiwan, and South Korea, and will eventually launch its online operations in those markets.

Browett scoffs at the notion of cannibalization among Tesco's channels. "If we were worried about cannibalization, we would never have moved from small High Street stores to supermarkets to superstores to hypermarkets. For us, grocery home shopping is just another format that delivers for a particular set of customer needs."

It's interesting to compare Tesco with amazon.com, which is its biggest online rival in the U.K. While amazon.com first developed a book business and then diversified into a variety of products including groceries (with its investment in homegrocer.com, which was later acquired by Webvan), Tesco approached product diversification from its grocery base. Browett asserted, "Groceries are a better core to start with because you have a much closer and more frequent relationship with your customers. If a significant number of people go online to buy groceries, then we have a fantastic opportunity to sell them a lot of nonfood items because we know so much more about them."

San Francisco Giants

The San Francisco Giants baseball club is one of the oldest companies represented in this book. The team's history dates back to 1883, with the formation of the New York Gothams in the National League. On May 1 of that year, they played their first game at a field once used for polo matches at 110th Street and Sixth Avenue. The Gothams knew the value of promotion: On June 16, 1883, the team held the first "Ladies Day" in the history of Major League Baseball, when women—with or without male companionship—were admitted free to the game.

In 1885, the name of the team was changed to the New York Giants, who played in a stadium called the Polo Grounds until the end of the 1957 season. The following year, the Giants moved to the West Coast, joining their longtime rivals, the Brooklyn Dodgers, who had relocated to Los Angeles. Giants' owner Horace

Stoneham cited a lack of parking as one of the reasons for leaving New York. Also, the city of San Francisco promised to build the Giants a new stadium.

The two expatriate New York teams played the first big league ball game on the West Coast on April 15, 1958, at Seals Stadium, a former minor league ballpark, which was the temporary home of the Giants. Almost two years later to the day, April 12, 1960, the Giants first took the field at Candlestick Park, a stadium built on a piece of land on Candlestick Point, between downtown and the airport. Tossing out the first pitch was Vice President Richard M. Nixon, who pronounced Candlestick "the finest ballpark in America."

That statement may not have represented the most extreme instance of hyperbole in Mr. Nixon's career, but it ranks right up there. "The Stick," as it came to be called, was fraught with design problems such as leaky pipes and nonfunctioning bathrooms. The toilet in the Giants' dugout had no door, but one was quickly added—once it was noted that fans in some box seats could see into the dugout. But most of all, Candlestick Park was known for its ferocious, unpredictable wind that whipped off the Bay, making a night game even in the middle of summer a frigid affair.

Over the years, the Giants periodically changed ownership and their tenure in San Francisco was occasionally threatened. In 1976, Bob Lurie saved the team from a possible move to Toronto by heading a group that bought the Giants and kept them in San Francisco. In 1993, after failing numerous times to get a downtown ballpark built, Lurie agreed to sell the team to a group that intended to relocate the franchise to the Tampa–St. Petersburg, Florida area. But a local investment group, led by Peter Magowan of the Safeway supermarket chain, saved the day by buying the team and keeping them in the Bay Area. After years of political and financial wrangling—including failed bond issues and threats to move to San Jose—the team and the city agreed to construction of a new 40,000-seat stadium on 3rd Street in a downtown waterfront area known as China Basin. On April 11, 2000, Pacific Bell Park opened. In its inaugural year, thanks to the novelty of the new stadium and an excellent team that won the National League Western Division, more than 3.3 million filled PacBell, which was sold out for every game. By comparison, in the last year at Candlestick, the Giants drew 2.1 million in a stadium with 60,000 seats.

The move from Candlestick to PacBell was made easier by the Giants' management's commitment to a multichannel approach that united its spectacular new physical facility with the power of the Internet.

"At Candlestick, we were in a ballpark that held 60,000 seats, but only a small percentage of those seats were sold before the season started," recalled Jerry Drobny, director of interactive marketing. "Back then, we were a very different company. We did a lot of guerrilla marketing, selling every ticket we could possibly sell to whomever, at whatever discount rate, in order to get bodies into the stadium."

The Web site, which was launched when the Giants were still at Candlestick, initially provided basic information, such as schedule, game times, and ticket availability. But as the Giants prepared to make the transition to PacBell, the Web site became a valuable tool to inform the fans and, of course, to sell tickets.

Not surprisingly, it was a challenge to sell season tickets and corporate licensing fees for an unfinished stadium. As a tool to convince corporate customers to pay for a seat license or invest in the new ballpark, the Giants invested in Web technology that offered clients a virtual view of their seats from their PCs. Using a model developed by the team's architects and graphics designers, a client could select the section he wanted to sit in and be shown a virtual picture of the view from that seat.

"The virtual view was a great tool for our salespeople to direct people to our Web site, which helped us to sell the ballpark and build the momentum that we needed to get this facility built," said Drobny. Dispensing essential sales information on the Web made potential customers more comfortable. "They didn't have a sales person pushing them. They could look do it on their own time at their own pace. On the Web, we gave them the ability to say, 'Yes, I'm interested. Contact me.' We found it was easier to close the sale with many of our best-qualified customers."

During the construction phase, fans could log on to the Web site's Webcam to watch the park being built. The Webcam was fully directional, enabling fans to view the progress on the field or in the stands.

The Giants' Web-related activities worked brilliantly in attracting customers. The 2000 season was completely sold out for every game—quite a change from the Candlestick days, when "we were in a very intense customer-acquisition mode," recalled Tom McDonald, vice president for marketing. "Once the season-ticket base was developed [for PacBell], the marketing department moved into 'a client-retention mode.' We asked ourselves: 'How do we do everything possible to retain customers long term?' The result was a coordinated effort to give fans a seamless customer service experience, from Web site to parking lot to the ballpark food concessions to the game itself."

For the 2000 baseball season, the Giants and the 29 other Major League Baseball teams independently ran their own respective sites. At the time, MLB had been slow to capitalize on the growth of the Internet, particularly compared to other profesional leagues. But for the 2001 season, MLB centralized its Internet assets and created a separate, for-profit limited partnership called Major League Baseball Advanced Media. All 30 teams share any revenue. MLB controls all team Web sites—including editorial content. Despite MLB's control, the Giants have been able to create a unique Web site that gives its fans the kind of customer service that they expect.

Nordstrom, Inc.

In 1901, two Swedish immigrants, John W. Nordstrom and Carl Wallin, opened a tiny shoe store in downtown Seattle, called Wallin & Nordstrom. The shop was financed by the $13,000 Nordstrom made prospecting for gold in the Alaska Yukon Gold Rush of the late 1890s. First day's receipts: $12.50. By the early 1960s, the company that eventually changed its name to Nordstrom became the biggest independent shoe retailer in the United States. Today, Nordstrom, which sells men's, women's, and children's apparel and shoes, and cosmetics, has 116 stores in 16 states, with sales in excess of $5.3 billion. It has an international reputation for outstanding customer service.

Nordstrom had been in the direct mail business with full-blown catalogs since 1994. This operation, which was based in a division called Nordstrom Direct Sales, was separate from the special promotional mailings traditionally sent out by department stores to announce a sale.

In 1993, the company began experimenting with interactive television, which, at the time, the business media had designated as the hot new thing. But by late 1994, it became apparent that interactive TV wasn't going anywhere. Nordstrom also experimented with a system for customers to be able to order by e-mail, 24 hours a day, with a personal shopper in the chain's downtown Seattle store.

At the same time, the Internet was seeping into public consciousness.

"The day I understood that people would be shopping electronically is when I knew we needed a Web site," recalled Dan Nordstrom, chief executive officer of nordstrom.com. "It was apparent that the Internet would become what interactive TV had wanted to be. It was only a question of when this was going to happen. It was a matter of bandwidth—most people had only 9,600-baud modems. At that point, we decided to focus on direct-mail catalogs and wait until enough consumers had modems that had enough speed. There also had to be enough usage. You had to have people who wanted to do it. It was a matter of supply and demand. If there wasn't a large enough offering, people wouldn't think of the Web as a place to shop."

Dan Nordstrom identified "the tipping point," in terms of meaningful Internet apparel sales, as holiday 1997, when The Gap and other sites began to attract significant traffic. "At that point, we decided we wanted to get our Web site together and have it launched by the holiday season of 1998 because that seemed when things were going to take off." In the fall of 1998, the retailer went back to its roots—footwear—and launched nordstromshoes.com. With 20 million shoes available on the Web, the company proclaimed itself "the World's Biggest Shoe Store," and ran a sweepstakes, giving away shoes for life. "During that holiday season, online was very successful, and at our offline Nordstrom stores, shoes had their largest year over year increase of any category. So, we knew we had a multichannel effect."

Nordstrom ultimately incorporated its shoe site into the company's overall nordstrom.com site.

"The Internet is not much different than the telephone," Dan Nordstrom mused. "When the telephone was introduced, companies had to develop a telephone strategy, to incorporate it into their business. Then the day comes when you don't think about it; a store without a telephone doesn't make sense." But the Internet is different because, "you don't have much of a road map. In this business, software becomes your store, and the ability to effectively execute software becomes similar to effectively using the store environment, whether you're displaying merchandise or serving the customer. You're in a perpetual state of invention, which is both exciting and sometimes frustrating."

Nordstrom.com topped Forrester Group's consumer-based PowerRankings for 2000, just beating out two-time winner landsend.com as the U.S.-based e-tailer providing the best online experience, thanks to the site's superior features (including name-brand boutiques), customer service, and delivery.

800-CEO-READ

In 1983, David Schwartz, owner of Harry W. Schwartz, a Milwaukee, Wisconsin, bookstore chain, hired Jack Covert, a former advertising sales executive and record-store owner, to launch a new project called Schwartz Business Books, which would sell business books directly to businesses. On the day he was hired, Covert and David Schwartz stood at the back of the book store at 5th Street and Wisconsin Avenue, where there was a warren of books on computers (covering topics such as DOS and CPM), medicine, technical topics, and business. "This is your store," Schwartz told Covert. "You will buy and you will sell. And you will make mistakes, but I will never tell you that you are wrong."

Free to build his own business, Covert began making cold calls to hundreds of major corporations. He filled the trunk of his car with business books and began making road trips to Wisconsin businesses, some of which became his first customers. He made day trips to the Fox River Valley in central Wisconsin, where he cultivated customers as varied as Menasha Corporation (which manufactures products such as material-handling containers and promotional displays) and the Aid Association for Lutherans. "I could sell $1200 worth of books on a trip. In those days, that was huge," Covert recalled. "I got to know my customers and they got to know me."

That personalized customer-service approach remains the hallmark of the company, which eventually changed its name to 800-CEO-READ, a division of Dickens Books Limited, the parent company of the Harry W. Schwartz bookstore chain.

Today, 800-CEO-READ is America's leading direct supplier of business literature to businesses, offering a broad range of published works, books, maps, papers, treatises, microfilm, and audio, video, and digital works. The company provides digital ordering, e-mail and 800-number telephone support, and collaborative account administration to more than 6,000 national and international clients, including businesses, nonprofits, and government services organizations. Covert and his staff of 10 employees, each sitting at a workstation in the downtown Milwaukee office, offer delivery of any business book anywhere overnight. The company has designated-supplier relationships with several Fortune 500 companies.

Back in the early days, 800-CEO-READ's primary channel was the telephone. Today, coupled with its Web site, the company has taken, in Covert's words, "a classic two-channel approach. You can't have one without the other. The site would be flat without the customer contact. The customer contact is old hat, unless you have something high tech that the customers can use."

Nevertheless, Covert doesn't neglect the most important channel—the face-to-face variety. He still makes a half-dozen road trips a year to visit clients.

Recreational Equipment, Inc.

Recreational Equipment, Inc. is a distinctively Pacific Northwest creation. REI combines the region's love of its natural treasures (particularly Mt. Rainier) with its left-of-center tradition of consumer cooperatives. In 1938, REI was established as a consumer cooperative in Seattle, by a group of mountaineers who joined together for the purpose of acquiring ice axes, crampons and other climbing equipment at affordable prices. Jim Whittaker, who in 1963 became the first American to climb Mt. Everest, is a former chief executive officer of REI. In Seattle, having an REI membership card with a low number is a sure sign that you are a long-time native.

Today, REI, which is based in Kent, Washington, sells authentic outdoor gear and apparel for a wide variety of activities, including camping, hiking, climbing, skiing, and biking. The nation's largest consumer cooperative, with more than 1.8 million active members, REI operates 60 retail stores in 24 states. Rei.com is the Internet's biggest outdoor retailer, offering more than 78,000 individual items, more than 45,000 pages of detailed product information, expert gear advice, online clinics, an interactive community system, and a complete adventure travel service, REI Adventures. REI also operates rei-outlet.com (http://www.rei-outlet.com). Sales in 2000 were $610 million, giving REI a healthy piece of the $5-billion-a-year outdoor-goods market. REI, which sells into more than 40 countries, offers versions of its site in French, German, and Spanish.

Because it is a cooperative, REI remits a portion of its profits back to its customers, who pay a one-time $15.00 lifetime membership fee. Membership confers literal ownership. Owners elect the board and at the end of every year are entitled to a patronage dividend—a rebate based on a percentage of how much they spent with REI during that previous year. The percentage ranges from 5 to 10 percent or more, depending on how profitable the company is.

Its relationship with that membership—a community of people with similar interests—was one of REI's biggest advantages as it contemplated its entry into electronic commerce. Another advantage was the six-decade history of REI's direct-to-consumer mail-order catalog—with some 10 million catalogs mailed annually—so its order-fulfillment system was already in place.

When REI began to look at a Web site in earnest in 1996, the team was assembled from virtually every department—marketing, merchandising, information services, adventure travel, retail, real estate, accounting, and public affairs. By bringing in people from all over the organization, REI tried to eliminate the fear that the Web site would cannibalize existing REI channels. "Many businesses have been like deer frozen in the headlights because of their channel conflicts," opined Matt Hyde, who was REI's vice president of online sales and is now senior vice president of merchandising and logistics. "They see the Web as competing with their other lines of business. But we take Web orders from customers who drive by our stores every day. We have many multi-channel customers. We can't choose how our customers want to shop. So we offer any product, anytime, anywhere."

Hyde was selected to head up the Web site project by Dennis Madsen, who was then chief operating officer and who is now chief executive officer. Like every REI employee, Hyde knew the merchandise because he was an REI member/customer. Prior to joining the co-op in 1986 as a part-time employee, Hyde had owned and operated his own guide service for climbing. In addition, he understood both retail and Web technology.

Because the Web was going to be an essential part of REI's business, the decision was made to develop everything in-house—at a time when most companies were outsourcing their Web sites. "It must be a core competency, just like service," said Hyde. "You don't outsource service. Online stores are not a project; they are a business," and must be expected to meet the service and financial targets of a real business. From the beginning, the site was treated as "a profit center rather than a marketing expense, which was highly unusual at the time."

REI has a common inventory and pricing database for in-store, catalog, and Web-site operations. In 1997, rei.com's first full year of operation, the site brought in about $30 million in sales—above what the company expected, and the equivalent of one of REI's smaller physical stores. By 2000, online sales were $92 million, a 125 percent increase over the previous year.

Today, few retailers have a better understanding of how to integrate online and offline operations. The Web site consistently ranks among the top 10 in both apparel and sporting goods, thanks to its onsite resources, ease of use, and customer confidence, and was selected to *Forbes'* "Best of the Web" and *Time's* "25 Best E-Commerce Sites."

REI's multichannel strategy has not been without missteps. Along the way, REI has taken its financial lumps. The cooperative decided early on to spend the necessary money on the launch and marketing of the site, and to absorb the losses. The Web site turned a profit in 1998 and 1999, but slipped into the red in 2000, owing to planned losses to pay for improvements and expansion. That brought about the first net loss—$11.4 million—for REI since the cooperative was founded in 1938. But Madsen said the losses were worth it in order to achieve REI's objective of being "the last man standing within outdoor recreation on the Internet."

❖   ❖   ❖

The overarching theme of the book is coordination: How can you align the various channels of your business to provide that highest level of customer service? We will learn how to make the virtual channel work with the physical channel; how to customize and personalize the Web site for the customer; how to ensure that the brick-and-mortar aspect of the business remains a crucial element; and, by training your people, how service can be seamless at every step along the way.

The companies represented in these pages have responded to the challenge of delivering seamless, multichannel customer service with their individual business models. They reflect and represent a model that can be applied to virtually any business—anytime, anywhere.

✧   ✧   ✧

Takeaways

Each of these companies has demonstrated a boldness that's often lacking among businesses, especially when they face a challenge as disruptive as coordinating multichannel service. Early on, they were willing to commit money, time, and resources to their multichannel approach. They have been willing to make mistakes. They have been willing to fail. And they have always been bold.

- To develop channel synchronization, make sure every division and discipline in your company is involved in decision making.
- Identify and capitalize on your existing competencies.
- Don't outsource service. Online operations are not a project; they are a business.
- Be prepared to fail before you succeed.
- Put value directly into customers' hands.
- Customer service is not the department; it's the company.

Anytime, Anywhere, Anyhow

Multichannel Synchronization

Choose always the way that seems the best, however rough it
may be; custom will soon render it easy and agreeable.

—PYTHAGORAS

With the growing popularity of Web sites in the second half of the
Nineties, so-called "traditional" companies questioned the direction they needed to take. Some manufacturers worried, if they
sold directly to consumers via the Web, about how their retail
partners would react. Retailers wondered: "If we sell online, will
fewer people shop in our stores?"

Some retailers were reluctant to launch a Web site for fear that
failure would tarnish their brand. Perhaps that apprehension was
justified. In early 2001, some 70 percent of 1,900 American shoppers polled by Jupiter Media Metrix of New York indicated they
would spend less money at a retailer's brick-and-mortar store if
they were unhappy with their experience on the retailer's Web
site. Yet, research shows that customers who shop through more
than one channel tend to spend more money.

Back before the Internet bubble burst, companies such as Wal-Mart Stores, Toys 'R' Us, Barnes & Noble, Charles Schwab, and Staples found several compelling reasons to put together an online operation, make it a separate company, and spin it off. The brunt of the risk was assumed by outside investors. Ever-rising valuations helped finance deals, and visions of stock options lured Internet talent.

At that time, savvy companies separated their online and offline operations. Wal-Mart, based in Bentonville, Arkansas, located walmart.com in the San Francisco Bay Area and hired mostly non-Wal-Martians. That move didn't work very well. Despite great expectations, the Web site of America's biggest brick-and-mortar retailer has not received high marks. In July of 2001, Wal-Mart bought out the minority stakes in walmart.com, which was held by Accel Partners, the California venture capital firm, and brought it back into the corporate Wal-Mart fold in order to strengthen the link between the Web site and the 2,800 Wal-Mart stores in the U.S. At the same time, rival Kmart did the exact same thing—after buying the 40 percent of its site, bluelight.com, that it did not own. Both retailers recognized that they lived in a multi-channel world.

Companies that spun off their Internet business found themselves faced with two problems that were ironically related to each other: the unintended promotion of "channel conflict" and the unexpected need for "channel synchronization."

By separating online and offline operations, firms inadvertently built rival factions that found themselves in internecine competition in the acquiring, pricing, and selling of products. Some firms adopted different compensation systems to reward online and offline managers. The result: the brick-and-mortar managers feared that the opposing Web forces would "cannibalize"—i.e., take sales away from—their established business. Not surprisingly, the two operations were not in synch; neither side knew what the other was doing.

An even bigger problem was the perception of the customers who didn't know—or care about—the internal dynamics of a Charles Schwab or a Toys 'R' Us and their Web sites. Barnes & Noble customers who purchased books on bn.com initially were not allowed to return them to B&N stores. But when it found that its biggest spenders were multichannel customers, the giant bookseller integrated its operations.

B&N and other companies learned a valuable lesson: Customers don't make the distinction between your channels. They see you as one brand. And that's how you should see your own business.

Shop the Way You Want

"It doesn't matter whether or not the customer comes to shop with us online, or over the phone or on the Web. What I want is for the customer to come," said John Browett, CEO of tesco.com, the online division of the U.K. supermarket retail chain. "Therefore, we don't see any channel conflict whatsoever. It's all about driving the overall traffic of all the businesses we have that touch our customers—grocery shopping, financial services, online shopping, etc."

In 1999 and 2000, while the press was predicting that Internet-only banks would eventually replace traditional store banking, Wells Fargo found the opposite to be true, according to Wendy Grover, vice president of corporate communications and director of public relations for the Internet Services Group. "After advertising on the Internet, we found that the majority of sales were actually fulfilled in branches. It was clear that [the Web site] was complementary to the branches, and that the overall customer-retention goes way up when they go online. So, our Web site reinforces our branches and our brand. Being on the leading edge of the Internet is a positive lift for the whole brand."

Recreational Equipment, Inc. (REI) never spun off rei.com because, according to CEO Dennis Madsen, "When customers think of REI, they don't think of us as a dot-com business or a catalog business or a brick-and-mortar business. They think of our brand as encompassing all of those channels of distribution. And the expectations they have of us are identical no matter how they shop from us."

REI has found that a multichannel knowledge of its customers enables the Seattle-based consumer cooperative to discern whether rei.com is bringing in new business or taking a bite out of existing business. Senior vice president Matt Hyde emphasized, "Because we've been able to take a look at customers shopping across different lines of business, we have found that, overall, multichannel shoppers drive growth and are not necessarily cannibalizing the primary line of business. A lot is added business. Every time we've sliced and diced this data, we've found that cannibalization isn't really happening. What we are doing is converting multichannel customers. We are giving them more choice and they in turn are giving us more share of their wallet."

As far back as 1996, when REI was preparing to launch its Web site, Hyde recalled, "We realized very quickly that you don't get to choose how your customers shop. This wasn't our choice; it was the customer's choice. We're the retailer. We just need to be there to service them. If you're not online, customers are going to shop somewhere else. Any thinking other than that is pure arrogance. We decided that we were going to be accessible to our customers in any way that they wanted to access us—the phone, the catalog, the Internet, in-store kiosks, and our physical stores, and whatever else evolves in the future."

Brian Unmacht, vice president of REI's retail division, noted there was initial resistance by in-store personnel over who would get credit for sales generated by kiosks that are located within the brick-and-mortar stores. Customers can make purchases from the kiosks, which are linked to rei.com. So, if a purchase was made via the in-store kiosk, was it a store sale or a Web sale? REI management solved that problem by having the direct-sales and retail divisions jointly share those sales. Promoting that kind of interchannel cooperation is "important for setting goals," said Unmacht. "We want people to realize that these sales help all of us."

REI closely tracks what channels customers are using because those buying patterns determine where the company earmarks its resources in the future. As a membership organization, REI has a powerful built-in mechanism to gather information. By tracking a customer's purchases made either in a physical store, online, or by mail-order catalog, "We can see how our customers are behaving differently and how their shopping habits are changing," said Hyde, "and from that, we understand how we need to invest in the future. This just makes sense. We have twice the product selection online than we have in our physical flagship store. We have entire categories of products that you can't buy in any online store. We have rei-outlet.com, which is product that exists only on the Internet. We have these great physical stores and we have an 800 number. As a customer, not only can I buy my favorite gear in our physical stores, I also have these other choices. If I have an affinity to REI, I can buy my scooter or fly-fishing outfit from REI. These are additional sales that we hadn't been getting from the customer."

REI calls that philosophy "Shop the Way You Want," said Unmacht. He pointed out that no matter from which channel an item has been purchased, the technical experts at REI's brick-and-mortar operations are ready, willing, and able to provide their technical product knowledge. "It's not uncommon that someone purchases a bicycle or another technical item online, and calls the store for additional support. We send people out from the stores, or the customer can visit the store for more help with the item."

Lands' End is another retailer that doesn't swallow the cannibalization line. Ever since it launched landsend.com in 1995, it's been the company's position that it makes no difference where an order comes from—it's still going to be sorted, packed, and shipped from the same 800,000-square-foot facility in Dodgeville, Wisconsin.

Lands' End took that approach because the company has always seen the Web as a channel; not a business. "It's one company and one set of customers," said Bill Bass, senior vice president of Lands' End. "Sometimes the customers will shop through the Internet and sometimes through the catalog. Most of them shop both ways, so they are mutually supporting. Each channel has its own strengths and weaknesses, so you try to play to the strengths of each; you let customers decide which way they want to shop. Sometimes they want to shop online, and sometimes through the catalog. It depends on what they are trying to accomplish and what their mood is. There are things you can do on the Internet that you can't do in the catalog and vice versa. Browsing through an Internet site is not a great experience. It's more fun to browse through a catalog, which has much better photography."

Striking a balance between catalogs and cyberspace is tricky but worth it. In 2000, some 25 percent of its online customers were new to Lands' End, and many were younger than its core demographic of 35- to 54-year-olds.

"We don't care how we get the sale, as long as we get it. Cannibalization is good," declared CEO David Dyer.

Dyer made one particularly smart move to avoid channel conflict: He put all Lands' End executives and salaried employees on a single-bonus program, solely based on the performance of the *entire* corporation. "So, if we don't sell a dime on the Internet for the rest of the year, it's not going to affect my bonus at all—other than to the extent that it affects the total company's bonus," explained Bill Bass. "If the bonus of the president of the store division is tied into how the stores do, he's not going to be very helpful in getting the online operation up."

As it evolves its channel synchronization, Frederick's of Hollywood is finding ways for its Direct Division (online and catalog sales) to work closely with its 200 brick-and-mortar stores. Customers can locate a store or order a catalog from fredericks.com; they can also receive e-mail notification on events that are happening at a store near where they live. Gary K. Landry, president and CEO of fredericks.com, stated flatly, "There is no territorial ownership on the sale to a customer. It's a Frederick's sale."

As an example of Frederick's divisions working together, Landry cited a problem that the company faced at Christmas 2000. While the Direct Division had run out of a particular style, the store division had plenty of it. To solve the dilemma, the online division took the orders for that style, manually printed them out, and then sent the orders to the stores, where the items were boxed and sent out to the customer. "We included a letter to the customer that apologized for the order taking a little bit longer to arrive," Landry recalled. "We told our customers that the item was being shipped from the store because we didn't want them to miss out on their Christmas holiday. Afterwards, we received many letters from customers who said they couldn't believe what we had done, and that they were very appreciative. So, whenever we have the opportunity, we try to have cross-channel solutions for the customers."

Cross-Marketing: Attracting New Customers

By synchronizing their channels, companies can link and integrate their marketing efforts to reach their customers with a consistent message. Cross-marketing channels attract new customers. Home Shopping Network can leverage its presence in 70 million American homes by driving traffic to its Web site at virtually no expense by permanently placing the hsn.com graphic on the television screen. On-air hosts and celebrities regularly mention the Web site while they hawk their costume jewelry, appliqued sweaters, and exercise machines. At the conclusion of their televised segments, the hosts and celebrities sustain the sales pitch via HSN's Chat Café online chat room.

Ever since Wells Fargo launched its Web site in 1995, "I have heard over and over from customers that they changed banks because we were on the Internet," said Executive Vice President Gailyn Johnson. "I ask them where they opened the account. They tell me that they walked into a store to do it. That's the power of having all these different channels."

Wells Fargo intends to make available on its Web site any product or service that is sold in the branches. Wells Fargo has been one of the few banks to be able to cross-market and cross-sell those items to existing customers, which the company believes is the key to increasing products.

Wells Fargo offers a far-reaching assortment of banking services on its Web site. Consumers can pay bills to anyone in the U.S., trade securities, view their account information, and transfer money between their Wells Fargo checking, savings, credit card, line of credit, and money market mutual fund accounts. They can apply for new accounts and products, find the nearest ATM or branch, change their address, and order traveler's checks, foreign currency, cashier's checks, new checks, account statements, and copies of cancelled checks. The site offers discount trading, real-time quotes, online company research, and news. Wells Fargo's ShareBuilder IRA allows customers to fund their IRA accounts and purchase stocks and index shares with monthly contributions through an online investment service. Through Portfolio Tracker and Task Tracker, online investing customers can manage their capital gains tax liability and reduce the amount of time they spend preparing tax forms. Wells Fargo is the first major financial services company to integrate these kinds of portfolio- and tax-management tools directly into its online brokerage Web site, allowing customers to more effectively manage their ongoing capital-gains tax liability throughout the year.

Wells Fargo also has a Resource Center for Small Business Owners that features a comprehensive set of online services including banking services, advice, and market intelligence. For its middle-market and corporate customers, Wells Fargo offers Commercial Electronic Office, with a comprehensive financial services portal with services including Foreign Exchange Online, which allows businesses to access the global foreign exchange market to buy and sell currency.

Eddie Bauer uses signs in the dressing rooms of its stores to encourage customers who were unable to find what they were looking for in the store to try eddiebauer.com. The signs underscore features such as convenience, a wider selection of merchandise, and the capability to track purchases.

Lands' End has found that the largest source of requests for its catalog is a designated area on landsend.com. At the same time, every Lands' End catalog carries advertisements promoting the features on the Web site. Again, each channel has its own strength. While everything in the Lands' End warehouse can be seen 24/7 on the Web site, only edited and targeted merchandise is available in specialized catalogs, such as the one dedicated to children's merchandise. Online, "you can slice the database many more different ways," said Bill Bass. "When you put things into the catalog, you pick one way of presenting the products—all tops and bottoms together; all the blue products together. At some point, you have to make the decision of how you are going to group the products. Online, you can let the customer decide: do you want to see all the tops, all the short-sleeved stuff, etc.?"

REI annually mails out 10 million copies of its catalog, which are used to direct customers to rei.com, which provides more detailed product information and a wider product selection. The Web address is featured on the front and back covers and on almost every page-fold. On the Web site, the home page includes a blurb that says: "Order our new catalog!" The Web site, in turn, pushes people back to the stores by not only listing store locations but also promoting the in-store events at each of REI's 61 stores. If there is a meeting of the Bicycle Coalition of the Delaware Valley in the multipurpose room of the Conshohocken, Pennsylvania, store, or a lecture by a wilderness guide on traveling safely in bear country, you'll find out about it on the Web site. This feature not only drives people back to the store, it also gives them the opportunity to socialize with like-minded people. REI says that the in-store event and clinic pages are among the most popular features on the Web site.

The companies who have solved the channel-synchronization conundrum have found that they can use the Internet to reach a new market. At REI, "We have many brand new customers who don't live near a physical store," Hyde pointed out. "Obviously, those folks have the Internet and the 800 number as their only options. We have a number of customers that use our online store for information and then they come into our store to actually purchase it. That's okay by me. Customers walk into the store with printed information from the Web site. What I find interesting is that we have a small, but growing, number of customers whose first REI purchase was from our Web site, but who then shop in our physical stores."

In Michael Powell's mind, the Internet expands the market; it doesn't substitute one form (online sales) for another (store sales). A good portion of Powell's internet buyers, who visit his site from all the world, generally are searching for out-of-print books on specialized topics. The rarer the book, the higher the price. The in-store customer is usually more of a generalist.

A visitor to a Tesco store can't miss references to tesco.com, which are all over the place. "We use the stores as a major recruiting mechanism for people doing grocery home-shopping online. We are trying to use all those channels to be complementary," explained John Browett. "You hope that, over time, you will be driving people into the stores—which are the base of [Tesco]— because of the great experiences they've had. We have evidence where people started to shop for groceries with us online and liked the range of products we offered or the experience they had. When they discovered that there is a Tesco nearby, they then came into the store. There are customers who used to shop in the stores and now shop online."

Tesco's position is that even if those online sales come from established offline customers, "it doesn't matter," said Browett. "Over all, you end up in a net-net position." Well over half the sales that come through the grocery home-shopping business are new to Tesco. The remainder come from existing customers who increased their spending. "We are not cannibalizing sales from stores. We are expanding market share, which is hard to do in our business."

The Web is another channel that needs constant customer-service support. "Because the Web is global, time zones do not matter," said Browett. "If you offer only traditional nine-to-five support, you have instantly alienated half the world's population. People shopping online locally also need out-of-hours support because many log on after work or after completing household chores."

Return to Sender

Returns have been the bane of retailers ever since the dawn of commerce. The easier a retailer makes returning a product, the better relationship that retailer will have with the customer. Returns are a challenge when channels are not integrated and synchronized, or when different operations have different computer systems, different management teams and sometimes even different merchandise. That's a prescription for alienating today's demanding consumers, who, according to a Jupiter Research survey, want to be able to return online purchases to a brick-and-mortar store and to be able to order a product on the Web site and pick it up at the store.

Customers are getting spoiled. They assume that when they make a purchase, the record of that purchase will be readily available, regardless of the channel it came from. But until recently, few retailers kept purchase histories. You can't get away with that anymore. All systems have to be synchronized. "That's taken as a given in our business," said Browett of Tesco. We wouldn't think about it in any other way. If I bought a product online, I could take it back to any Tesco store. We make no distinction whatsoever."

The ability to seamlessly deal with returned merchandise is an enormous edge that multichannel retailers have over pure-play Web retailers.

About $8 billion worth of apparel is returned to catalog and e-retailers every year. An estimated half that amount is due to poor fit, owing in part to brands and designers not standardizing sizes. For companies like Lands' End and Frederick's of Hollywood, which sell only their own branded product, that is not so much of an issue. To help customers choose correctly, they include size charts with both their catalogs and their Web sites, and they thoroughly explain and illustrate how best to take your own measurements. Nordstrom and Tesco, which sell their own branded merchandise as well as that of other companies, do the same thing.

Nordstrom has had an unconditional money-back guarantee ever since John W. Nordstrom opened the doors of the first brick-and-mortar store in downtown Seattle in 1901. When the specialty fashion retailer launched its catalog in the early 1990s, it immediately gained customers' attention by never charging for shipping costs on returns. Dan Nordstrom, president of nordstrom.com, recalled that rival direct mail companies "thought we were crazy and that we didn't understand the industry." Turns out Nordstrom's return rates were no higher than the rest of the industry. Even more important, "When you make returns easy, they don't increase—you just sell more."

When Nordstrom launched its Web site in 1998, the company instituted the same no-hassle return policy. Every package mailed out with a nordstrom.com order comes with a pre-addressed mailing label and postage-paid envelope—in case the customer wants to return it. A $4.95 processing fee is charged to the credit card or deducted from the refund check.

Nordstrom offers free exchanges. If customers are not completely satisfied with their orders, they can send them back.

Nordstrom pays the return postage and ships the new items with no additional charge. Not surprisingly, such service is costly. Although the return rate on Nordstrom's Web site is less than that of the catalog, some categories have much higher rates of returns—dresses, for example, run close to 40 percent. Nevertheless, the company believes that such a generous policy ultimately makes good business sense.

"If a customer is in possession of a good they're dissatisfied with, it doesn't do you any good to have them keep it," Dan Nordstrom reasoned. "Every time they look at it, it gives them a weird, negative connotation that filters back to where they got it. We'd rather get it out of your closet and give you something you feel good about."

Frederick's offers an unconditional money-back return policy for whatever reason within 90 days of purchase, regardless of channel. But Frederick's stores can *not* take back merchandise purchased from its Direct Sales Division. Gary Landry said the primary obstacle is the crazy-quilt of state sales taxes. Frederick's catalog and Internet divisions charge sales tax only in the state of Arizona, where the company has a physical presence—a distribution center. When this book went to press, Frederick's did not yet have one common inventory system for both divisions. It did, however, have the capability of sharing a customer's transaction history with all channels. Landry acknowledged that Frederick's will ultimately synchronize its channels. "This is the start of the journey," he said.

FedEx is doing its part with its NetReturn, a service that enables customers and merchants to electronically process package returns by letting customers print a shipping label authorized by the merchant and generated from their own personal computer. The system notifies the sender of the closest FedEx drop-off locations, where they can send back the return package, which also can be

turned over to a FedEx driver. The location of the returned merchandise can be followed using FedEx's own package-tracking
capabilities.

REI strives to give consumers the same message across its Web
site, stores, and catalog. Customers can buy products online or via
the catalog and return them in stores, if they wish. Brian
Unmacht, vice president of REI's retail division, said, "If people
buy something in a store, they can mail it back. Being able to
return an item in whatever way you want is a matter of figuring
out internal issues and deciding what's best for the customer. We
have a long history of mail order and retail, so it was not uncommon for someone to buy something from mail order and return it
to the store and vice versa. So, when rei.com came along, we just
adopted that into the same procedure."

Know Your Customer
Across All Channels

Rather than worry about channel cannibalization, smart retailers
try to know their customers across all channels, and learn how
those customers behave across all channels. Armed with that
information, they can anticipate what they need to satisfy and
keep their customers. The day has arrived when customers will
not accept the fact that a company won't have complete access to
their entire purchase history, be it via store, catalog, or online.
That means that companies must invest in systems that enable
them to integrate this information to more effectively cross-
market products and services.

"Customers are not going to tolerate retailers that don't understand them across all the channels," said Matt Hyde, senior vice
president at Recreational Equipment, Inc., who characterizes
most REI customers as single-channel shoppers. "There is

another subset that are double-channel customers. Others shop with us all three ways. Our most valuable customers are the multi-channel customers, who will shop online for a certain need and then go into the store for another particular need. For convenience, they might shop online for a known item, such as a tent, to be shipped to their house. But if they want to buy a pair of running shoes, they're going to go to the store and try them on."

Key to REI's multichannel strategy has been to provide a "strong value proposition," said Hyde. "We believed we could be successful if we differentiated our online store from our physical stores, and gave people a different reason to shop online. We always talk about *any product, any place* and *answer any question*—that's the breadth, convenience, and strategy."

REI is so committed to communication among its channels that when the co-op expanded its headquarters and the dot-comers were moved to another building on campus, the company invested in 24 scooters to make sure that the Web staff was connected to the rest of the business.

In that spirit of cohesion, REI has a unified customer database, "so the information that I have about you in the stores is something that I will be able to access via the Web, telephones, etc," said Joan Broughton, vice president of online and direct sales. Previously, she was rei.com's executive site producer, responsible for defining and driving the design, content, and community aspects of REI's e-commerce sites. "Some of that comes from the personalization and customization that we offer on the Web. Some of it comes from interaction when a customer visits an REI store. When we ring up your purchase and we see that you recently bought a bicycle online, we can mention to you: 'Do you know we are offering a bicycle clinic this weekend?' That kind of attention is not Orwellian. It isn't bizarre that you're at an REI store and we know what you just purchased. But it would be nice to be able to have that information and to offer you something that you are interested in. You have to be smart without being too clever." (Customization and personalization will be examined in great detail in Chapter 4.)

In the future, "We want to be able to tailor experiences in a way that really gives customers a sense of how valuable it is to be a member. If you are a good customer of REI for a long time, we should be able to recognize that, and reward you appropriately," added Broughton. Eventually, a sales associate at an REI brick-and-mortar store will be able to run a customer's membership card through the cash register and instantly see through a Web-enabled point-of-sale system that she is, for example, a snowboarder, and be prompted to offer her a personalized discount on ski wax.

While some retailers put all of their stock-keeping-units (SKUs) on their Web site, Nordstrom takes a different approach. Nordstrom.com offers only a third of the more than one million SKUs that are carried in an average 180,000-square-foot Nordstrom store. The reasoning is simple: Nordstrom has found it impossible to make a profit on orders of less than $80.00. (Many retailers have faced the same problem. One reason Wal-Mart cited for cutting back on walmart.com was the fact that the Web site carried too many low-priced items.) Nordstrom's Web site emphasizes exclusive brand-name merchandise in clothing and cosmetics, which provide higher margins and an average order size of $150. Nordstrom.com features several boutiques from brand names such as DKNY, Kenneth Cole, and Ralph Lauren, with generally 30 or 40 items apiece.

By knowing its customers across all channels, Nordstrom presents a look and feel that are uniform across all channels. Browsing nordstrom.com, customers don't quite get the aesthetic experience that they would get in a warm, cleverly designed Nordstrom store on Michigan Avenue in Chicago or in the

Horton Plaza Mall store in San Diego, but they do see lots of clearly marked merchandise and, when needed, plenty of attention in the form of a tab on the Web site for Customer Service and Live Help. This unified image is a recognition on the part of management that, "Customers are not all that interested in our channel operations," said Dan Nordstrom. "They are interested in a relationship with a retailer."

Catalog Channel

Multichannel companies must present a rich, consistent experience on every channel where they do business. For some companies that experience starts with their catalogs.

Before there was the Web, there was the mail-order catalog. Merchants like Sears, Roebuck and Montgomery Ward built their businesses on catalogs before they branched out into retail stores. In the late-19th century and the early-20th century, these catalogs were certainly a form of family entertainment that brought the material wonders of the world into living rooms across America. Eddie Bauer, a Seattle hunter, fisherman, and inventor, who opened his first sporting-goods store in 1920, started a mail-order business for authentic outdoor gear and equipment in 1946. His first mailing list came from the letters and postcards—which he stored in a shoebox—from satisfied customers, including Charles Lindbergh and Zane Grey.

Taking a page out of the Eddie Bauer playbook, Jack Covert started the first mailing list for 800-CEO-READ in a similar fashion. In the early years of the company's existence, the staff collected business cards from customers who previously had made special orders. Those business cards comprised the customer base for its first catalog, the *Business Book Gazette*, which included the company's own best-seller list. "Being an old music guy, I knew that people like to know what's new and hot," recalled Covert. The information-packed *Gazette* grew to be a semiannual, 30- to 40-page, 75,000-copy mailer. The four-color *Gazette* was eventually replaced with a two-color newsletter, called *The Keen Thinker*, which goes out nine times a year to a target mailing list of 10,000. The result is a much more personal selling and marketing tool, which represents another *touchpoint* with the customer.

Covert has a reputation in the business-book publishing world as a champion of titles that he helps turn into national bestsellers. "Jack is not simply a bookseller; he's a tracker and a prophet," said author Harriet Rubin, a former book editor. In recent years, Covert has added to 800-CEO-READ's anytime, anywhere approach with two subscriber newsletters—*Jack Covert Selects*, a compendium of reviews of business books, and *The Airplane Read*, a monthly recommendation of a novel or business book that would be ideal to read on a flight. Both are available as opt-in e-mail services.

"That's the true outbound marketing," said Covert. "I want to be the 'rubbish filter' for people who are looking for business books."

Lands' End has long been sending out well-designed catalogs that are put together with a sense of fun. For example, a February catalog highlighting Valentine's Day featured a short but informative history of the sending of Valentine's cards. The catalog features occasional editorials written on a wide range of topics by well-known authors, playwrights, and celebrities, including a humorous essay on Christmas by Garrison Keillor, a short story by Jacquelyn Mitchard, and a tour of the Scottish Isles by William Least Heat-Moon.

The Telephone Channel

Working hand in hand with the catalog is, of course, the telephone. You remember the telephone, don't you? It's that instrument that people used to use to talk to each other. Today, it's often a tool for exchanging voice mail messages—not for conducting an actual conversation. But in the multichannel world, the telephone is more important than ever. Most of the companies featured in this book have call centers where customer-service representatives use the good old-fashioned telephone to help answer the questions of catalog and Web site customers.

Lands' End tries to re-create the kind of one-to-one service that a customer receives in a fine brick-and-mortar retail store. One of the first catalog retailers to offer a toll-free number, Lands' End has long understood that even in the age of the Internet, online customers don't want to be left fending for themselves out in cyberspace. Customers on landsend.com feel more comfortable speaking by telephone to the staff of friendly, knowledgeable, and highly trained customer service representatives. On an average day, some 300 telephone lines handle between 40,000 and 50,000 calls. In the weeks leading up to Christmas, over 1,100 phone lines handle more than 100,000 calls daily. Every year, Lands' End customer service reps field 15 million calls and 231,000 e-mail messages. In an effort to offer more personalized wardrobe advice, Lands' End introduced a "live chat" feature that combines the best features of the telephone and the Web. (Lands' End Live will be discussed in greater detail in Chapter 3.)

Nordstrom is also using live chat to more fully capitalize on the expertise of its telephone customer service representatives. At the same time, Nordstrom is finding ways to use the telephone to better meet customer needs. For example, Nordstrom discovered that one of the top 10 search phrases on nordstrom.com was for "Kate Spade," the designer of shoes and handbags. There was just one problem: Kate Spade shoes and handbags weren't available on nordstrom.com, but they were available at Nordstrom stores. So, to make sure customers don't leave the Web site unhappy, Nordstrom redirects them to make a telephone call to a personal shopper in a Nordstrom store that carries the Kate Spade line.

At 800-CEO-READ, "We have 20 years of experience at Call Center, which is integral to the customer service we offer. Customer service is too important to lose that voice contact," said Covert, who saw "very little difference between our customer-service channels for Web and voice." A half-dozen people take orders over the phone, from 8 A.M. to 7 P.M. Central Time, five days a week. "We're all in the same room. So, when one of our Client Services people sees a book that is mispriced, he fixes it. We have that kind of nuts-and-bolts communication."

Powell's Books' telephone channel operates from 7:30 A.M. to 8:00 P.M. PST on weekdays, 9:00 A.M. to 7:00 P.M. on weekends, Powell's will do book searches for up to seven titles at a time. After searching for the book, Powell's will call back if any are found. Powell's also does special telephone orders from publishers both domestically and overseas.

The telephone is extremely important at The Geek Squad because, said founder and CEO Robert Stephens, "You have to give a damn about everything. You have to be a control freak. You have to be anal retentive. I knew [The Geek Squad's techs] could fix the computers and solve the technical problems. But what I wanted to make sure was that they returned their phone calls— *quickly*. We are in the business of being on call. We use our out-going voice message as an advertisement. When a customer calls the company, they hear the following voice message: 'You've reached The Geek Squad. 24 hours on-site computer support. If you have a problem we'll be there right away. Press 1 and we will have your call returned in less than 7 minutes.'" Stephens explained: "That tells you everything about me: I'm clear, concise, quick, and standing by. Why do I say seven minutes? Because I want to be specific."

By capitalizing on its telephone channel, The Geek Squad has been able to expand its operation to Los Angeles, where the company has a virtual office. "When somebody from Santa Monica has a computer problem, he calls 1–800-GEEKSQUAD, and the phone rings in Minneapolis. We answer it and then send the text message to the employee in Los Angeles, who goes straight to the job," Stephens said. "Our tech guy fixes your computer, takes your credit card, processes it on their cell phone, prints you an invoice on your printer, and leaves—with no paper."

The Geek Squad does little troubleshooting over the phone, preferring to take care of problems in person. Trying to do computer repairs over the phone is "like walking a blind person through a tracheotomy," Stephens quipped. "We can't see it. We can't touch it. A lot of our support is personal. You can only be so personal over the phone. It takes two hours over the phone for what we could do in ten minutes in someone's home."

The telephone channel has long been essential for customer service at FedEx. The overnight package-delivery company employs about 3,500 customer service representatives working in 18 call centers throughout the U.S., with another 42 internationally. Although these centers are located in different cities, "We operate as if we are all in one city, just on different floors. We have in the U.S. one network schedule that's created based on the incoming call volume, which has produced a cost savings," explained Vice President Sheila Harrell. "Our call centers respond to whatever customer issues come up, be it ordering supplies, scheduling the pickup, tracking the packages or providing location information. This information is also available on the Web."

Using technological innovations, FedEx created a customer-friendly virtual environment. But company founder Fred Smith was fearful that the customer service people "were not getting the same level of attention in terms of upgrading," recalled Senior Vice

President Laurie Tucker. In the late Nineties, FedEx embarked on a three-year project to restructure and retool its call centers, "so our customers could be served by our multiple operating companies in a seamless way," said Tucker. "We quickly moved to do something radical, which we love to do at FedEx. We pulled all the sales forces out of the various operating companies. We pulled out the marketing groups and the IT, and we put them all together in a single services company to face the customer seamlessly."

It has been a huge task for FedEx to integrate the transactional histories of millions of customers. "We are providing the people in our call centers with a very enriched set of data that we are mining. Not only do we know our customers as company names or individuals, we also know the actual people inside the companies. We can mine this massive amount of information so that we can get to the actual individual and find out what that individual's needs are," said Tucker. "We can respond much more specifically and actually make the transaction go much faster."

Exploiting this rich vein of information, FedEx representatives can more easily solve specific customer problems—from how to get a shipping system installed in their company to how to get their package out of customs in Ireland. FedEx reps can also be more *proactive*. For example, if a customer ordered a large amount of supplies—and had never done that before—he might receive a phone call from FedEx asking if he's introducing a new product and is getting ready to send it out. If so, FedEx will offer suggestions on how to make shipping easier.

Recognizing that customers want FedEx services to be available "anytime, anywhere, anyhow they want access," said Karen Rogers, vice president of electronic commerce marketing, FedEx has expanded into wireless technology, so "We will be able to proactively push that information to you and you will be able to pull the information from us." Using their personal digital assistants, Web-enabled cell phones, and two-way pagers, FedEx customers can access real-time package-status tracking information, get a rate for a package, and locate the nearest drop-off location. Couriers and contractors can update package-status information while they are away from their delivery vans. FedEx salespersons can gain faster access to databases while out on sales calls.

At Wells Fargo, only a small number of customers want to bank exclusively online. The bank has found that routine transactions on the telephone drop off by 17 percent when people use the Internet for checking their balances or transferring funds. "While the majority of our online customers make fewer phone calls, they still make phone calls. They make fewer branch visits, but they still make plenty of visits," said Avid Modjtabai, executive vice president of Wells Fargo's Consumer Internet Group.

Moving Customers to the Web Site

When using a multichannel approach, companies must be sensitive to the needs, whims, and insecurities of the customer. For the companies, there are obvious and meaningful financial incentives for moving customer contact and transactions to the Web, which is the most efficient channel. It costs a couple of cents to process an order on the Web, compared to a couple of dollars with a catalog order. Jack Covert is trying to move customers to the 800-CEO-READ Web site by offering substantial discounts for ordering, which can be done 24 hours a day.

Powell's Books at the end of 2000 began to move as many telephone orders as possible to the Web. "By examining our phone bills, we found that two-thirds of the customers who call our Burnside [flagship] store are from out of state. We were able to shift that much business from a hands-on, labor-intensive process to a streamlined, automated process. That process was already in place and had proven itself over three years," said Sheila Keane, corporate strategic project manager. Powell's also gathered books from its warehouse and its six other stores in the Portland area, in order to offer customers more choices. The goal is to let them choose at which Powell's store they would like to pick up their book orders. The bigger challenge was to offer that service to Internet customers.

"What surprised me was the extent to which local people would use the site," remarked Keane. "They would see if we have a book and then come down or call the store." Local customers who use powells.com then want to pick up the book at the most convenient store. This presented some challenges to Powell's customer contact center because "that's not how we were organized." Initially, Powell's simply shipped orders to its Internet customer. "We discovered, however, that a significant number of local people were coming in with lists that they had generated off of the Internet. Or they would call us with lists and ask if we could ship them the book or if they could pick up the books at the Powell's store closest to them. I suspect it's a small minority of customers who are asking us for this. But they are in significant enough numbers that they need good customer service. They would not understand our inability to do this, and would not be terribly patient. Saying, 'This isn't how we are organized,' would not thrill the customer."

To satisfy those customers, Powell's added another feature to its Web site. When a customer clicks on a particular book on powellsbooks.com, he or she sees a box next to the book that lists the number of copies of that book at each of the various Powell's stores in the Portland area, and in what section of the store the book can be found.

Keane said that she spends a few hours a week monitoring calls at the main store. She was surprised at the large number of local Portland customers who tell Powell's staff people that they first saw a particular book on powells.com. "They went about getting the information in one manner, and then chose to actually make the transaction in a different manner. But they are still going to drive downtown to pick up the book." Right now, local customers order over the Internet and get their order shipped. "If you come to our Web site and you see a book that you want, and you don't want to put your credit card across the Web, you can call us up; we will place the order for you," said Keane. "If you want to pick it up at our Hawthorne store, we will get it there to you. We will figure out how to do all those internal operations to make that happen."

Ever since it launched its Web site in 1996, Powell's has looked for ways of combining its brick-and-mortar and Internet businesses, in order to "keep the company as a whole," said Michael Powell. "One of the points behind seamless service is giving the best service possible however the customer can access you. We are not going to ask our customers to contact us only through a certain method or venue. They can use all methods and venues interchangeably; we can service them however they choose. We have agreed that we want to keep the whole company together in achieving that goal."

At Powell's, seamless service means establishing a central, flow-through contact center for all the non-walk-in customers, by phone, fax, e-mail, or Internet. "My strategy is follow the example of the success of our whole Internet operations," said Keane. "Because we've built everything in house, and we have a very hot programming staff, we are able to very quickly make changes and enhancements. Back-end operations are more sophisticated. Anything that can possibly be automated is automated. Our primary short-term strategy to get results quickly is to do everything we can to make our customer service—particularly the catalog sales and phones—piggyback on the back-end operations of our Web site. The long-term strategy will certainly be a unified system, but whether it's going to continue to be on the back-end of our Web site remains to be seen."

Powells.com is working on a system that—like amazon.com's—will track the customer's purchase history and communicate with the brick-and-mortar business in terms of inventory. One way to bring those systems together is through the PC registers in the stores that are connected to the Web site, so sales people can check the entire inventory and other databases. If the store doesn't have the book, an employee can tell the customer a variety of things about the book, including whether it's in print, and the price it's being sold for in a variety of venues.

"Right now, we are at the point where you can access us any way you want," said Keane. "Down the road, when we become even more sophisticated, there may be ways that we can tag or identify callers or e-mail that are very sales-specific. That information would be sent directly to a customer-service person, rather than go through our system. I've always had this vision that any time a customer is on our Web site and their shopping cart is full, and they decide for whatever reason to leave before completing the whole transaction—that's the key place where we want to make sure we have customer contact. If we received an inquiry that can be answered by a Frequently Asked Question, then we will send the customer an automated e-mail. By whatever way that we are accessed, we are going find a cost-effective way to respond to our customers."

Customer service at Powell's was not always so mindful of efficiency and cost-effectiveness, according to Darin Sennett, whose business card reads "Director of Webbish Things" and who has worked at powells.com site since 1995 (almost from the beginning), when the site was getting just 10 to 20 orders per day. Operating out of Powell's Technical Store, the site featured a searchable database, which was used primarily by math professors who were searching for books on their specialty. "The customers would search the database, find the book, copy the information, paste it an e-mail and send it to us," recalled Sennett. "One of us would then go down to the store and get the book. The customers would have a number of questions, and we would send e-mails back and forth before the book got sold. We would even sit there and type out tables of contents." That was typical of the Powell's staff, which "would go through extreme and ridiculously inefficient lengths to please the customers. A customer would ask us to put the book aside for him, which we would do. A couple of days later, he would order another, and then another. Finally, he'd ask how many books he had on order. We'd have to add them up manually. We took great pride in that."

For almost a year, Sennett was the entire customer service department, answering e-mails 8 hours a day. "I just plowed through customer e-mail," he recalled.

Sennett's story aptly shows how primitive and basic was Powell's initial Internet foray. The early Web staff was composed of three people, including one staffer who wrote the software for the operating system.

"The technology was not that complex," said Michael Powell. "We didn't have to invest hundreds of thousands of dollars in the hardware. I suspect we invested $10,000 or $20,000 in a small server and whatever else one needed."

Today, Powell's online operations have a dozen employees, and about 35 people who fill orders.

"The lesson here," said the pragmatic Mr. Powell, is that, "we have five programmers and one systems administrator. That's our affordable resource base. There are four or five people who work on the marketing side—the look and the features—of the Web site. So, we have about a dozen people. That is our commitment to our Web site. It's what we can afford to do. These are not inexpensive people. We live in a business with certain fixed margins. But what's fascinating to me, and the lesson I would offer that would inspire other people is this: We have a 40-hour work week here. With that kind of disciplined commitment, I am constantly amazed at how we can get such very successful solutions out of those 12 people."

Sennett reflected: "In retrospect, it was the frugality that is almost my greatest point of respect for this company. It's certainly not always easy, but it is why we are where we are."

Powell's is in a pretty good place. Forbes rated powells.com the best bookseller on the Web, ahead of the likes of amazon.com and barnesandnoble.com—"people who spend tens of millions of dollars on those functionalities," said Powell.

Powell believes that spending that kind of money can be a huge mistake. "Someone asked me recently: 'Does size matter?' I said, 'yes, you can be too small.' In this environment, if you don't have the money for the infrastructure, you're dead. If you can't spend $50,000 to $100,000 a year investing in equipment, software, and people prior to sales and marketing initiatives, it's very difficult to be a player, to be a successful Web presence," said Powell. "On the other hand, there is a lot of literature on how you can blow through tens of millions of dollars and be a fond memory in the cemetery of dot-coms. So, there is something about being too big that I don't understand. You would think they could harness all that creativity in a virtual network and get the job done. But, somehow, they fail. Is it because of their size or the nature of the beast? I don't know."

Provide the Most
Economical Sales Channel

At Frederick's of Hollywood, "In an ideal world, the Internet is absolutely the channel that we are trying to move our direct customers to because we want to give them the most economical channel in today's world," said Landry. If a catalog customer calls the Frederick's 800 number and is put on hold waiting for a customer service representative, a recorded message "promotes the fact that all of these styles, and more, are available for you on the Internet—very convenient and very easy." Frederick's offers the same prices both on the Web site and in the catalog.

To Landry, the purpose of the Web site is "to provide the most economical sales channel for all products. We are able to leverage the technology to replace human capital whenever we are trying to make a sale. Instead of having a sales associate on the floor greeting the customer; instead of having to have a customer service representative on the phone taking an order, the Web site allows us to use and leverage technology to provide the most efficient and cost-effective channel. Compared to the catalog, it provides virtually free real estate. We can take the product down in smaller increments and therefore squeeze out more gross margin dollars. We can list products that are out of season from a selling perspective but not necessarily from a fashion perspective. For example, we could have a quantity of an item that sold well. We can continue to sell that item, which gives us a more orderly liquidation than we could get with a dramatic blow-out sale or clearance sale."

Frederick's has a policy that a customer can order anything from any of its 100-plus previous catalogs, which are available online. Anything that is currently in the catalog is on the Internet. Some 20 to 30 items, which are among Frederick's racier items, are available only on the Internet. "The Internet customer acknowledges that he/she wants to look at that item," explained Landry.

Avoid Technology for Technology's Sake

Clyde Ostler, group executive vice president of Wells Fargo's Internet Service Group, has noted that the bank may eliminate bank officers having to answer mundane questions, such as the status of wire transfers or interest rates, so they can focus on more value-added tasks. "We hope that with the Internet, we can do in one step what now takes two or three." That makes financial sense for banks. A typical teller transaction can cost a bank between $1.00 and $1.50, compared to Internet transactions, which cost less than 5 cents, according to Gartner Financial Services.

Wells Fargo's goal is to have customers be able to access services where, when, and how they prefer. The bank offers them many channels—stores, ATMs, phone banking, and the Internet—but they are all part of a single face of Wells Fargo. Seamless service is available 24/7 by phone and e-mail.

But Wells Fargo does not believe in using technology for technology's sake. "We must make sure that the experience the customer is having on the site or across multiple channels makes sense," said Avid Modjtabai. "It's very much of an integrated, multichannel approach. We're not trying to force people to go one way or the other. We want to give them choice and let them decide what channel is best for them, and what products and services they choose to access. At the end of the day, it's the customers' choice. The focus is on the customer. That strategy drives how we organize and approach our business."

Many banks have been discontented with the Internet because it has failed to deliver on the promise of significantly lowering costs. Although the estimated cost of online transactions such as checking account balances or transferring money is about a penny, while in-person transactions cost about $1.00 each, most online customers prefer visiting their money at their bank branch or ATM. That's why Internet bank operations are not profitable on their own. Wells Fargo found that customers with any kind of online banking services are 50 percent less likely to leave the bank; the benefit is even greater for customers who make online bill payments. Gomez Advisors estimates that people who use a bank's Web site at least once a month have a median household income of $57,800, compared with $44,800 for non-Web bankers. More than a third have household incomes greater than $75,000, compared with 19 percent of non-Web consumers.

In order to keep its customers coming to—and getting more comfortable with—wellsfargo.com, the bank is working on providing a consistent experience across the sites, whether the customer using the site is a small business owner, a private customer with personal accounts, or an investor. "To make sure the experience is consistent and logical, we are leveraging synergies across the four lines of business and across the four customer segments—investment, small business, and wholesale," said Avid Modjtabai. "When we put teams together, we have representation from the four lines of business on each one of these teams so that we are meeting everyone's requirements. We have guidelines regarding the look and feel of the brand, the navigation, and the nomenclature, in order to make sure what the customer sees on the site is consistent. Our infrastructure and platform allows us to create consistency across the four lines of business, so we are all using the same personalization engine, the same content management system. The technology is also helping us implement some of those requirements to make it consistent."

Wells Fargo thinks of itself as a financial services company, with several channels to serve the customer. "We don't treat it as a separate stand-alone business and we don't have differentiated pricing on the Web," said Modjtabai. "Only a small amount of people want to bank only online. The majority of customers want to have multiple channels. We have created the best of both worlds in a hybrid organization that keeps our focus on the Internet, but then leverages the strength of our traditional business. Now all banks that once had separate Internet operations have folded the Internet into their core business.

❖   ❖   ❖

At Enron Energy Services, "We actively cannibalized ourselves and migrated transactions that were more mundane to the Web, and let our clients self originate those," according to Vice Chairman Marty Sunde. "Guess what? It didn't make the customers go away. It allowed Enron people to spend their time solving much more complex problems. Plus, overall transaction volume went up. There were people in our division who were doing 100 to 500 transactions a day. Then they migrated those to Enron Online and are today doing 2,000 transactions a day."

FedEx is faced with the question of how to move to another channel a routine transaction that the customer has been doing for years and takes for granted. "You need to educate the customer on the best channel," said Cynthia Henson, vice president of customer service at FedEx. "To make a pickup call, for example, it might be best for the customer to go to the Web."

Laurie Tucker neatly encapsulates what companies such as FedEx face when it comes to satisfying customers "who ask us to make their life easier, to give them time back. That's going to be a challenge because brick-and-mortar companies are not engineered for personalized service. We're engineered for efficiency—to keep that customer on the line for the shortest amount of time possible. We budget customer service by how many seconds we're on the phone with a customer; we have a constant desire to make that number smaller and smaller. Today, we are focusing on moving customers to fedex.com to give them more and more value online. Fedex.com handles all of a customer's routine transactions, including shipping. Thus the customer experiences enriched telephone interactions because our customer service people can spend more time solving the more complex questions. As customers go to fedex.com to find information on their business and their account, the calls to the call center will lessen, but will increase in complexity. The more routine queries are better handled on the Web site. We'll continue to provide more tools on the Web to take on more complex tasks."

Although it's much more cost-efficient for FedEx's customers to use fedex.com, "We would never force the customer. We have found that you can give customers incentive to do business on a particular channel," added Tucker. "We won't eliminate paper airbills or penalize customers for using them. The onus is on us to create the enriched experiences online so that customers prefer our online services."

❖   ❖   ❖

Takeaways

Synchronizing channels is a mighty challenge. Your customers expect you to know them across all channels—and will accept nothing less. They expect to be able to exchange or return an online purchase at a brick-and-mortar location. Part of the multichannel challenge is to do two things simultaneously: (1) listen and respond to your customer across all channels, and (2) subtly move your customer to the most effective channel.

- Cannibalization is good.
- Customers don't make the distinction between your channels. They see you as one brand. That is how you should see yourself.
- Customers have the same high service expectations regardless of where they shop.
- All channels should be promoted by all channels, because they feed off each other.

The Web Channel

Everything should be made as simple as possible,
but not simpler.

—ALBERT EINSTEIN

There is no clearer example of online customer service than a Web site that is simple, straightforward, and easy to navigate. Your Web site is your *relationship* channel with your customer; it is the fulcrum of your multichannel customer service strategy.

Today's demanding customers want a site to provide attractive visuals, thorough product information, efficient checkout, and fast delivery. If there's a problem, they want to be able to easily contact someone who can help them. For example, at Wells Fargo "You are one click away from help by sending us an e-mail," said Executive Vice President Gailyn Johnson. "Every e-mail has to be answered within 24 hours, if not sooner. There is always a phone number that can help you." Your Web site should be built around what your customers actually want to accomplish—not what you think might be technologically sexy. Because most Web sites are visited by customers with varying levels of computer sophistication, design your site with them in mind.

It's not critical or even necessary for you to be on the leading edge. Some retailers want their site to be as familiar as other sites, just as most brick-and-mortar stores share the same basic physical format with other brick-and-mortar stores. After all, if you were designing a physical store, you wouldn't make it radically dissimilar from other stores; you wouldn't put the cash registers in the back; you wouldn't install departments that are not clearly identified.

"In navigation, layout, and function, we don't want our Web site to be different," said Gary Landry, CEO of fredericks.com. "We want our shopping cart to be like other shopping carts. We want to make improvements over other sites, but we don't want to be radically different. A change can't be something that surprises the customer when they click on. We want someone who shops at the gap.com or landsend.com to be very comfortable and to understand the navigation at fredericks.com."

In this chapter, we will look at the elements of good Web design and what makes a satisfying Web experience. We will see how individual companies use the Web to aid their customers, and how they make their Web site essential to coordinating seamless service in a multichannel world.

Web Site Design: The KISS Principle Rules

Many Web sites were initially the creation of people who understood the complexity of technology but not the simplicity of commercial interaction among human beings. Those sites were festooned with cool technological doo-dads and graphics that often were irrelevant to the experience. Non-technical customers are looking for an intuitive experience. When they log on, they need to be taken by the hand, to be shown how to use the site, and to be shown how to navigate their way through the site.

"People like to be treated like people, even if they are online," quipped Joan Broughton, vice president for online and direct sales at REI.

"Customers are not on the Internet to be entertained," said Dan Nordstrom, president of nordstrom.com. "They don't particularly care how a site looks, other than that it should look nice. They are not evaluating the design, good or bad."

"Customers don't come to a Web site to browse as you would a store or catalog," agreed Bill Bass of Lands' End. "Customers are not looking for a shopping experience. They don't want music playing in the background. They don't want little dancing bunnies on the screen. They want to get in, do what they want to do, and get out."

Laurie Tucker, senior vice president of FedEx, heartily stressed that when a company creates a Web site, "they need to be smart, but not fancy. Gee-whiz bells and whistles are not useful. They aggravate users."

Early on, focus groups of customers told FedEx that they wanted basic information and they wanted it fast, simple, and uncluttered. "Along the way we learned that fedex.com initially was a very Information-Technology-driven Web site because it initially came out of the IT group," said Karen Rogers, vice president for electronic-commerce marketing at FedEx. "Our marketing department partnered with our IT department to combine functionality and design. They gave us insight into how we serve up a very rich experience and yet enhance the speed. Now, we have one of the fastest Web sites. Before we redesigned the site, we weren't even on the radar screen in terms of speed."

Enron's clickpaper.com division is designed so that customers can quickly and efficiently buy or sell a forest product at the click of a mouse, according to Greg Piper, president and chief executive officer of Enron Net Works, which oversees clickpaper.com. "We tried first to do Step One correctly—quickly and efficiently capture the order. To us, seamless service means that customers can enter our secure Web environment and be able to know what they are getting, at what price, under what quality specifications, and at what location it will be delivered. They want to know quickly whether they can transact the deal. They want to be able to see how the order is captured and how the transaction goes through their system and our system. And when they leave, they want to be done."

At Tesco's Web site, where customers are ordering dozens and dozens of grocery items, "it's not so much how pretty it looks; it's about speed and ease of use," explained John Browett, CEO of tesco.com, which features a simple economical layout. "If you are buying an average of 72 items in a basket, you need to go through those things very fast indeed. We've worked on trying to make that process as easy as possible for you by making the site really quick. That reflects a fundamental understanding of the customer experience. It's very easy to get wrapped up into graphics and three-dimensional images. Those are all great things, but they make the download time so slow that they no longer make the site a functional one. Some people in the states have criticized our Web site. But we know it's fast; it's quick and it works easily and logically for our customer."

Tesco customers can shop in a couple of different ways. They can browse departments that are laid out logically or they can use the individual customer's "Favorites List," which includes what that person has previously bought both online and in the store. "That's a huge customer benefit because that means she doesn't have to search through 20,000 to 40,000 items to find the things she usually buys," said Browett. "That's very seamless for the customer because she doesn't have to worry about whether her favorites are always there. We are doing all that behind the scenes for her." If she wants to buy items that are not on her Favorites List, she can use "Express Shopper," by typing in a grocery list that goes into the Tesco database. When she types in "bread," she is given all the bread alternatives, and then clicks on her selection.

The Geek Squad, the iconoclastic computer repair firm based in Minneapolis, offers customers a simple, no-frills Web site because, "We assume our clients are not computer-sophisticated; otherwise, they wouldn't be coming to our site," reasoned owner Robert Stephens. "The site loads quickly. We make the log-in simple. We don't want you to create another damn user name and password to access The Geek Squad." Perhaps most important, The Geek Squad has its telephone number and office address shown clearly on the site. The Geek Squad uses its site as a marketing tool and a lure for customers. The site clearly displays a list of help topics—everything from how to deal with power surges and with spam e-mail to how to buy a computer or a Palm Pilot. In a feature called "5 Tips for Buying a New Computer," there are links to the Web sites of the four computer manufacturers that The Geek Squad recommends: Dell, Gateway, Micron, and Compaq. "We're trying to increase our customer base by offering easy-to-find help right on the site. The information was designed for a customer to print it out and fax it to a buddy," said Stephens. "The site is there to help, educate, and entertain."

Once the San Francisco Giants built Pacific Bell Park, the notion of "customer service" on the Web site was dedicated to answering questions that customers would have about the new facility: transportation, directions, maps of the neighborhood park, seating, amenities, food and beverage options—all the things that were different from their experiences at Candlestick Park, which had been the home of the Giants since 1960.

"A good site creates a lot of efficiencies for the organization," said Tom McDonald, senior vice president of consumer marketing. "It reduces the number of phone calls, questions that you get on the day of the game. We felt that it had a profound impact on people's education curve in the new facility."

One of those efficiencies helps to sell tickets.

"As we move forward with single-ticket buyers, computer-generated views from the seats are very helpful," said Russ Stanley, vice president of ticket services and client relations. "You are not buying blindly anymore. It gives more confidence to people buying on the Internet. They used to buy tickets at the ballpark because they thought that the seating inventory was better here. It's all the same, whether you are here at PacBell Park, one of our dugout stores or outlets around the Bay Area, or on the Internet. Now, we are using the expertise of our ticket sellers on the Internet so people don't have to come here and they can buy the tickets from their homes."

Speed Thrills

For most of us—particularly those with a 56K modem—the first criterion we use to judge a site is how quickly it downloads. We can't emphasize too strongly that cute animation and flashy splash screens are great for showing off, but not for doing business. Sorry, we don't have the time.

Dan Nordstrom envisions the day when people will have access at home to fast, broadband Internet connections because "That's the point at which we expect fashion products to really take off. With most people now using 56K modems, you have to have a pretty spare presentation on the Web site. The things that are going to increase business online are more speed, better search tools, and an environment that's merchandised in a way that makes sense."

FedEx's Laurie Tucker emphasized that, "We need to understand that the world is not on a T1 line like we are in our offices. We must build Web sites to meet the needs of the customer who is still on the slowest dial-up." If you engineer your Web site for looks and not speed, you are putting your customers on notice that you are an egotistical, self-centered company that thinks that it's more important that you flash your logo in five colors than provide them with speed. "It's very important to us at FedEx that we be very quick because that shows sensitivity and respect for the customer."

You show that sensitivity and respect for the customer by putting yourself in the shoes of your customers so that you can anticipate their every step. Virtually every department—not just marketing or information technology— in your organization should be involved in fine-tuning your Web site.

Your home page is where you make your initial impression. It is the most crucial *touchpoint* to your customers. Consequently, you want that first page to be downloaded quickly. Online consumers have been found to wait as long as 13.2 seconds before abandoning a lazy-loading home page, according to a study by Boston Consulting Group, which also found that almost 21 percent of impatient shoppers will go somewhere else before the home page is fully loaded. Can you imagine losing one-fifth of potential customers because they couldn't reach you on the telephone or couldn't push their way through the doors of your store? Your home page should tell users where they are, who you are, what they'll be able to do, and where on the site they'll be able to get it done. That's it. The rest will follow.

Now that I've arrived at your home page, I want to be greeted as if I've walked into a brick-and-mortar store or the reception area of a firm. When I'm online, of course I'm not looking for a human being to acknowledge my presence, but I do hope to find clearly marked signs to point me in the right direction. I don't want to be distracted by clutter and noise. One good strong message with some ancillary messages will be fine, thank you very much. Rather than compel me to keep scrolling down pages, please confine and minimize your home page to a couple of screens below what I first see when I log on to your site.

And while we're talking about minimizing, please lessen the information you want from me. I know you'd love to have my age, income, likes, dislikes, favorite color, etc., but, sorry, I don't have time right now. If I want to fill out your forms, I'll do it later—I promise—but don't prevent me from trying to give you my money—now!

REI's Joan Broughton emphasized the point that retailers must realize that "you are not selling to techies." When a customer logs on to rei.com, the back-end support operation of the Web site is retrieving customer information, such as previous purchases, credit card number, etc. Even though, by having this information, REI makes it easier for the customer to shop, "The customer doesn't care. You want to make it easy for them. But, at the same time, you want to be able to replicate the good parts of the [brick-and-mortar REI] store experience. Online, if there are points at which you have to ask for the information, you need to at least let people know that this too will pass, and they will be able to get what they want, and go on."

Amazon.com's site has gone—and will continue to go—through many changes. Even though amazon.com is a pure-play Internet retailer, its Web site provides valuable lessons to multichannel companies. When, early on, amazon.com began expanding its product line from purely books to CDs, DVDs, videos, etc., in the process it added a bevy of new tabs until the home page was a bit of a cluttered mess. The company eventually cleaned up the muddle by reducing the main tabs down to two—"Welcome" and "Store Directory"—and provided links to product categories. "When you come into a store, you need a soft landing where you can take a breath and orient yourself, as opposed to getting assaulted by a barrage of offers all at once. We wanted to create that soft landing online," explained Maryam Mohit, vice president of site design for Amazon, who told the *New York Times* that her design team was influenced by the book *Why We Buy: The Science of Shopping*, by Paco Underhill, founder of Envirosell, a marketing research firm that studies shopping behavior. According to Underhill's book, "In the world of cyberspace, everywhere is an exit. You have the capacity to bail out at any point, and an enormous number of people do."

Amazon.com has always offered a text-only version of its Web site. This version has been developed so that it works for people with certain disabilities, such as impaired motor skills, as well as customers who prefer the quicker download time. Luxury retailer Neiman Marcus's Web site also offers text-based information, which quickly directs the customer to the designer boutique they are looking for.

EnronOnline, the largest business-to-business e-commerce site in the world, caters to a sophisticated commodity-trading community—mostly large market-making houses in the energy business, which have T1 lines and state-of-the-art computers. These companies aren't averse to downloading applications that allow Enron to paint their screens with lots of visuals and information.

But with its clickpaper.com division, Enron is catering to the forest products industry, where many users are located at a mill or a lumberyard, with a laptop and a 56K modem. Consequently, Clickpaper is short on visuals but long on text-based information. Clickpaper's primary goal is to transmit its base prices to customers "in less than a second," said Greg Piper, president and CEO of Enron Net Works, which includes clickpaper.com. "We also put out a lot of data-based information, such as industry news and historical information. It's got to get to the customers quickly."

Recreational Equipment, Inc. was faced with a particular challenge for its home page. Because the rei.com site was tailored to members of the consumer cooperative, the first question new users were asked was their membership number. "The member number provides REI with a lot of information about you, and helps you an awful lot. But when you ask that of somebody who has never seen or heard of REI before, that person will probably leave because he will say, 'I didn't know this was a private site,'" said Joan Broughton. "For someone who is a pro at shopping REI, that doesn't cause a moment's hesitation. But we certainly want people who are going through our site for the first time, and who like what they see, to not be scared off by something that is not meant to scare them off. We needed to reorganize that information. But the way that our process is set up with our back-end, that was more difficult than it sounds. It's built from the code up, so we had to change the code underneath it to make it work." When customers first log on to rei.com, they are no longer asked for their membership numbers. That comes in later, when they order a product.

Navigation:
The Little Search Engine That Could

Okay, now that I'm on your Web site, how do I find what I'm looking for? If your search technology is lacking, you'll be chasing away potential customers. The Web site for the QVC television shopping channel, iQVC, discovered that more than 50 percent of its customers used the search box to maneuver through the site. QVC transformed the search function so that customers could search for items such as rings by color, brand, size, and price. With a smart, intuitive search tool that capitalizes on your database, you can slice and dice that database in an infinite number of ways that will help customers make decisions—quickly.

Consistency in purpose and design are prerequisites of a user-friendly Web site. Customers feel comfortable negotiating a site that features consistent elements. On sites such as powells.com and rei.com, the categories for products and services are always listed on the left-hand side of the screen, regardless of where you are on the site. Users want to be able to navigate the site as they feel, and not have to worry about retracing their steps, like Hansel and Gretel dropping bread crumbs to mark their trail back home.

"Customers come back because they find what they are looking for," said Dan Nordstrom, president of nordstrom.com. "We think the Web shopping session needs to occur in five minutes or less. You need to get to the Web site, find the item, and check out in five minutes." Before Nordstrom could offer this kind of experience, "We first had to understand what service was online. It's not necessarily like service in the store. Service is whatever the customer needs it to be at that moment. That was something that we learned, that was not self-evident on Day One. The idea of a fast Web site is the equivalent of a store with ample parking."

REI has done the unusual thing of developing in-house its own product-search engine and has worked on improving it ever since it launched rei.com in 1996. "You can't go out and buy a generic search engine that's going to understand your hierarchy—the things that are important to your customers revolve around brand, price, etc.," said senior vice president Matt Hyde. "All of the elements are so essential to the delivery results that the search engine has to match the way that our online store was set up and match the logic that we use around the specialty shops and product categories."

Bill Bass of Lands' End believed that most customers were logging onto the site not to look for recommendations but rather to find items that were already predetermined before they logged on. "They know what they are looking for—'I want snow boots for my kids'—and they want to know how quickly they can get in, get the snowboots, and get out." Shoppers on landsend.com can move quickly from one area to the next because navigation is made easy with tabs for each product category, which are located across the top of the page. With a couple of clicks, shoppers can easily move with their shopping cart from women's shorts to kids' shoes. Permanent site features, such as requesting a catalog or tracking an order, remain fixed on each page.

Faster pages are a byproduct of smart design. "You need to be a minimalist in style when you're designing a Web page," said Bass. "Thumbnail graphics, which are a lot heavier than text, offer more visual information and appeal. You don't need to have a lot of pictures, and the pictures that you do have must be there for a purpose. Make them small. Everything you put on a page makes the page bigger. The bigger the page, the slower it is. The design principle is to make a site fast, and there are a thousand techniques to accomplish that. Speed kills; that's the most important thing." Lands' End, REI, and other firms use a "caching" technique pioneered by Akamai Technologies, Inc., which speeds up the downloading of frequently requested pages (that don't change very much) by pre-storing their Web site's graphics on Akamai servers around the world and then quickly distributing them to the customer via their Web site. For example, if a landsend.com order comes in from Rome, Italy, Akamai has servers in Rome that are storing the graphics on Lands' End's pages, "so the customer from Rome doesn't have to get the graphics from our U.S. site, and then cart them back to Rome. The graphics are right there in Rome. He goes through the Lands' End site, but it is sitting physically on a box, right next to our landsend.com box. It's hosted right here at our headquarters in Dodgeville, Wisconsin."

Although the downloading of product photos slows down the process, photos are essential when it comes to products such as clothing, where the crucial elements are the attractive visuals of the items and the elegant prose that is used to describe those items. Nordstrom was faced with doing its own photography for the products it sells on nordstrom.com, just as it does for its print catalogs. But when you have 60,000 images, at a price of $300 to $500 each, you get costs that are "out of control," said Dan Nordstrom. To help solve this problem, Nordstrom uses software from a company called TrueSpectra, which specializes in scalable imaging solutions. TrueSpectra enables a Web site to display a single image at several different sizes, allowing shoppers to get a closer look at the item by zooming in or panning across. A site needs to load only one image of an item because with a simple click, customers can change the color of the item.

"Ease of Use" Should Be Your Mantra

Just as the door to your place of business should be easy to use, so should your Web site. "'Ease of use' is our mantra," said Karen Rogers, vice president for electronic-commerce marketing at FedEx. "We researched different designs in order to create the most usable experience. We wanted to be able to find what functionality our customers wanted. We didn't want to offer our customers something that was self-serving. Instead of asking what was important to us, we decided to take the customer approach and find out what was important to them. On our Web site, which is our primary channel for servicing our customers, we are providing them with the speed of the information and the richness of the content. We have found that the customers are using this channel far more than even our 800 number, primarily to track their packages. They are also shipping their packages, checking rates, ordering supplies, and looking for their drop-off locations— basic access to all the information you could ever want to know about FedEx."

Wells Fargo is a strong advocate of keeping a site simple. This philosophy is summed up in one key guideline for the site: "You are one click away from anything you want to know," said Executive Vice President Gailyn Johnson.

Most of the companies featured here are catering to an unsophisticated audience, so they try to make things as simple as possible. At Oncology Therapeutics Network, the Web site uses minimal graphics, lots of white background space, and no clutter on the screen. There is only one clear action on every screen. "We design it in the way the customer uses it," said Chief Information Officer Sue Dubman. "An advisory board of doctors and administrators give us feedback on what's useful or not useful; what they like; what they don't like. For example, there is a section on when upcoming invoices are due. We tell the medical practice that we will give them a certain amount off of their bill if they pay within a particular period of time. We'll also let them know when one of their contracts [for ordering oncology medication] is about to expire."

Some of the Web sites of the companies included in this book are pretty slick and professional. One site that is purposely unslick—reflecting the funkiness of its physical flagship store—is powells.com. "The spirit of Powell's comes out in whatever we do in every direction," said Darin Sennett of powells.com. "That's because we are cheap. We won't go into debt to finance something crazy, so we have to do everything ourselves. The Web site is a true physical manifestation of what we are as a company—the people who work here, the books that we buy, the way the store looks, the way the shelves are stocked."

Sennett proudly pointed out that no one who has worked on the design of the site has ever taken an art class. "What's always struck me about our site is its lack of professionalism in design," Sennett said, tongue partially in cheek. "I find that good design is sometimes asphyxiating in that there is an airtight, seamless, perfectly well-designed piece. For some sites, that works pretty well. Over time, we have been able to turn our lack of professionalism into an asset. We don't want to lose that fun factor. We don't want it to look too nice. We're not about perfection. We're about that old weird used book that you couldn't find anywhere else."

Shop With(out) Abandon

Just as in any good brick-and-mortar store, online stores should clearly distinguish their product departments and checkout stands. The shopping cart, clearly identified, should always be on the same spot on the screen, preferably the upper-right-hand corner, and it should display the most current added item. That feature enables customers to keep a running account of what they have purchased.

Throughout the experience, the help button must always be present and obvious. Customer service information, such as a telephone number, mailing address, and e-mail link, as well as answers to frequently asked questions, should be prominently displayed. The business-to-business site clickpaper.com does this as well as any site. At the bottom of *every* page are the words: "Call our toll free number for customer support. The Americas: +1 800-986-3837 or +1 713-345-4357. Europe & Other Regions: +44 (0) 20 7783 3434 or email us at: customersupport@clickpaper.com." No matter where you are, you know you can be rescued anytime, anywhere.

Multichannel retailers are working to coordinate their inventory systems for all channels, so that online customers will be able to access the same merchandise sold in the brick-and-mortar stores. If an item or a size or color is out of stock, the best sites have already grayed it out, so that it will not be sold. And of course, the transaction must be accurate, i.e., what the customer expects to buy had better be what shows up in the mailbox on the day it's expected, and at the price that the customer expected to pay.

As customers shop your site, you are keenly aware that they could abandon you at any time. Some surveys show that as many as 75 percent of Internet shoppers vacate a Web site before making a purchase. At REI, "We have tried to improve upon all of the places where people are likeliest to abandon the process, such as the checkout," said Joan Broughton. Checkout needs to be fast, short, and easy; if not you'll lose sales from frustrated or impatient customers. There are potential pitfalls in any area "where you are asking people to do a self-service version of what would be taken care of seamlessly in the stores. Almost every site that has been around for any length of time was initially built from the code up. If you have a Web site sitting on a legacy [pre-existing] store [inventory] system—as many multichannel retailers do—then you have a process that you have to somehow duplicate online—a system that was based on what works in the store. So, you have to be careful not to put customers through their paces in a way that is onerous or confusing."

Sometimes, the final obstacle to a sale is shipping costs—but not if you've explicitly spelled out your shipping terms on your home page, or at least supplied a clearly marked link to your policy on shipping costs that your shoppers can readily locate. The importance of being clear on this is supported by a study conducted by the Yankee Group, which showed that 56 percent of customers surveyed cancelled their order when they found out the shipping charges were too high.

Ordering and Fulfillment:
Getting It Together

At least 70 percent of online shoppers make at least one query about the status of their order, according to a survey by the Ernst & Young accounting firm. Consequently, companies need to have their systems in place so that the customer gets the merchandise ordered. (I know that this is painfully basic advice. But great customer service is built on paying attention to the basics.)

That's where many companies fall down on the job, according to Matt Hyde of REI, who has seen "so many businesses focused on the front end and they didn't understand the back end. I liken a Web site to an iceberg. What you can see is the tip of the iceberg. All the work that you do, all the programming and the resources and the customer service is 90 percent of your infrastructure." Unlike many companies that rushed to establish a Web presence and cut corners by limiting—or even skipping—integration with their existing systems and fulfillment operations, REI integrated the fulfillment for all its channels. Because co-op members needed to be able to get credit for whatever orders they placed, wherever they placed them, REI in 1997 became one of the first retailers to provide a common inventory and pricing database for in-store, catalog, and Web-site operations. And why not? REI's new distribution center in Sumner, Washington, with six miles of conveyor belts, was already taking care of store and catalog fulfillment out of the same inventory.

Hyde has found that the package-delivery expectations of online customers differ slightly from those of their catalog counterparts, and REI has had to react accordingly. Online customers have "electronic expectations. They were not satisfied with the regular shipment time that we have for our mail order business. People who shopped mail-order were used to paying shipping, and waiting for packages and back orders. Today, a lot bigger universe of people are shopping online. A lot of those people aren't used to mail order and they don't like paying for shipping. They don't like waiting for packages. They don't like back orders. We had to address that. So, we made a major investment in our distribution center to increase ship times. We went from about 5 to 7 days nationwide service to 1 to 3 days nationwide service at a flat shipping rate of $3.99. That's expensive. We subsidize our shipping. But the month that we did that, our customer-performance rating instantly went from 8.5 to 9.4. It's amazing how you can impact service and customer satisfaction in this medium and see it so quickly."

Feedback: The Customer Speaks

The most user-friendly Web sites have been designed and redesigned based on the feedback they get from their users.

To get feedback on what its customers wanted in its Web site, Frederick's of Hollywood used a series of surveys that customers filled out to enter contests. Frederick's learned from its customers that they liked navigating Web sites that featured "pull-down" menus, which is the basis of many offline applications such as Microsoft Office and all e-mail programs. With a pull-down menu, when users place their cursor on the icon or word for a product category, all the products in that category appear as a linked list, directly under the icon or word.

"Customers are used to using that [pull-down] metaphor in dealing with technology and with computer screens," said Gary Landry. "So, if you continue to reinforce that metaphor, then they become comfortable with that." He cautioned that new versions can't be radically different from their predecessors. "We started with a pulldown menu that had a "SHOP" button, and underneath that were the categories you currently see on the Web site. Customers said they wanted to see the categories up all the time, and then have the subcategories on a pull down. So, we migrated from one pulldown mini-structure to another. We didn't radically change everything. We made that one change."

Frederick's makes major navigation changes to its site every six months; minor changes every month or two. The company will often do a soft launch of a feature without announcing it. "We make sure that it's working and the customer likes it," said Landry. "Then we do a press release or e-mail or highlight it on the Web site. We tell the customer it is an experiment and may or may not be a permanent feature. We want their feedback and comment. We like to have friends and family—people who are not so close to the products—test them out. We have them run through any new feature that we are adding. We try to make sure that all of our wording is understandable to the lay customer."

Wells Fargo also extensively uses online surveys on a regular basis "to give us customer feedback when we are trying to prioritize our projects. We ask them what is important to them. We have focus groups for usability testing. They tell us what features of functionality they care most about," said Wendy Grover, director of public relations for the bank's Internet Services Group. "As we bring up new functionality, we need to know what the experience is like from the customer perspective. We must make sure that the experience the customer is having on the site or across channels makes sense."

Karen Rogers, vice president for electronic-commerce marketing at FedEx, emphasized that her company is fanatical about getting customer feedback on design improvements, such as the size and efficiency of images on the site.

Rogers's boss, Laurie Tucker, said that getting feedback from customers about adding new features is the best way to understand customer thinking and to create value for those customers. "If you are in an environment where you have large competitors, who have done a good job of nearly duplicating your services, then the only way that you are going to differentiate yourself and hold up your price/value ratios is to keep adding value—without adding a lot of costs. Before we add a new service, we first get feedback from our customers. We ask them: 'Would you give us more business if we offered you this service?' If we don't get a 'yes,' then we question whether we should do it. If we ask customers if they would be willing to pay more for a service and the answer is 'no,' then that tells you how much value there is in that service. We have to be careful not to do cutesy things just because we can. We need to look at the things that are going to add value."

When REI launched its site in 1996, the first customers, the early adopters, were Internet savvy and were "extremely vocal" regarding the site, recalled Matt Hyde. "When they would find problems with the site they would e-mail us code fixes. Today, people are not as tolerant or as likely to give you the feedback. Right up front, you have to be right. To this date, we take every e-mail that the customer sends us, we categorize it as far as suggestions or places where customers are getting stuck, and we put it into a job list to fix. I have mixed emotions about every e-mail. On one level, I look at each one as a gift. Every negative e-mail is also a little failure. We have to figure out how to remove that particular burden from our customers."

REI and other companies have found that the Web is an inexpensive way to create and test new businesses or offer new products and categories—because it doesn't have to touch the finite space in its 60 brick-and-mortar stores and in its catalogs. Responding to feedback from focus groups, rei.com began offering an assortment of products in flyfishing and fitness—two categories that don't exist in REI's physical stores or catalog. It took REI ten weeks to construct the online fitness store and five weeks for the fly-fishing shop. By contrast, if REI installed these departments in a physical store, it would have taken at least six months to achieve. Based on successful online sales, REI introduced into some of its stores fitness products such as scooters, rollerblades, and running shoes, and rolled them out into other stores because they were so successful online.

"In a physical store, we're confined by a box," explained Hyde. "The Internet allows us to grow and expand business."

Based on feedback from customers, Enron's clickpaper.com added a feature that enables customers to calculate currency from Euros to dollars.

Features: Setting Your Site Apart

Each one of the featured companies is chock full of features that set their site apart. In some cases, it's not just having the feature; it's the way that you use it that counts. In this section, we'll discuss some of my favorite features, which serve the purpose of utilizing the technology that makes the Web an essential channel.

Earlier, we discussed how two out of every three online shoppers abandon their shopping carts before making a purchase. Many online retailers believe the chances of retaining those customers markedly increase when they provide those customers with personal contact with a human connection, either through a toll-free telephone number or live chat online. According to a survey by Jupiter Research, 90 percent of online customers prefer some form of human interaction during an e-commerce transaction. To those customers, it's not enough that a site offers direction through text-based information and frequently asked questions (FAQs). This is especially true on sites that sell clothing because of the myriad of variables in determining fit, size, and color.

Lands' End Live

Through "live chat," questions can be answered and purchase suggestions can be made instantly by customer service representatives who know the merchandise because they've been trained in how to sell it, and because usually they have the merchandise right at their fingertips in the call centers. Live chat is also more cost effective for a retailer like Lands' End, which can have one well-trained employee deal with as many as four online chats at one time. Some sites feature software that enables the company's personal shoppers to transmit digital images of the items to a customer's screen, which allows buyer and seller to view the same item at the same time.

Lands' End (as is REI) is one of the premiere proponents of live chat, with its Lands' End Live feature. As Bill Bass explained it: "Lands' End is committed to providing customers with the most personal and responsive shopping experience available anywhere online. We constantly ask ourselves: 'How can we use technology, this new tool that we have, to do better customer service? What could we do online that we couldn't do in the catalog, because we are limited by the form of the catalog?' Every year, we try to roll out something that nobody else has done before, something that we think will affect how people shop on the Internet. In 1999, we added Lands' End Live."

Lands' End Live synthesizes the company's e-commerce, customer service, and telephony infrastructure by enabling shoppers to browse the site while they are in real-time communication with service representatives by phone or text-based chat, 24 hours a day, seven days a week. Customers click on the Lands' End Live button on their computer (no special plug-ins or software required) and enter their name and phone number. An electronic signal is transmitted from the customer's computer to a Lands' End Live personal shopper. The signal immediately calls back the customer and simultaneously connects a personal shopper to the customer by phone and Internet browser. They can talk through text messages while pushing Web pages to each other, and can simultaneously view the same Web pages.

"To me, [the communication] works better if you choose the phone because it's a more natural conversation than chat," said

Bass. "Initially, it's a spookier experience for the customer if she uses the phone because we answer so quickly. Our standard of service is the same as we have for the main telephones—to answer within 20 seconds. It's been running about 7 seconds. Seven seconds after you push the Lands' End Live button, your phone rings: 'This is Sally from Lands' End Live. May I help you?'" Lands' End has found that 80 percent of customers who use Lands' End Live prefer to use live chat rather than the telephone, perhaps because most people shop from work, where they often have access to high-speed connections and a separate phone line.

Lands' End has trained several hundred sales reps to answer specific questions live online about product features such as size, color, how to complete a purchase, shipping options, and how to navigate to other areas of the site. Reps can also help the customer put together a wardrobe by splitting the browser to show the customer a pair of cotton shorts and a T-shirt together. These personal shoppers have the capability and background to make multiple sales because they have an average of nine years' experience assisting Lands' End customers by phone on the catalog side, and have completed an average of nearly 500 hours of training, including 70 to 80 hours of product, customer service, and computer training when initially hired and an additional 24 hours each year thereafter.

This extra attention to the customer is paying off. According to Nielson Net Ratings, Lands' End converts more than 10 percent of its Web visitors to buyers—compared with the industry average of 4.9 percent.

San Francisco Giants' Double Play Exchange Window

When the Giants first began selling season tickets to its stadium, Pacific Bell Park, which opened for the 2000 season, the team offered customers only one plan—to buy full season tickets. But few people can attend all 84 games—81 in the regular season; three in the exhibition season.

With that strategy, "We were shifting the burden to the ticketholder," conceded Tom McDonald, vice president for consumer marketing. "They would have to either broker those tickets or get a cluster of friends to split them up. After putting in all that effort to make the sale, the worst thing for us would be to lose that customer because he had a bad experience trying to manage his investment in those 84 tickets."

To resolve that situation, the Giants did two things. First, they allowed customers to partner with friends, family, colleagues, business contacts, etc. to share a season ticket.

The other innovation was something that could have been done only on the Web. The Giants provided a handy little bit of technological wizardry to help fans peddle tickets that they couldn't use. The team borrowed a low-tech idea from the Baltimore Orioles baseball team, which instituted a "scalp-free zone"—a physical location at the Camden Yards ballpark where a season ticket holder can legally sell a ticket without a premium. "We thought it was a nice service, but it's a lot of trouble because you have to show up to the ballpark for a game you're not going to attend," recalled McDonald. "We figured that there had to be an easier way through technology to do this."

So, the Giants devised the Double Play Ticket Window—a place where a season ticketholder puts up the game ticket for sale on the Giants Web site, sfgiants.com. The team established a floor price—the face value of the ticket—but it decided not to establish a ceiling price. If the game date is fast approaching, and the fan is concerned about selling his ticket, he is allowed to modify the price. When another fan agrees to buy the ticket at the posted price, he types in his name, phone number, address, and credit card number. The seller is notified by e-mail that the ticket has been purchased and that his account has been credited. The seller doesn't have to return the physical ticket to Pacific Bell Park.

The buyer is sent the ticket's five-digit code, and is given the choice of either having the ticket mailed to him (if it's far enough in advance of the game) or going to Pacific Bell Park to one of the on-site ATM machines, which have ticket-dispensing capabilities. The buyer uses the credit card used to purchase the tickets in the ATM and the ticket (with a unique 12-character security code) spits out of the ATM. As soon as the transaction occurs, the ticket held by the season ticketholder is voided. The barcode for the new ticket is read by the ball park's electronic turnstiles, and the buyer heads to his seat to watch Barry Bonds hit another home run.

The Giants put in place some precautionary mechanisms to keep everything under control, and to make sure there weren't too many offers out there. A seller couldn't have more than five offers up at any given time. The team released the games on a month-by-month basis.

"We didn't want it to be a situation where scalpers were selling their full season's tickets," said McDonald. "We wanted to limit supply to the upcoming games that were the most topical. Let's say you have two $36 tickets that would sell for $72, and you put them up for $100. The seller had to monitor it, if he wanted to make sure his tickets were sold. Typically, if there was a huge premium, the tickets wouldn't sell. Then, you would have to go back in and reprice them. If you put them up for $150, they usually wouldn't sell. There was no bargaining and no feedback."

The Giants maintained control of the situation throughout. The team didn't start the service until mid-June 2000 and only with the very best seats, which were held by 5,000 charter season ticketholders, who controlled about 16,000 seats in the Charter Seat program. Then the team opened it up to another 4,000 season ticketholders, representing about 12,000 seats, toward the end of the season.

For the team and the fans, it was a win-win situation. "It was absolutely the right process and was very successful," said McDonald. For the Giants, "it opened up our ticket universe. Some people who are visiting San Francisco feel they can't get a ticket. But this supplies an avenue for them. They may have to pay more than face value, but they don't have to go to a broker. We couldn't have done that anywhere other than the Web. It was the perfect place to do that."

Promoting a Sense of Community: We're All in This Together

REI has several features on its Web site that help promote a sense of community among the consumer cooperative's 1-million-plus members, who share a love of outdoor adventure. REI customers use message boards to swap tales of their experiences, discuss the relative merits of products, or post photographs of their adventures.

With a link on rei.com called "Learn & Share," customers can find out more about in-store REI clinics on topics such as backpacking, hydration, and bike maintenance, and are provided with a selection of gear for whatever and wherever their adventures take them. For example, in the "Learn" section, under "How To Fit a Backpack," the Web site has detailed instructions on how to choose a pack well suited to the individual's dimensions and how to customize it based on body shape. In the "Share" section, customers can find hundreds of articles on virtually every aspect of outdoor life: camping, hiking, snow sports, cycling, climbing, etc., as well as read posted comments from other member customers. From those articles, there are links back to REI products that are specific to that particular activity.

"It used to be that we were very good at providing product knowledge. We are now moving more to helping people purchase the product," said Brian Unmacht, vice president of REI's retail division. "We talk today about a 'selling culture' at REI. In the old days, we were good at providing the information, but that didn't necessarily end in a sale. Today, we are trying to help people figure out the product they need, where they want to go, how they want to use it—and help our sales people sell."

Community has become part of Tesco's strategy. In July 2000, the U.K. supermarket chain joined in a 50/50 joint venture with iVillage, Inc., the operator of the U.S.-based women's network, to form ivillage.com, for the purpose of communicating with—and creating an online community among—women shoppers in the U.K. and Ireland. Because women are expected to account for 60 percent of all online users by 2005, Tesco feels that it can get closer to those customers through iVillage's formula of practical solutions and everyday support for women, and its commercial tie-ins across 16 interactive channels covering topics such as astrology, beauty, computers, diet and fitness, and relationships.

The San Francisco Giants have a natural community composed of fans of the team. The Web site has a lineup of features that promote and exploit the fans' interest in the team. There are chat rooms and message boards for would-be managers and general managers to second-guess and offer their opinions on how the team should be run, who should play or not play, and who should be traded. The site offers news of the team and the ballpark; auctions for items such as autographed bats and balls; and an online store, where a fan can buy an "authentic" Barry Bonds All-Star Game Batting Practice Jersey for $129.50 or a San Francisco Giants Ladies Spaghetti Strap Tank ("What better top to wear to the game on those muggy July and August nights?" reads the Web site description).

Frederick's of Hollywood's "Ask Amanda"

As it has been reconfiguring itself from a retro purveyor of feminine cheesecake to a hip and contemporary multichannel retailer, Frederick's of Hollywood has been appealing to young, with-it women who share a particular slant on life. One of the ways fredericks.com is creating a community of like-minded women is through a lifestyle column called "Absolutely Amanda," an Ann Landers–like slant on—among other things—how to buy the appropriate lingerie. "Amanda" is spokeswoman Amanda Frank, who answers questions from women who e-mail her about topics such as how to be fitted for a bra or what to wear after the Super Bowl to get the attention of a football-addled husband.

Frederick's has had "absolutely phenomenal feedback on the Absolutely Amanda column," marveled Gary Landry, president of fredericks.com. "The single biggest point of feedback is that customers are completely taken aback that there really is an Amanda, and that she does personally answer their e-mail. These are not stock answers. They ask very detailed questions, such as, 'I bought this wedding dress with this type of neckline, and I'm wearing this color. Can you tell me the things that I'm missing? What type of corset would look best?'"

Amanda also writes a weekly column that talks about not only the merchandise that Frederick's sells but also fun fashion things, such as what women are wearing at the Oscars and Grammys and the new trends in fashion. "Even if we don't sell that trend, we will probably be selling something that fits under that trend," said Landry. Customers subscribe to the Ask Amanda column and have it e-mailed directly to them.

The Frederick's Web site also features a link called fredericksflowers, powered by proflowers.com, which ships long-stemmed roses, tulips, or a "carnival of color" bouquet to a loved one in seven days. "Flowers really are the ultimate gift of love, and eventually we plan to have gift shipments that will include flowers and lingerie, as well as other romantic items like videos, books, electronic greeting cards, chocolates, gourmet food, wine, and romantic getaways," explained Landry. "A customer can get all of this on one site for one-stop shopping. Part of our strategy is that we want Frederick's to be your trusted one-stop shop for romance, special occasions, and gift giving between a man and a woman."

FedEx: A Community of Small Businesses

"We're always looking for services to offer small businesses in order to create loyalty," said Laurie Tucker of FedEx. "We believe small businesses will grow into large businesses if we help them become successful. As we begin to understand what the customers are using on our Web site, we can direct information to them. We have found that the small customer needs the low price and ease of access; the larger customer wants to smoothly integrate a solution into the way they already operate."

Fedex.com offers small businesses a wide variety of featured services, beginning with the Small Business Center link, which offers a broad spectrum of information on topics such as management advice on managing cash flow or deciding which software to buy. The site presents how-to articles covering business management, taxation and finance, sales and marketing, computers and technology, and human resources. Small business operators can download presentations and tools, receive special FedEx offers (such as saving up to 7 percent on popular IBM products and solutions), or find customized forms to print and use immediately.

"The site is constantly kept up to date in terms of the richness of new information for small business," said Tucker. That's what is so unique about the Web experience. You can provide much more to the customer than you could in the person-to-person experience. This is not to take away from the person-to-person experience. We will never, ever eliminate that; it will always be there. Our vision is that, over time, both experiences become enriched as a result of our technology. We don't use technology for its own sake. We use it to truly enhance the customer experience."

Another feature tailored for small businesses is the FedEx eCommerce Builder, which helps companies build and manage their own online store. Customers can choose whether they want a simple, basic site; whether they need a site for electronic commerce; or whether they want to add e-commerce capabilities to an existing site. Customers have the option of either building the site themselves—with the help of FedEx's programmers—or having those designers do all the building of the site.

Customers who need to learn how to ship a package internationally can log on to FedEx's Global Trade Manager, a one-stop online resource for simple, international trade tools and resources. Global Trade Manager provides U.S. customs import/export documents for shipping to or from the United States, Canada, Hong Kong, the United Kingdom, Puerto Rico, and Singapore. Through Global Trade Manager, a shipper can find the documents needed for shipment to a particular country, and a document library that provides printable import/export forms. Another tool allows the customer to permanently store relevant information, which makes return visits to Global Trade Manager that much quicker and more efficient. A feature called "International Resource Center" provides, among other things, daily news briefs, a currency converter, and customs regulations. "We can tell the customer if there are any problems in shipping a particular commodity to a particular country. It will even tell you if the individual you are shipping to is a restricted party," Laurie Tucker pointed out.

Beyond Your Borders: Building an International Business

In the mid-1990s, the native language of 80 percent of Web users was English. By the year 2004, that figure will fall to only 33 percent, according to estimates from Global Reach, Inc., a market research firm. As the World Wide Web truly becomes world wide, companies are broadening their scope beyond the confines of North America. The retailers who do international business stress that it is important to have a consistent look and feel to all areas of the site.

But there are many obstacles to constructing an e-commerce site that is multilingual. First of all, it's expensive—costing from tens of thousands to millions of dollars, depending on the size and scope of the site. Besides the subtleties of language, the site must be able to process orders in different currencies, characters, and size measurements. "If you can give customers the size conversion and currency conversions, the ability to understand how to order, and explain how those orders are processed in their native language, then the description of the item itself is not as important, because every item has a picture," said Landry of fredericks.com.

One of the other key challenges that Lands' End and other multichannel retailers face is adapting their product lines to local preferences for color and style. Although the apparel retailer will sometimes produce special items for the European market, it generally offers the same selection as it does in the U.S.

In late 2000, Lands' End launched country-specific Web sites in France, Italy, and Ireland, rather than create country-specific catalogs, which are much more expensive. The company had the ability to take this approach because the Internet is an inexpensive technique by which to enter a new market. If Lands' End customers in those countries also would like to have the catalog shopping option, Lands' End will launch mail-order catalogs in French and Italian. Lands' End already has established catalog/Internet joint ventures in Japan, Germany, and the U.K., and owns a British-based warehouse to distribute products across Europe.

Frederick's of Hollywood's Web site is increasingly popular overseas, particularly in England, Australia, Japan, and Germany. Not surprising, because many of Frederick's orders come from military personnel stationed overseas.

The lingerie retailer has learned to be sensitive to cultural differences and mores. "We are learning what might be offensive to the German culture or Japanese culture," said Landry. The company is also learning about holidays celebrated in other countries that might provide a tie-in to Frederick's merchandise. The Absolutely Amanda column can discuss a German holiday in German to make Germans "feel more a part of the community."

At Powell's Books, a big percentage of early online customers were overseas shoppers looking for technical books, which were difficult to get. Today, about 4 percent of Powell's sales come from international shoppers.

"It's been in my head since we started the Web site that we want to be the global bookstore. I've been pushing for foreign-language versions of our Web site," said Michael Powell. "But we don't mean it as a virtual bookstore like amazon.com. We want to be *the* global bookstore rooted in a brick-and-mortar environment—and carry the quality of that brick-and-mortar feel to the Internet."

Powell shows that a company doesn't have to be the size of FedEx or Lands' End to have an international business. Sometimes, you can do it by pure serendipity. Mike Powell knew a German wholesaler. A Powell's employee had a friend in Germany who offered to contract to develop a site for Powell's in Germany, to make sure the site was "culturally correct," recalled Powell. "My criteria was that it shouldn't read like it was written by an American learning German. It should have some of our idiosyncratic feel to it in German."

Powell believes that the small size of his company is an advantage to pulling off a project like this. "What I like about our setup is that I can ask, 'How can we get in Germany?' and the five people who can make it happen are sitting there talking to me. It wouldn't work for me if I had to ask that question in an e-mail environment. It would be hopeless. Human beings can't work that way. I don't know how Barnes & Noble or amazon.com handle that problem. We are always trying to create a sense that you are dealing with people whose normal life is involved in the bookstore, and that the Internet is an extension of that, rather than a virtual replacement for the bookstore."

Powell claimed that his was the first American company to have a legal trade relationship in Vietnam, because books were never embargoed. Later, when the company ventured into doing business in China, "I thought my fortune had been made," Powell wryly recalled. "We sold a container-load of one single title: the Sears catalog. But the week I shipped that container of catalogs over to China, Sears canceled the catalog."

FedEx currently offers its Web site in 204 countries in 13 languages, but the design is consistent throughout. The reason, Laurie Tucker told me, is that, "many Web sites look different as you go from country to country. But we know that our customers travel, and they have global operations. So, it really helps them know that 'tracking,' for example, is always in the same place on the screen, regardless of the language. It's important that we provide that seamless integrated experience around the world."

Add Value:
Form Alliances & Partnerships

Alliances and partnerships will help you distinguish yourself from the competition and add value to your site, as well as your entire company. "What it all points to is that companies are going to be successful by partnering. It's not a strange thing anymore," said Laurie Tucker. "Companies who successfully use alliances create unique product value for their customers. This is counter-cultural. We are not going it alone any more. We're going to partner more and more so that we can create more channel access and new product variations."

In order to deliver that extra value to the customer, to make the customer's online experience better, "you've constantly got to take risks," added Tucker. "Sometimes, we've gone online with an alliance partner and it didn't turn out like we thought it would. The nice thing about the Internet is that if something doesn't work, you can pull it back; it doesn't have to be there tomorrow."

FedEx has had a relationship for many years with Kinko's, the Texas-based retail chain that specializes in visual communications services, document creation, and copying. Kinko's has 1,100 retail locations in the United States, Canada, the Netherlands, Japan, South Korea, Australia, the United Arab Emirates, China, and Great Britain. FedEx operates its full-service "World Service Centers" in 150 U.S. Kinko's branches, each offering the latest document drop-off time available in that zip code area. With the

Kinko's-FedEx relationship, the documents can be created, copied, and shipped in one location.

Exploring how it could extend its relationship with Kinko's in the virtual world, FedEx came up with an idea that played to the strengths of both companies.

In fall 2000, kinkos.com and fedex.com launched a link from fedex.com to kinkos.com for same-day delivery and overnight delivery for most of the U.S. and select international markets. In a single transaction from their desktop, customers can prepare documents in multiple finished formats, such as black and white copies, bound color presentations, and color transparencies, and ship the finished documents to multiple recipients via FedEx, of course. The sender can even include personalized memos with each package and specify various arrival times, including same-day and overnight delivery. Customer support is available 24/7 via email and a toll-free telephone number. To offer customers even greater flexibility, documents can be printed and shipped online until 9 P.M. EST for next-business-day delivery or 8 P.M. local time for same-day delivery in specific markets.

Not surprisingly, this feature is popular with people who travel a lot. "If you are on the road, preparing a document, you can upload it as soon as you get to your hotel room, download it to Kinko's and have a bound, professional-looking document out to your five top customers within 24 hours," said Karen Rogers of FedEx.

                    ✻   ✻   ✻

As a popular, winning baseball team, the San Francisco Giants are constantly being approached by a roster full of corporate sponsors who would like to participate in promotions with the team and its star players.

"Our watchword for those kinds of partnerships is, we will do something if we feel strongly that the offer provides value to our customers, and our customers will perceive that value as a benefit to being a season ticketholder. If not, they don't have access to our mailing list." One regular partner has been the Automobile Association of America, which sponsors a cruise line tour for fans who get to meet Giants players. That tour is marketed to season ticketholders, who have first crack at signing up.

Oncology Therapeutics Network has been involved in an alliance with cancereducation.com since 1999, to provide full-service online oncology-drug information and continuing medical education and training for physicians, patients, and nurses. The business alliance links the two Web sites to provide medical professionals with the first fully integrated, comprehensive online source for oncology pharmaceuticals, education, and information. OTN's drug-ordering system is directly linked to cancereducation.com's Web site for the exclusive provision of cancer-related educational presentations and extensive informational services for oncology professionals. OTN is cancereducation.com's exclusive channel for the ordering and distribution of oncology pharmaceuticals and services for office-based oncologists.

According to Tom Ludlam, president of OTN, "Office-based oncologists are under tremendous time constraints from increased caseloads. That makes it ever more difficult to stay abreast of the latest treatment modalities and diagnostic procedures. By partnering with cancereducation.com, we are able to provide convenient access to up-to-the-minute information and educational programming, as well as other resources and tools customized for the oncology professional."

Cancereducation.com's video educational content connects users with major cancer centers, round-table discussions with thought leaders, symposia and medical conferences, and other live and archived multimedia educational events. The content is supported by a vast suite of online resources and tools to assist oncology professionals in their day-to-day practices, including a drug information database, Reuters Health News, online access to medical journals and other frequently consulted professional references, medical conference schedules, treatment guidelines, and a search engine for clinical trials.

OTN also has an alliance with an alternative medicine company called One Body, a source for treatments that go beyond traditional chemotherapy. So-called "traditional" doctors, who are not trained in alternative medicine and treatments, use One Body to learn about the alternatives that their patients might be using. "Usually a patient won't tell a doctor about this," said Sue Dubman, OTN's chief information officer. "We are giving more information to the patients who want more information. But, at the same time, we are giving the doctors the opportunity to know about what the patient is doing, so that they can advise them."

By offering an informative, well-designed Web channel, OTN is able to bring together various philosophies and points of view to help people get the treatment they need to save their lives.

❖   ❖   ❖

Takeaways

There is no clearer example of online customer service than a Web site that is simple, straightforward, and easy to navigate. Your Web site is your relationship channel with your customer; it is the fulcrum of your multichannel customer service strategy. Today's demanding customers want a site to provide attractive visuals, thorough product information, and fast and efficient performance.

♦ Because most Web sites are visited by customers with varying levels of computer sophistication, design your site with the least sophisticated in mind.

♦ The Web is essential to coordinating seamless service in a multichannel world.

♦ In Web site design, the KISS principle rules.

♦ Customers are not on the Internet to be entertained. They don't particularly care how a site looks, other than that it should look nice.

♦ Customers don't come to a Web site to browse as they would in a store or catalog. They say that want to get in, do what they want to do, and get out.

♦ Use your site to help and educate the customer.

♦ Demonstrate sensitivity and respect for the customer by putting yourself in the shoes of your customers so that you can anticipate their every step. That means using your Web site yourself to see if it's working the way you want it to.

♦ Virtually every department in your organization should be involved in the fine-tuning of your Web site.

♦ Your home page is where you make your initial impression. It is the most crucial *touchpoint* to your customers. Consequently, you want that first page to be downloaded quickly.

♦ The idea of a fast Web site is the equivalent of a store with ample parking.

♦ Faster pages are a byproduct of smart design.

♦ Ease of use: Just as the door to your place of business should be easy to use, so too should your Web site.

♦ With a smart, intuitive search tool that capitalizes on your database, you can slice and dice that database in an infinite number of ways that will help customers make decisions— quickly.

- The most user-friendly Web sites have been designed and redesigned based on the feedback they get from their users.
- It's not sufficient to have a particular feature on your Web site. You must also use that feature in a way that benefits the customer.
- Regardless of the language of your Web site, when you are doing international business, it is important to have a consistent look and feel to all areas of the site.
- Continually add features and services that add value to your Web site.
- Alliances and partnerships will help you distinguish yourself from the competition and will add value to your site, as well as to your entire company.

FOUR

Customize and Personalize

Enriching the Web Channel Experience

> Knowledge is the only instrument of production
> that is not subject to diminishing returns.
>
> —J. M. COOK

My father, Fred Spector, owned a butcher shop in an outdoor farmers' market in my hometown of Perth Amboy, New Jersey. His stock-in-trade—other than steak, chop meat, and head cheese—was personal and personalized service. He knew his customers' tastes, their likes and dislikes; how thin they wanted their salami sliced, how thick they wanted their steaks cut.

His greeting to his customers was his metaphorical home page. Each regular customer was acknowledged individually, and with a slightly different opening offer, or perhaps a little joke. I'll never forget the time he spotted a particular female customer, a regular, on the other side of his showcase, and he greeted her excitedly: "I had a dream about you last night!" Surprised, and perhaps slightly embarrassed, the lady quickly glanced over to my mother, who was nearby, and by the time the lady turned to look back at my

121

father, he was elegantly presenting to her a cut of meat resting on a bed of wax paper and, without skipping a beat, declared: "I dreamt I sold you this beautiful leg of lamb!"

All the customer could do was laugh—and, of course, buy the leg of lamb. A sale was made because my dad personalized his approach. He knew the customer had a good sense of humor and he customized his presentation because he remembered her previous purchases, which were stored in his memory's data bank. He also knew how to sell a product that he wanted to move.

✿   ✿   ✿

In the 40 or so years since that story took place, the essentials of customer service have not changed very much. We just have more and better high-tech tools to work with.

One thing that has changed is that customers are more demanding than ever. According to the results of a bevy of studies, about 50 percent of all the customers who log on to a retailer's Web site will quickly look at the home page and then head off to another Web site because they didn't find anything to catch their interest. So, it stands to reason that the more a site is customized and personalized to the individual customer's interests, the more likely that customer will stay.

Because customers are calling the shots, smart companies are doing all they can to learn how to customize and personalize their services to meet those demands. These companies are *proactive*. They anticipate customers' needs by capitalizing on information and relationships. The better you know your customers—by collecting and mining information on their tastes, purchase histories, etc.—the better you can develop and capitalize on long-term relationships, enhance the customer's experience, and target the customer's needs.

Although this sounds obvious, most companies have been slow to grasp the importance of information-gathering. Consumers consistently tell pollsters that they want e-tailers to provide personalized online shopping programs that send them a reminder to buy a gift for a special occasion or an important date such as a birthday or anniversary. Yet, less than 20 percent of retailers have access to a customer's online and offline purchasing history, according to a poll by Jupiter Media Metrix.

Tesco is a retailer that understands the importance of personalization. When the mother of a toddler logs on to tesco.com, the Web site sends her a personalized home page featuring a special offer for a baby stroller. The home page for a customer who is a wine connoisseur announces a bargain price on a favorite Chardonnay.

This kind of personalized direct marketing campaign, when done correctly and smartly, can replace the forests of paper circulars and fliers that companies send to our homes in hopes of getting a tiny percentage of us to reply. To quote Mark H. Goldstein, former chief executive officer of bluelight.com, the e-commerce site of Kmart Stores, which sends out 3.6 billion paper circulars and fliers each year: "The Web can do a better job delivering the right types of offers to targeted segments. These fliers are a blunt instrument, and we want to be a surgeon."

Getting to Know You, Getting to Know More About You

When I wrote *The Nordstrom Way*, I interviewed many of that company's outstanding salespeople to divine the secrets of their success at building long-term relationships with their customers. One of the ways they did that was by collecting a huge amount of information about those customers.

All top sales associates rely heavily on the tools that Nordstrom gives them. One of those tools is the personal customer book, which helps them keep track of every customer's name, telephone number, charge account number, sizes, previous purchases, vendor preferences, likes and dislikes, special orders, and any other characteristics, such as being a difficult fit or preferring to shop during sales events. These expandable, loose-leaf personal books also contain, among other things, daily, weekly, and monthly calendars; a to-do list; and the phone extension for every department in every Nordstrom store in the country.

"Everybody in this company needs to have a book like this. It motivates you to keep you going for more," said Kazumi Ohara of the Chanel department in downtown Seattle, whose voluminous personal books (a reflection of the magnitude of her clientele) are the company standard. A top Nordstrom suit salesman found it essential to record all of his customers' purchases in his personal book because he serviced so many downtown Seattle businessmen. With a client list that included 40 attorneys in the same law firm, he had to make sure that two men who work in the same office, or who were likely to run into each other, didn't wear the same outfit. No matter how many customers he had, he knew he had to take care of each one of them as an individual.

Sometimes, in order to convince customers to provide you with helpful personal information (such as demographics and buying habits), you have to entice them to sacrifice a little bit of their time to fill out a questionnaire. Bluelight.com has convinced almost 7 million customers to fill out such a questionnaire in exchange for free Internet access. By combining this information with Kmart's existing database of the purchasing histories of 92 million households, BlueLight can recognize customers when they log on to the site and personalize their home page.

Customization vs. Personalization

Customization means giving customers what they have already told you they want. It's not a new concept. Information sites such as Yahoo, Excite, and MSN have long enabled a registered user to create a home page that displays preferred information, such as the performance of stocks and forecasts of local weather.

Personalization, on the other hand, is about collecting so much good historical information on customers that you can anticipate what they want. This is popularly known as "one-to-one" or target marketing.

In order to create a system that can deliver a high level of personalized attention across all channels of communication and distribution, a company must be willing to make the requisite investment in hardware and software to the tune of anywhere between several hundred thousands dollars and several million dollars. This requires integrating in a firm's central database the customer's various and sundry facts and figures, purchasing history, and previously viewed Web site pages. That information is then coordinated with customer resource management (CRM) software technology, which analyzes the data and searches for behavioral patterns that tell marketers how a certain group of customers should be catered to. By using an accurate content-delivery system, retailers make sure that the right targeted offers or suggestions find their way to the screens of the customers who will be motivated to buy.

Amazon.com has been one of the pioneers of such personalization, based on a customer's purchasing history. When a returning customer logs on to the amazon.com Web site, he is greeted by name ("Hello, Robert Spector. We have recommendations for you"). Some of the recommendations are uncanny.

I once ordered a CD called "Bleecker Street," which consisted of cover songs from artists who were denizens of the West Village of New York in the '60s. One of the 20 or so artists on that CD was John Gorka. As I wrote this, I clicked on to amazon.com, and there on the home page was a recommendation for John Gorka's latest CD. Amazon.com even has a link called "Why Was I Recommended This?" to explain their reasoning. There is also another section on the home page called "New For You," which features other recommendations. (I've always gotten a kick out of the message underneath: "If you're not Robert Spector, click here.") Amazon's technology, which was essentially developed in-house, uses algorithms to weigh factors such as the ratings customers give to products they purchase (I didn't bother to give "Bleecker Street" a rating) as well as, of course, the customer's buying history and the buying history of customers who have a similar profile.

Now, I also buy products on amazon.com for my 14-year-old daughter, Fae, who is an avid fan of "Sailor Moon," which is a cartoon program done in the Japanese style of animation known as anime. So, what amazon.com does is allow me—if I choose—to eliminate from my profile "Sailor Moon" or anything else that would stray from my personal buying patterns.

As a multichannel bookstore, Powell's is developing systems so that it can know its customers across all channels. Powell's can access a database that holds information on all customer contacts and transactions—from problem solving to package tracking—at each of the points where the customer has contacted Powell's. The bookseller is able to match customers' likes, be it a favorite author or a subject of interest. Despite the popularity of this technology, Powell's has been hesitant to fully integrate this information because, "We've never been a business that has pushed the customer. For example, on our Web site, e-mail is opt-in," said Sheila

Keane, corporate strategic project manager. "We carry that philosophy across the lines. But, if we want to use that information— whether a customer wanted recommendations—it's already there."

Regardless of whether the information is there to mine, Michael Powell is still "skeptical of taking that to the next level." He cites as a potential scenario: "You bought a book from me about whaling, so I think you ought to read *Moby Dick*. There are people who want that. But there are a lot of people who don't. Or you can be wide of the mark [in making a recommendation]. You only have to fail the customer once. So, I think there should be a lot of caution, particularly concerning something as idiosyncratic as books, where you don't know the person; you can't read their body language; you can't bore down into their request. If you ask them, 'Have you ever read *Moby Dick*?' and they say, 'Yeah, I tried it and I hated it,' that tells you something about where you've got to move next."

(By the way, Powell's has sold many editions of *Moby Dick*, ranging from a used $1.95 paperback to a $12,000 first edition.)

Michael Powell does believe that if a customer says he or she has just finished a Tom Clancy novel and is a big fan of the "techno-thriller" genre, and asks for recommendations for anybody who writes like Tom Clancy, "that's a perfectly legitimate question and one we should be able to respond to." But there is another caveat: "If the customer who bought the Tom Clancy novel doesn't request that information, then I think you are treading on pretty thin ice when you start trying to push books on people without knowing more about them than you are apt to discover over the Internet. If you say to the customer, 'You bought a Tom Clancy novel. Have you thought about Ken Follett?' that can be very irritating. Even worse than irritating is if they follow up on your advice and it's not right. You pushed a book on them. They didn't ask for it. They took your word for it. The customer is going to trust you only once."

REI has found that, "The more that e-commerce retailers can mirror in-store shopping experiences online the better," said vice president Joan Broughton. Like Mike Powell, she cautioned against being too clever. "For example, a customer named Jennifer enjoys climbing. So, when she comes to REI, I'm going to be really smart and show her only climbing equipment. But she might be coming to the site to buy something for her brother, who is an avid fisherman. If she sees only climbing equipment, I've probably annoyed her or confused her—and I will have lost the sale."

So, how does a retailer find that balance so that a site does not become too personalized? Broughton answered simply: "When people come to your site, ask them what they want to see."

Information Please: I, Me, Mine

For twenty years, FedEx has made major investments in creating software and a massive digital network to directly link its customers to its operations. FedEx boasts that its team of 1,500 in-house programmers writes more software code than virtually any other non-software company.

Central to the customer-service philosophy at FedEx is the doctrine that the data on each shipment is as valuable as the shipment itself, and is as important as its fleet of trucks and planes. Using NCR's multi-terabyte Teradata Warehouse, FedEx creates a 360-degree view of each customer that enables it to better serve that customer's individual needs. By collecting information about its customers' shipping patterns across all its subsidiary companies, FedEx is better able to forecast the unfolding flow of freight and to better allocate assets to manage it.

Like many Web sites, fedex.com enables each customer to create his or her own personalized "My FedEx," which adds more customer value to the site. According to fedex.com Marketing Vice President Karen Rogers, "We created My FedEx not because it's the cool thing—My Yahoo, among others, has been out there for a while—but rather to proactively serve up essential information to the customers and to speed up their experience on the Web. Because we know so much about the customers, when they log in, we can tell them about such things as the [package] drop-off locations that are closest to them." Without filling out a shred of paperwork or making a telephone call, customers can orchestrate their entire transaction from the fedex.com site, beginning with placing the order and ending with notice of the delivery of package—and every step in between.

Personalization of the site greatly assists customers in tracking their packages. Once they key in the tracking numbers at My FedEx, fedex.com will remember that information, thereby saving the customers time by not having to re-key the tracking number. The FedEx tracking system can electronically provide the status of any package at any point of its journey. When the recipient signs a handheld device carried by the delivery person, the signature and the delivery information are automatically entered into the FedEx central tracking system. Customers can obtain tracking information in a number of ways. They can designate whether they want to receive an e-mail notification that their package arrived, or they can have the e-mail sent to the package recipient. The signature proof-of-delivery can be printed right off the Web site. This time-saver reflects FedEx's long-time belief that a convenient, hassle-free package-tracking system is key to its strategy of providing customer service in the multichannel world. FedEx has installed special computer terminals for more than 100,000 customers and given proprietary software to another 2.6 million.

Some observers believe that the tracking system is so good that it has become the most crucial competitive edge in the FedEx arsenal. In fact, FedEx has farmed out its services to design and operate the high-tech inventory, warehousing, distribution, and customs clearance for a host of leading international manufacturers and retailers.

"We are all thinking very hard about personalization at FedEx," said Senior Vice President Laurie Tucker. "We are opening up our precious information about our customer and turning it back to the customer in a secured, accessible way. We house a lot of data at FedEx, but we want to craft it into information. We want to begin to use that information to personalize the experience by knowing you well enough to anticipate your need. For example, if yesterday you used international shipping to send a package to the U.K., then today, you would get an e-mail from FedEx. It would basically say, that, 'Since you used us to the U.K. yesterday, would you like more information about the products that we offer to the U.K.? Are there any other companies that you'd like to know about? How often do you plan to use this? You might be eligible for a discount. Have we introduced to you our Global Trade Manager Web site?' We don't want to do this in an obnoxious way, but in a helpful way so that we can personalize the experience."

FedEx helps companies who employ a Web channel to better manage their inventory levels by selecting the shipping and delivery options that are most timely and cost effective. Good inventory management minimizes how long an item is stuck in a warehouse. The logistics units at both FedEx and its rival United Parcel Service operate warehouses for major e-retailers. For example, Koninklijke Philips Electronics NV moved its semiconductor warehouse operations from California to a facility near the FedEx Superhub near Memphis. By executing all of Philips's U.S.

orders and coordinating overseas deliveries, FedEx has trimmed transportation time from two weeks to less than five days, resulting in a major improvement in customer-response times.

Coincidentally, FedEx has been of major assistance to another featured company, Oncology Therapeutics Network. According to OTN Customer Service Manager Mary Seguine, FedEx helped OTN become a pioneer in shipping refrigerated products of oncology medication. OTN moved its warehouse from Rancho Cucamonga, California, to Memphis, "to remove one more variable for our customers' benefit. We are among the first group of packages that get on a FedEx plane."

Show Me the Money

Wells Fargo offers wellsfargo.com customers Single Sign-On service, which combines both their consumer banking and their investing into one user interface. The service provides a seamless integration of online financial services, including one-stop access to banking; bill paying; mortgage, student, personal, home-equity and auto loans; full-service and discount brokerage; and credit card accounts. It allows the more than 3.3 million Wells Fargo customers to access all of their account balances, loans, and investments in one convenient location. Previously, Wells Fargo customers wishing to check balances, loans, or investments online were required to sign on multiple times through separate parts of the site. This new service is a more simple, intuitive procedure. From the Single Sign-On page, customers can link directly to many different views of their financial data, including a one-page account summary listing all their Wells Fargo balances with individual account totals and category totals and have immediate access to trading, banking, and brokerage accounts, which allows for faster navigation of the site.

Like many other banks, Wells Fargo is a big proponent of *aggregation*, a big buzzword in the industry. Aggregation is a process for gathering all of a customer's financial accounts and collecting them on one single Web site, in one account with one ID and one password. So, rather than being forced to go to several different sites or peruse a variety of monthly statements to track all their accounts (retirement, checking, savings, credit card balances, interest rates, stock portfolios, etc.), customers can view them all in one place at one time—even if those accounts are with many different financial institutions.

Customers like aggregation because it makes their lives easier. Banks love it because it opens up a wide variety of marketing possibilities, enabling them to entice customers with a central location for all their financial accounts. The one-stop Web site provides the stickiness that marketers love because when customers visit the site often to pay bills and watch the performance of their stocks, the bank is in a position to offer products and services such as a loan for a new car or an opportunity to refinance a mortgage.

Wells Fargo hopes the provision of these kinds of services will translate into greater customer loyalty, where people will stay with Wells Fargo and consolidate more of their banking with Wells Fargo. "We track our customers over time," said Avid Modjtabai, executive vice president of Wells Fargo's Consumer Internet Services. "As they come online, their use of online increases significantly, although they still use the other channels. But once they get used to seeing their accounts every day, that application is very sticky." Online users represent an attractive demographic because they tend to hold higher balances, and use more products, and once they go online, they hold more products and deepen their relationship with the bank. "Routine transactions on the telephone drop off 17 percent as people substitute using the Internet for checking their balances or transferring funds," added

Modjtabai. "Fifty percent of customers say that their perception of Wells Fargo has become more positive after using us online."

Gather Information in One Database

REI's philosophy is that offering personalization for people who want it is akin to getting help from someone on the sales floor. The consumer cooperative's 35 Web developers are continually finding ways to personalize views of products based on customers' tastes, which REI expects will lead to greater sales.

By being a consumer cooperative with an active membership base of nearly 2 million, REI is building on the vast amounts of information it has in order to further customize and personalize its Web site. That membership accounts for about 85 percent of in-store transactions and about 50 percent of online transactions. The purchasing histories of customers from all REI channels are stored in a single database, which also includes information on where the customer lives and what sex and age group the member belongs to. The purchase history is the window into each member's spending habits and product preferences.

In 2001, REI installed a Web publishing platform from content management vendor Documentum that lets the retailer more easily personalize the site's 45,000 content pages. Eventually, all regular customers with shopping histories at REI will be greeted by their own home page. Using customer-segmentation software, rei.com is able to present product pitches that are more targeted. By reorganizing the data that is stored within REI's back-end systems, and using software that reflects a customer's preferences and buying patterns, REI can more effectively deliver personalized pages to a customer's computer screen. This approach borrows a page from the strategy book of catalog mailers—such as

REI—who have long sent different catalogs to different customers, based on past purchases. These direct-mail companies
commonly test product offerings, package designs, and other
presentation elements as a way to hike rates of response. REI also
tracks how customers alter their navigation on the site, noting
specifically whether they purchase more from one page as
opposed to another page.

REI uses an *extranet* channel—with secure access—that allows
wholesalers to supply information directly into its database.
Eventually, when a customer logs on, he will see the tent and
portable stove that he'll want for his next camping trip, based on
the data REI has collected. Because REI has been working on
gathering all this cross-channel information into a single database,
the consumer cooperative is light years ahead of most retailers in
the move toward multiple sales through personalization. And why
not? The research reveals that multichannel customers spend
more money.

Tesco has been working on "building the single customer view,"
said managing director Tim Mason. The U.K.-based grocery
retailer has taken it slowly because, "We wait until we understand
the customer more fully. Because of the frequency that people
shop with us and the amount that they spend with us, we have a
lot of tools to develop an understanding of the customer."

John Browett, chief executive officer of tesco.com, pointed out
that, "There are different levels to personalization. On the site, a
customer is able to choose what is relevant for her. We have been
able to do that within the Web site itself. For example, when you
are browsing the wine department and buying Chardonnay, we
might put up an advertisement or suggestion on the top row of the
Web site that says, 'How about strawberries?' There are some
quite amusing links." Tesco has "played around with some links"
based on individual customer shopping patterns that show that

customers who buy a particular item might "therefore be interested in other elements of" that item. Nevertheless, Browett did concede that, "With food, it's hard to do what amazon.com does in recommending books by authors you have previously purchased. With food, it's not yet so straightforward." That's an element of personalization that Tesco is working toward.

To further its push to personalization, Tesco is using a software program from Autonomy called My Web. Offered free to tesco.com's offline customers, My Web is downloadable from the Tesco site and "sits" on the user's PC. My Web responds to the shopping habits of customers by suggesting to them that they visit a list of selected sites that are related to subjects or products they are interested in. It understands key concepts and ideas contained in those documents and automatically suggests relevant web pages or news stories on the Internet. When Tesco customers are surfing other sites on the Web, My Web will prompt them and remind them about Tesco products and prices. For example, for a Tesco customer who has visited another Web site on nut allergies, My Web will make suggestions about products on tesco.com that are nut free.

Business-to-Business Personalization

The people who use Oncology Therapeutics Network's services are not technologically sophisticated. OTN caters to small office-based oncology practices that treat cancer patients. Although OTN is on the leading edge of technology for the health-care market, "We have a number of accounts that have no access to the Internet," said Customer Service Manager Mary Seguine. Many of those customers use the OTN site to order drugs for more than one practice. "When you are managing a diverse group of clients, simplicity is important: The nurses want to get on, place the order, and get off."

When the company, which is a wholly owned subsidiary of Bristol-Myers Squibb, launched its Web site in 1998, "We wanted it to be highly personalized for what our users needed, explained Toto Haba, OTN's user interface developer. "We wanted to design it to make it easy for that one person who orders or does the accounting for several practices. They could look at invoices for all the sites that they take care of."

OTN offers an exclusive free service called Lynx2OTN, which provides convenient, round-the-clock ordering and access to many of OTN's services. Lynx2OTN offers secured access to individual account information, data on financial reimbursement (from insurance companies), and reports on clinical trials and products. Clients can view OTN's complete catalog with pricing that is specific to their account—or accounts, if they centrally place orders for more than one medical practice. They can place drug and supply orders 24 hours a day, 7 days a week with an order form that is customized for each practice. The system verifies product availability for each item at the time of order and confirms delivery status. Whenever they choose, clients can access, in real time, their account information, such as order status, invoices, and credit history. They can view OTN's complete oncology-medication catalog at the touch of a button.

To add more personalized value to its site, OTN offers essential services such as a choice of payment terms, customized fax-order forms, real-time verification of product availability, extended ordering hours, reimbursement support, non-biased clinical-research information, updated information such as approvals of drugs by the Food and Drug Administration, and the latest reports on legislation affecting their business.

Speeding up invoicing and ordering has been a key initiative at OTN, which works closely with office managers, some of whom order medication for several medical practices. It used to take the OTN accounting department five days between taking an order and mailing the invoice. Now the invoices are sent online within 24 hours after the order is placed. Customers also receive a copy via snail mail. That has been an enormous help for the people managing multiple practices. OTN customers can review their status in the order section, which gives them a history of its last 14 days of orders through every OTN channel. They can see the order they placed within 90 seconds. Because most of these practices order almost every single day or a week at a time, it's critical for them to get that timely information. In the pre-Internet days, OTN customers had to wait until the end of the month before receiving their previous month's sales information. Printing those reports was extremely time consuming.

When the order is received, the client immediately receives an e-mail with a confirmation number, and another e-mail when the manufacturer drop-ships a product from the warehouse. Because OTN keeps the product in its own warehouse, it is easy to check on inventory. If the customer's order exceeds OTN's inventory, OTN will alert the customer. They can indicate if they need a product by a particular time or where to ship the order, and OTN will respond by e-mail.

OTN puts together a personalized list based on the contracts that the practice negotiates with manufacturers. Because some contract prices for drugs are based on the order volume of each practice, it's essential for these practices to have this personalized information readily available. Clients can review invoices and the contract expiration dates, as well the last 90 days of invoices for every product they order. As they have gotten used to using online technology, OTN has found that many customers prefer reviewing their order history online, rather than with paper invoices.

Office managers can use the information for trending analysis, because the information includes the average wholesale price—the price at which the practices are reimbursed from their insurer. (They make their money on the margins between what they pay for the drug and what they sell it for.) When they are negotiating contracts, they can use that information to show manufacturers that they purchased X amount of a particular drug a year ago, and, therefore, should be eligible for a discount this year.

OTN collects and processes a massive amount of information and puts it all in one place on its Web site to help clients better manage their practices. "We are cleansing and standardizing this data and presenting it back to the client, so they can compare their practice with other practices in terms of how they are using drugs to help their patients," said Patrick Walsh, manager of inside sales. "A lot of the information content we provide helps the practice sift through very difficult and complex rules. It will help the manufacturers establish proof that this drug has been used successfully to treat a particular diagnosis or indication."

OTN presents assortments to customers based on what practice they are in, their purchasing history, suppliers in which they may be interested, and business relationships. In 2001, the company added a program-management feature that enables it to contact customers via e-mail, Web, paper, and fax to alert them on the latest news, such as a new product launch or an upgrade to its Lynx System on-site drug-dispensing technology.

Make Your Primary Goal
Be "No Surprises"

At clickpaper.com—the first true online trading site dedicated to the forest products industry—customers can customize the site for themselves. After they register with the site and receive their user IDs, they can enter the space on the site where actual physical and financial transactions take place and they can customize and filter what they want or don't want to see. For example, if a customer buys and sells only newsprint, chances are that customer is probably not interested in lumber. The customized page offers updates on the industries the customer trades in. Some customers want to see news only concerning North America; others are interested solely in Europe. With new enhanced filter options, customers may sort by multiple categories to create their own subsets of forest products, which are organized in a format that meets their needs.

When a Clickpaper customer logs on to his version of the site and makes an order, he sees on the screen a "Today's Transaction" box that instantly reveals a summary of his transactions for that day. A feature called "Positions" calculates the customer's net buying and selling position with Clickpaper. As the customer looks at the screen, a red flashing price indicates that the price has just fallen. A green flashing price indicates that it has just risen. The customer then knows whether he should now order.

When Clickpaper fills the order, the details of the transaction immediately appear under "Today's Transaction." The message summarizes the order, the amount, the price, and the location. Clickpaper will later send an electronic confirmation or, if the customer prefers, a confirmation via fax.

The next step is fulfilling the orders, which are overseen electronically by Enron Net Works' back-office staff, which includes one group that handles invoicing and another that deals with logistics and scheduling. These teams make sure that the customer gets the right product in the right quantity at the right price at the right place at the right time—all the while giving personal attention and personal interaction with the customer.

"At the end of the day, there are no surprises," said Bob Crane, vice president of forest products trading for Enron Industrial

Markets. "The product shows up on time, where it's supposed to be. Our goal is 100 percent accuracy on every invoice. We can't schedule only 90 percent of the product right. It's got to be 100 percent."

Part of Clickpaper's commitment to personalized customer service is making sure that the financial transactions are completed smoothly. The trade area requires a credit evaluation to transact. When a party requests a password to make transactions on clickpaper.com, the credit group of parent company Enron Corp. examines the party's financial statement and establishes the level of credit exposure. When the party is about to close a transaction, the system measures in real time the level of credit risk allowed. "If you are good for $1 million in exposure and try to order $2 million, the trade will be rejected," explained Crane. "We then tell the party to contact us and we will explain why the trade was rejected. The credit group looks at its database every day to see how much credit exposure we are willing to have with each client, and they look at the value in the deals that we have with them every day. We do that because the market moves every day."

Clickpaper.com has a comprehensive, clearly marked, and easily accessible "Contact Us" tab, which can be used to send directly from the website an e-mail to the Help Desk, where there are people on duty to answer calls personally. If a customer has a question regarding a specific product, he can call the trader specified to the right of the product's long description or on the page where the buyer/seller confirms his bid/offer on a transaction. Although the goal is to make the Web site the entire medium for the transaction, Clickpaper makes sure there are customer-service people to quickly take care of any problems.

Clickpaper.com account managers can administer their whole portfolio of buy and sell positions by telephone, fax, or e-mail.

"But when he has a tool like Clickpaper.com, he can manage a lot more products and services than he ever could have dreamed of before the Web was there—and a lot faster," said Greg Piper, president and CEO of Enron Net Works. "With Clickpaper, he has a tool where anyone with a browser can look at what he needs to do. When he's trying to buy, he's admitting that he needs to buy; and when he's selling, he's admitting that he needs to sell. On the Web, he can reach thousands of customers and instantly better manage his portfolio of what he's trying to do. In the these platforms and sites, the Web has taken our ability to handle transactions and increased them 7 to 10 fold in some markets because of the way it removes points of friction, and gets you out to so many people in real time. The Web sites like Clickpaper dramatically improve his ability to be the best buyer and seller in the whole market. The site is the center for all this activity."

Provide Clients with One-Stop Shopping

800-CEO-READ made its major commitment to the Internet in 1997, but its first emphasis was working with client companies to develop *intranet*-based ordering systems. The Web site offers a customized interface that is tailored to the learning and information needs, service specifics, and billing options of individual clients. The interface gives an employee of one of 800-CEO-READ's corporate customers the option of searching, browsing, and buying books and other materials in the conventional way.

If the employee wants to order non-book items, or needs additional information on a book, or just wants to save the time of searching and browsing, she can click the "Quick Order" option. There are four instances to use the Quick Order form: (1) when you need something other than a book; 800-CEO-READ also offers videos, training guides, treatises, microfilm, government publications, and much more; (2) when you know the book you want, but can't find it in the database; (3) when you don't exactly know the complete title or author's name; (4) when you know exactly what you want and don't need to search the database of books. The customer is asked to enter as much information as she has, send the form, and, as the Web site states, "leave the rest to us." For special services, such as, to quote the Web Site, "needed it yesterday; need it here, there and everywhere; need a brochure enclosed, etc.," customers are asked to call "our Client Services experts or use the Quick Order Form and get real service!"

If the customer places an order for a book, but it doesn't come up in the search, she is directed to go to Quick Order where, "she can type in that she's looking for, for example, a blue book on leadership from 1976, and she thinks the author was McClain. We do our research and then ask: 'Could the author be named Mc*Cain*? Could the book have been published in 1986 instead of 1976?'" explained Jack Covert, president of 800-CEO-READ.

If the customer prefers to speak to a human being, the site clearly says "Need an expert NOW? Pick up the phone and talk to one of our Client Services Associates: 800–236–7323." And, in another section, the site reassures the customer: "Our friendly staff of Client Services Associates will make getting the knowledge resources you need exceptionally easy. Did we mention fast . . . on average placing an order on the phone takes less than 4 minutes." That is where, Covert said, "we apply our do-whatever-it-takes telephone philosophy to our Web site."

To make life easier for its clients, 800-CEO-READ also offers customized invoicing, statements, billing, and management reports that sharply reduce costs for both 800-CEO-READ and its clients. "The client gets the statement any way they want it, whether it's digital or on paper or purchase order," said Covert.

"They get one-stop shopping. They get one check at the end of the month. We try to make things as simple as we possibly can."

If the Shoe Fits, Buy It

There are few things in life more personal than getting the right fit for one's clothing purchases. Lands' End develops consistent sizing standards for clothing by testing the clothes on real people, not just models. For example, over 100 local children in Dodgeville, Wisconsin, fit and wear-test all types of products, offering their official advice to the merchandise team on fit, style, and comfort.

But even that is an inexact science, so Lands' End launched a feature called My Virtual Model, which "is designed to take the guesswork out of shopping for apparel online," explained Bill Bass, senior vice president of Lands' End.

My Virtual Model was developed by Montreal-based software developer My Virtual Model, Inc. Bass described these tools as representing "the biggest shift in the apparel direct-to-consumer market." My Personal Shopper (MPS) uses a technique called "conjoint analysis" to create personalized recommendations. After consumers answer a few brief questions, MPS suggests clothing based on personal preferences. With My Virtual Model, male and female users can create a more accurate representation of their bodies by incorporating data gleaned from a body-scanning procedure, which is executed in just 12 seconds and captures more than 200,000 data points of a body image. The technology is the first fully automated, Web-enabled body scanning system available in a broad-based consumer application.

Throughout 2001, landsend.com and ImageTwin Personal Body Scanning deployed more than 50 body scanners in shopping malls, health clubs, and stores in major cities throughout

North America in order to make the technology more widely available. To help people feel more comfortable about having their bodies scanned while being covered in flashing white lights, landsend.com created a "My Virtual Model tour," in which a 48-foot promotional trailer equipped with ImageTwin body scanners made stops in 14 major cities all across North America. In New York City, for example, the trailer was parked in crowded Lower Manhattan, where passersby were encouraged to become scannees.

Before a customer entered into the body-scanning booth, she had to change into a pair of tight-fitting shorts and a tank top and remove any jewelry and eyewear. The shopper was given a plastic card encoded with personal identification, which was protected by a password. When she swiped the card—as one would swipe a credit card at a cash register terminal—a mirrored door opened, unveiling the body-scanning device. The shopper placed her feet atop a pair of neon footprints, pressed the scanner-activation button with her thumb, and grabbed ahold of a pair of plastic "arms" that jutted out from the walls of the scanner. She stayed completely still while the scanner completed the procedure, creating a virtual model of her body. Once Lands' End recorded this data, the shopper applied clothing onto her vitual body by clicking "try on" buttons to see how the clothing might fit her.

Online, of course, you can't scan your body. But a virtual dressing room on landsend.com does provide two measurement options. For a quicker, generic model, shoppers can use pull-down menus that offer selections of hip size (small, medium, or large), bust size (small or large), and waist size (well-defined or not). For a more exact model, shoppers can use pull-down menus that offer exact measurements. Other features include color-coded charts to select hairstyle and color, face shape, and skin color.

Because more than half of the country's population doesn't fit standard sizes, Lands' End believes strongly in this revolutionary technology as a way to more effectively personalize the online shopping industry and become the future standard for how customers buy apparel online.

"Once consumers create their model, they can view themselves virtually as they try on outfits geared to their size and explore various clothing styles," said Bass. "With a click on the 'try on' button, shoppers can view on their model several hundred clothing items that mix and match to almost a million outfit combinations. The ultimate goal for the future is to offer almost every Lands' End apparel item for 'try on.' It's become hugely popular. It's one of the most visited parts of our Web site."

"Shop with a Friend" is another feature made popular by Lands' End, which debuted the innovation during the 1999 holiday shopping season. "Shop with a Friend" enables friends or relatives to meet online from separate locations and shop together via the Internet. Customers can "Shop with a Friend" 24 hours a day, 7 days a week from anywhere. Lands' End saw a demand for this kind of personal service when it commissioned a survey that showed that 52 percent of all respondents said that, if it were possible, they would shop with another person online.

Here's how it works: Two shoppers agree on a time to meet at landsend.com and decide on what password they will use for their private session. After they've logged on and entered that password, both cybershoppers receive a message that confirms that they are connected and the shopping trip can begin. For example, a mom and her daughter could converse via electronic chat or by telephone if the shoppers have a cell phone or a second phone line not connected to the Internet. The two shoppers are able to browse any and all of landsend.com while simultaneously viewing the same pages. Each shopper can point to a page on the site and the same page will instantly appear on the companion's screen, creating a fun, interactive shopping adventure for people who are in different states, perhaps even different countries.

"Shop with a Friend" has its own security protocol. The shopper initiating the "Shop with a Friend" session is the only one with the ability to purchase during that particular shopping session. This allows the one who started the session to finish shopping with one friend and then give the password to another friend so that they can continue looking for items by using the same shopping basket. For example, a mother could first shop with her college daughter for holiday gifts and then log on with her sister to pick out gifts for their folks. At the end of the shopping trip, the mother can check out all items at once.

Loyalty and E-Mail

When it comes to driving customers to a company's Web site and building and retaining loyalty, e-mail works. It's a cost-effective way to communicate with your customers, but the message has to be personalized, relevant, and timely.

For customer service, it's a great tool for FedEx to tell you that the package you sent has arrived at its destination. It works for Tesco, when the grocery retailer is filling up customers' shopping lists and wants to keep customers up-to-date with their orders. "Otherwise, you risk losing repeat business," said John Browett. "Customers will not be annoyed by e-mail telling them their order is confirmed, and then another telling them it has been shipped."

For retailers, targeted e-mail messages are important. Nordstrom employs a strong e-mail campaign that sends HTML messages to its existing customer base. The retailer has found that the e-mail campaign is probably the most effective and efficient of all the tools it uses to drive the customer to its Web site. At

Frederick's of Hollywood, "E-mail is very effective in getting a small amount of product, very particular items to the eyes of the customer," said Gary Landry, CEO of fredericks.com. "It's also very effective for target promotions, such as, for example, 20 percent off all bras. One area where it performs poorly is in offering a broad selection of products and letting the customers review them. Most customers want an e-mail that is short and to the point, with very few choices, rather than an entire department worth of information."

That's what the Internet is good for: targeted e-mails sent to customers who have given you their consent and have expressed a preference to be alerted for a particular product or service. Then you can concentrate on exactly what they are interested in.

At 5 to 15 cents apiece, targeted e-mail is inexpensive compared to mailing a paper catalog, which can cost $1 a customer, and a banner Web site add that can run to 50 cents or more per customer. Plus, e-mail is the most effective, with response rates of 20 percent to 30 percent, according to a report by Forrester Research. Ironically, that effectiveness is also the potential problem. Online companies are expected to triple their e-mail spending by 2004, when they will be sending out an estimated 210 billion e-mail messages. (I know. You're thinking, "Oh, great.")

E-mail's greatest virtue is that its effect can be easily tracked and readily quantifiable. William Park, the chief executive of Digital Impact, once told the *New York Times* that e-mail was "the most measurable marketing vehicle of all time. You know exactly who you are sending e-mails to, you know how they are responding—did they click, did they buy? People respond to their e-mails in a matter of days or they won't respond at all. So marketers can determine if their campaign was a success in 48 hours versus the four-to-six weeks it might take for a direct mail campaign."

But e-mail will quickly lose its luster if marketers abuse it. "Permission" is the key concept. Messages should be sent only to customers who have voluntarily opted in and provided their addresses. And you should not e-mail even those people more than once a week. Users don't want more clutter in their mailboxes. That's why they subscribe to spam-blocking services, or have their e-mail provider block messages for them.

❖   ❖   ❖

The San Francisco Giants have used e-mail very cleverly in communicating with their clients. For example, on the January day that was the official deadline for fans to pay for season tickets for the upcoming season, every customer who still owed money was sent a personalized e-mail from his or her customer-service representative as a reminder of the deadline. "We gave them an embedded unique URL that would take them straight to the payment page, with their account information already filled in, for them to put on their credit card," recalled Jerry Drobny, director of interactive marketing. In 2001, "We sent out 1,700 and got 200 responses. That's a huge service win for us. That's a phone call we don't have to answer. Not that we don't want to talk to our customers, but from an efficiency standpoint, it was a huge win/win."

The Giants have found this method has been well accepted by its clients. "Because the message comes from their customer service rep, it makes it easier for the customer to directly respond to their rep with any kind of issue they have," added Drobny. "You also have to have the support mechanism ready for when they do respond, so they won't be disappointed. We are figuring out how to handle the spikes in e-mail when we send out those reminders. You can't staff to the level where you can provide great service every day of the year. The more we can push the customer base to 100 percent e-mail communication capability, the better.

Nevertheless, Drobny cautioned, "You have to make sure you don't hit them too often."

Russ Stanley, the Giants' vice president of ticket services/client relations, said, "We have e-mail addresses for 70 percent of our customers and we send them e-mail reminders, such as a time change for a game. We used to send them a half sheet of paper in the mail. Now, we communicate a lot more with our customers and in a more professional manner."

❖   ❖   ❖

At Powell's Books, owner Michael Powell believes strongly that e-mailing can be overused. The bookseller offers customers an opt-in e-mail newsletter that is very basic, virtually all text, and very much no-nonsense. People can choose a generic newsletter that covers a broad cross-section of books, or a more specialized one that reflects a particular genre. Powell's newsletter is very informal. In fact, as Sheila Keane of Powell's pointed out, "At the end of every newsletter, it says 'Powells.com newsletter by Dave.' And [a staff member named] Dave is the guy who writes it. It's stuff that comes out of his head. We get a lot of e-mails from customers thinking, 'Is there really someone named Dave who is writing this?'"

"We want the newsletter to reflect people's interest," said Mike Powell, "You can still get the generic newsletter as well. If we have an offer on a book of Kentucky history, I'd like to send e-mail to a certain number of people in Kentucky who have opted in for information like that. But I would never dream of saying, 'We have this good buy on this book on Kentucky history. How many customers do we have from Kentucky? Quick, send them an e-mail.' I think that is an inappropriate way to do business. *There is too much customer service that transcends what people think are bounds of propriety*[emphasis added]. Make the services available to people. If people ask for them, make sure you do a professional job of supplying them. But don't push it down their throats. If you do, they won't come back."

Loyalty and Affinity

One way to get your customers' e-mail addresseses is by creating a free affinity program such as Frederick's of Hollywood's Star Club, which is a feature on fredericks.com. When a customer signs up to be a member, she gives Frederick's her e-mail address, which makes her eligible to receive an exclusive weekly newsletter, with specials, features, member-only discounts, sneak peeks of new merchandise, pre-order options, and invitations to private online events. Frederick's also gives the customer a discount code for 10 percent off her next purchase, valid for one week, and free shipping year-round on orders over $100, when she orders off the Web site. On its Web site, Frederick's emphasizes the point that joining Star Club is completely confidential. A request for membership must be confirmed via e-mail before the customer is added to the mailing list. Customers receive only the e-mails they choose.

Star Club is promoted on the inside back cover of the Frederick's of Hollywood mail-order catalog, which says, "Join our free Star Club to receive discounts and other benefits." Prominent on fredericks.com is a button to click to find out about Star Club. Fredericks.com also offers contest promotions on the Internet site to encourage customers to join Star Club. Said Gary Landry: "You're not required to join to enter the contest, but we heavily promote joining while you are entering the contest."

The weekly, personalized Star Club e-mail service targets a customer's product preferences, be they shoes, Water Bras, or thongback panties. Customers are sent special offers, as well as the

Absolutely Amanda online advice column—the "Dear Abby"–type feature, written by Amanda Frank, who is billed as "Frederick's renowned fashion expert," and who, according to the Web site, "discusses fashion tips, what's hot, how to get that perfect fit and more."

According to Landry, Star Club membership went from zero in Fall 2000 to almost 80,000 members. Between 500 and 600 people sign up each week. "It really ramps up when we run a contest, such as for three-day-and-two-night vacations in Las Vegas or San Francisco." The ultimate goal is to reach 500,000, which would match the number of people whose addresses Frederick's has. "We are looking to get numbers similar to the catalog because we definitely see a pop in sales with every e-mail that goes out," said Landry. "It's a matter of being top of mind with the customers. The bigger the number of Star Club members, obviously, the bigger the life in Internet sales with every e-mail."

❋   ❋   ❋

Almost every retailer has some sort of customer-loyalty program. Consequently, because there's no novelty to it, the onus is on the retailer to make those e-mails meaningful.

At a time when its competitors are broadening their Web sites, Tesco is still considered a leader in promoting loyalty as a way of retaining customers. The primary tool for achieving this is membership is Clubcard, tesco's customer-loyalty program. In fact, one can't order anything at Tesco.com without registering to get a Tesco Clubcard number, which Tesco uses to learn as much as it can about its customers. "We know lots and lots about our customers through the Clubcard database," said John Browett. Tesco knows how much a customer spends each month as well as more esoteric facts, such as where they live, the number of children they have, and the name of their favorite cheese. Tesco keeps track of how many online shoppers are already Tesco customers as well as how many customers are being lured from the competition. If a first-time online shopper already has a number, it will be recognized by the system. Tesco uses the extensive data it gathers about its customers' shopping habits to customize products and services on a broad demographic scale, comparable to the way that amazon.com recommends a title or an author for a customer who has purchased a specific book. For example, a tesco.com shopper who chooses a certain type of cheese may find suitable wine recommendations suddenly pop up on the screen.

"Once you develop understanding you can develop trust and a relationship," said managing director Tim Mason. "We have a natural desire to try to understand what individual consumers are doing and we have been able to do things where customers recognize the benefit." One example is to alert customers to the availability of organic products. Another is encouraging parents who are either expecting a baby or who already have a child under the age of two to join (for free) Tesco's Baby Club. Members can save up to £150 on a range of baby essentials, special treats, and exclusive offers. Members automatically receive a Clubcard, which makes them eligible to earn Clubcard points. Tesco also sends Baby Club members eight free print magazines that focus on the key stages of pregnancy, childbirth, and life with a toddler, and includes advice from Britain's leading child-rearing experts.

Clubcard holders are eligible for a broad range of deals that are explained, categorized, and color-coded on the tesco.com site. They collect points when shopping with a Clubcard at Tesco as well as with other outside companies that are Clubcard partners. Members receive Clubcard Vouchers with their Clubcard statements which are mailed out every February, May, August, and November. They gain access to Clubcard Deals through "Keys"—they earn one Key every time they spend £25 in a single visit to a Tesco store. If a member earns 50 Keys over one year, she becomes a Keyholder, which allows her access to Clubcard Deals. When she earns 100 Keys over one year, she becomes a Premium Keyholder, which entitles her to even more savings. Customers can select online the Clubcard deal that they want. For example, they can use their Clubcard Vouchers to earn a Tesco currency called Holiday Tokens, which can be redeemed for prizes such as a ship cruise along the Mediterranean coast or tickets to the theatre.

Wherever a customer shops, Tesco reminds them of the benefit of the Clubcard. Andy Cropper, assistant manager at the Kensington store in London, pointed out, "We always ask people in the store if they have—or want to use—their Clubcard, so that they can collect points on their purchases."

Some 14 million people have a Tesco Clubcard. The card is used in 85 percent of all Tesco customer transactions.

Tesco uses the loyalty card to amass information about its customers, "so that we can service them more effectively," explained Browett. "The card enables us to segment customers so we can send them relevant offers and promotions. We send customers vouchers through the post [mail] that they can redeem for cash. We have tens of thousands of variations. For example, if you like wine, we will send you a voucher that will give you money off wine. That's quite sophisticated. We consider Tesco the most sophisticated user of that kind of data." Tesco extends this segmentation to the print catalog magazines it mails out to customers. The print version that a customer receives is dependent on the information Tesco has about that customer.

Browett said Tesco is striving to "understand the total extent of the relationship we have with our customers."

The supermarket chain offers Clubcard customers financial services, free Internet access (a move that Marketing Manager

Helen Bridgett described as "the virtual shopping world's equivalent of free parking spaces outside stores"), mail-order catalogs,
and telephone customer contact through its call center in
Dundee, Scotland. And, of course, customers visit the stores.
Browett felt that this regular customer contact gives Tesco
(which offers customers credit cards and various forms of insurance) an advantage over U.K. banks "that don't know if a customer has a loan or current account because they are still operating with old systems. They have no customer relationship to
use as a management tool. We have that relationship with customers for our financial services. So, I'm very intrigued as to
how that will play out over time, because knowing your customer so intimately is a relatively new thing for retailers.
Retailers need to know their customers as intimately as possible.
How can you service them if you don't understand what they are
buying or not buying?"

Clucards help Tesco discern why a demographic segment is not
buying a product. "Then we do the diagnosis, talk to the focus
groups, do the quantitative research, and fix the problem. In the
good old days, you had no chance to fix the problem. You couldn't
get down to these very defined segments of the marketplace," said
Browett.

Because Tesco serves the vast middle of the mass market, strad-
dling some of the upscale market and some of the downscale market, getting the right combination of merchandise and price
points in the store is a complicated task. "The Clubcard for us is
absolutely central to doing that. I can't imagine that we could run
the online and the offline business, or anything, without the Clubcard loyalty data. If you don't have that, then you are flying blind.
You don't know why people are doing things."

           ❖   ❖   ❖

The San Francisco Giants in the 1997 season inaugurated a Pacific Bell Giants Rewards Club, which makes active club members eligible to win prizes. For example, for July 2001, the Grand Prize was "100 Giants Bucks," good for concessions and souvenirs at the ballpark. Other prizes that month included a baseball autographed by pitcher Shawn Estes and a set of pins—one commemorating the milestone 500th home run by Giants star left-fielder Barry Bonds and another marking the Giants as the National League West Division Champions. Other lucky winners got the opportunity to throw out the ceremonial first pitch at a Giants home game.

Over the course of the season, fans can earn 200 points for simply buying a ticket and attending the game.

Privacy and Security

The flip side—the devil's bargain, if you will—of the whole shmear—of targeted e-mail, contests, customer surveys, and loyalty programs—is a sacrifice of privacy on the altar of customization and personalization.

Many of today's customers already freely give out personal data online all the time, especially if there are prize incentives or gifts. "We long ago quit worrying about safeguarding every piece of information about ourselves," Bob Wientzen, president and CEO of the Direct Marketing Association, told *Business 2.0* magazine. Surprisingly, it seems that most consumers are not particularly concerned about online target marketing. According to the Pew Internet & American Life Project, 64 percent of Internet users have shared, or are willing to share, personal information such as an e-mail address or name in order to use a Website. The overwhelming majority of online users have divulged private information as a way of personalizing their site.

But a lot of customers do care. With so many people on the Internet, we are all becoming more savvy about how we are being watched, tracked, and recorded. Consequently, the task for smart companies who offer a high degree of personalization is to strike a happy medium between blithely giving consumers all the goods, services, and special offers they want and aggressively using all that personal information and risking frightening those customers right off the Internet.

Therefore, the best advice is the most basic advice: Be crystal clear on your Web site about your commitment to privacy with a clearly worded and easy-to-find policy that can be linked from every page on the site.

At REI, for example, the consumer cooperative plainly explains its privacy policy, covering how it collects and uses information such as domain names and *cookies*, those pieces of data a Web browser stores on a hard drive. REI, like other Web sites, uses cookies to recognize customers when they pay a repeat visit to the Web site, and to personalize the shopping experience based on the customer's preferences. REI does not, however, use cookies to gather any personal information on the customer, and it never makes a customer's e-mail address available to any other company or organization without the customer's permission.

To give your users even more assurances, prominently show the logos of consumer protection sites such as gomez.com or the Better Business Bureau that have rated your service. In addition, clearly explain your standards of encryption and how credit card information is sent to the servers of your site. Make it very clear and easy for customers to opt out of giving out personal information.

At Lands' End, "We are privacy fundamentalists," stated Bill Bass. "We don't use that data for anything, other than to build My Virtual Model. We are very clear on our privacy policy on the site:

We ask you information only for the expressed purpose of what we tell you we are going to use it for. And we only ask you stuff that we need to know in order to fulfill whatever service we tell you we are going to do. For example, if you sign up for e-mail—weekly or monthly (you can adjust the frequency)—we say, 'we need your e-mail address because we need to know where to send the e-mail, but we are not going to ask you for your name and address because we don't need that to provide you this service.'"

On its Web site, Lands' End clearly spells out its policies: Under the heading "Your Privacy at landsend.com," the company explains that any personal information that a customer shares with Lands' End is kept absolutely private. Shoppers are told that the the Web site is secure, and that the company has "invested in the most updated technology to ensure that customer data is appropriately encrypted."

On the security page of landsend.com, it is spelled out that customers' names and other information are not shared with, sold to, given to, or traded to any outside company agency. Lands' End guarantees the security of its transaction system and assumes total liability in the case of fraud. As a safety precaution, all credit transactions occur in a secure area of the Web site to protect the customers from any loss, misuse, or alteration of the data collected. (Since landsend.com went live in 1995, there have been no confirmed cases of fraud reported by customers as a result of credit card purchases made through the site.) Designed to enhance shopping convenience, each customer has the option to create a Personal Shopping Account where his or her information is securely stored and is accessible only to that consumer.

Lands' End stresses that customer information is safe because it asks for personal information only needed to provide a service. When a customer places orders by mail or phone, Lands' End might share that customer's name with other companies whose

products or services might—in Lands' End's estimation—interest
the customer. If customers prefer not to have their names shared,
they can contact the company by using the telephone or e-mail
address found on the Web site.

Frederick's of Hollywood offers customers a choice of either
"Double Opt-In" or "Opt-In with Confirmation," according to
Gary Landry. "For somebody to get an e-mail, they have to sign up
for the Star Club. Then they will get a confirming e-mail saying,
'Either you, or someone who was pretending to be you, signed up
for Star Club. If you wish to join, click here to confirm. Otherwise
you will *not* be a member of the Star Club.' Because of the nature
of our product, we have a lot of pranksters. Also, on every e-mail
we send out, there is always an 'unsubscribe' link that you can click
on, and you will never receive another e-mail from us."

Powell's Books has a strictly "opt-in" policy for receiving its targeted biweekly e-mail newsletters, based on previous purchases.
As of this writing, 200,000 people had opted in. If customers prefer not to receive the newsletter, they will receive only e-mail
directly related to their orders, such as confirmation and receipt
of an order. On the site, Powell's states: "We hope the opt-in
method will become the norm rather than the exception for commercial interests on the internet." This policy is spurred by
Michael Powell's belief that, "Just because you are a customer, we
are not going to assume that we should channel all this stuff to
you. That would get us some marginally more business, but, in the
long run, it would not serve us well."

Powell's Web site states categorically: "The personal information you submit to Powells.com will not be shared, sold, or dis-
closed to third parties in any form, for any purposes, at any time.
Powell's will not disclose your sales history to third parties for any
purposes, at any time. The items you purchase will not be shared
with other businesses or customers, period, online or off." Adding

a bit of a political note, Powell's adds: "When you purchase a book from Powells.com, you are voicing your support for one of the Internet's opt-in policy pioneers and a longstanding voice in the fight against spam. To join an ongoing conversation about opt-in, opt-out, and related aspects of spam theory, visit the news.admin. net-abuse.email newsgroup."

Darin Sennett, Powell's "Director of Webbish Things," considers privacy "a key customer-service issue with our customers." Although Powell's uses cookies in order to keep track of the items in a shopper's online cart, the bookseller does not use them to record a customer's name or phone number.

Online security is the companion of online privacy when it comes to establishing trust with your customers. Several of the companies featured in this book use VeriSign Inc.'s Internet Security Server Digital ID to offer proof of identity, to enable secure communications, and to encrypt transactions with site visitors through their Web browser connection. Many of them also use Secure Sockets Layer to encrypt credit card numbers, names, and addresses.

When Wells Fargo launched its site, "security was our biggest hurdle," recalled Gailyn Johnson. "We needed to change people's mindset and make them feel safe, so that they would use the Internet with comfort and security and see that we stand behind those transactions the same way we do when you are at the ATM or at the store [bank branch] or on the phone. We designed the original site specifically for security. For example, account numbers are Xed out. They are not even passed over the Internet. We had to teach customers that we were doing that intentionally. We never greeted them by name while doing online banking. We could do that, but we didn't."

Wells Fargo clearly spells out the security features of its Internet Banking site to ensure that customers' accounts remain private and secure at their desks, over the Internet, and at the bank. For example, on the customer desktop, the bank allows only Wells Fargo–approved browsers to access online banking. Wells works with browser companies to develop security features that meet its standards. A banking session times out after 10 minutes of inactivity. There is no automatic caching of personal information on a hard drive when a banking session is concluded. With its online customer guarantee, customers are covered 100 percent for any funds improperly removed from their account while Wells Fargo is handling their transactions—including funds removed from an account as a result of either online theft of account numbers or passwords or unauthorized online removal of funds from accounts.

Today, we have so many tools to customize and personalize the online experience. We must be careful not to be so enamored with those tools that we turn customers away at a time when we need them more than ever.

❖ ❖ ❖

Takeaways

As customers are faced with more and more options, they are looking to do business with companies that know them across all channels, and who customize and personalize the Web experience. The more a site is tailored to the individual customer's interests, the more likely that customer will stay.

- Know your customers as intimately as possible.
- Amass as much information as possible about your clients—without being too nosy.
- Promote loyalty with your customers.

- Stay in touch through targeted e-mails.
- But don't overdo the e-mails. They will quickly lose their luster if you abuse e-mail. "Permission" is the key concept. Messages should be sent only to customers who have voluntarily opted in and provided their addresses. And you should not e-mail even those people more than once a week.
- There is too much customer service that transcends what people think are bounds of propriety—so be careful.
- Once you develop understanding you can develop trust and relationship.
- Protect your customers' privacy and be clear about your policies.
- Security on your Web site should be paramount. Reassure customers that your site is secure.
- Make it very clear and easy for customers to opt out of giving out personal information.

The Brick-and-Mortar Channel

Let Me Entertain You

Let me do a few tricks, some old and then some new tricks.
I'm very ver-sa-tile.

—From "Gypsy," lyrics by Stephen Sondheim

Driving south on Interstate 5, just before reaching the exits for downtown Seattle, motorists looking off in the distance to their right can't miss the flagship store for Recreation Equipment, Inc. The first image one notices is a 65-foot-tall glass-enclosed building, framed by a set of 12 steel-pipe braces, highlighted by a mural of an ascending rock climber. The Space Needle and the Olympic Mountains loom in the background.

Once the car is parked by the store, the motorist morphs into a mountain climber or a hiker or a camper, who is ready to immerse himself in the REI brick-and-mortar experience.

Located on a 2.1-acre city block, the 116,000-square-foot store (with 80,000 square feet of retail space) is enveloped by a forest planted with 54 varieties of Northwest plants, shrubs, and trees. A walking trail emulates the feeling of treading on forest duff by using plants that thrive in lowland wet areas and sunnier, drier slopes. A 580-foot-loop bike trail, made of crushed rock, is a challenging course composed of obstacles, inclines, and drops. The trail, which drops 23 feet in elevation and has a variable grade up to 10 percent, is designed as an all-weather path for customers to test-ride mountain bikes. A still pond and a waterfall charged with recirculated rainwater add to the natural surroundings. The earth, water, and rocks are reminiscent of a stream cascading down a mountainside. The sound of water is all around.

Mammoth wooden doors at the store's entrance use ice axes as door handles—a tribute to REI's early history, when the consumer cooperative was founded in 1938 by outdoors enthusiasts whose first purchase was an ice axe.

Once inside, shoppers can easily find their way through the two floors of specialty shops by following signposts, inspired by trailhead markers, that point the way to the separate departments devoted to climbing, camping, bicycling, skiing, and paddling. The imposing interior features exposed beams, duct work, wood fixtures, and big windows to emphasize natural light. Interactive features can be found throughout the complex. A little pond of brackish water is used by customers to try out water-purification systems. Camping stoves are activated under a vent in the Stove Center. A sloping 25-foot-long gravel footpath is used for testing the 358 models of hiking boots and shoes. (Similar test equipment is found at stores in Denver and Minneapolis.)

On the restroom doors, the male and female symbols are both stylized in active climbing positions, rather than the usual woman in a skirt or man wearing pants. The symbol on the restroom for disabled accessibility is a figure in a racing wheelchair.

The signature feature of the store is the world's tallest indoor freestanding climbing structure—a 65-foot-high, 110-ton pinnacle enclosed by a glass rotunda at the north end of the store. With more than 13 climbing routes, the rock can accommodate 15 climbers of all abilities at one time. (Each climber is individually belayed for safety by assistants on the ground.) The pinnacle incorporates a wide variety of climbing features, including cracks, overhangs, faces, and knife-edges. From the top, there is a view just east to the I–5 freeway, and west to the Olympic Mountains beyond Puget Sound. The "cherry on the cake" is programmed theatrical lighting that simulates the path of the sun.

Clearly, REI has created a space that not only draws customers to the store, but also *keeps* them in the store. In addition to all the features for testing products, the upper floor of the store includes a 250-seat meeting room for use by outdoor clubs and a 100-seat deli/café that overlooks the courtyard.

The outdoor retailer is keenly aware that its brick-and-mortar channel is an essential component of seamless service. That's why, at the time when so-called experts were predicting the demise of brick-and-mortar stores, canny retailers such as REI were finding ways to enrich the in-person shopping experience. Even amazon.com's Jeffrey Bezos, the man who changed many people's shopping habits, has always expressed his feelings about the uniqueness of actually going to a physical place to shop. Bezos understands that people don't restrict their visits to bookstores just to find a particular tome. Sometimes, they just want to immerse themselves in a sea of books and while away a few pleasant hours. "We will never make Amazon.com fun and engaging in the same way as the great physical bookstores are," Bezos has admitted. "You'll never be able to hear the bindings creak and smell the books and have tasty lattes and soft sofas at Amazon.com."

Offering Customers an Engaging Space

That's the kind of experience that visitors enjoy 365 days a year at the aptly named "City of Books," which is Powell's Books' main store on West Burnside Street in downtown Portland, Oregon. At

68,000 square feet, the largest book store in the United States straddles an entire block. It is a literary melange of industrial buildings that once housed a car dealership that sold Nash Ramblers and a car-repair shop, which were fixtures on what had been Portland's auto row. With its concrete floors and 10-foot-tall wooden bookshelves, the quirky, utilitarian building has never shed its industrial roots. A first-time visitor can be overwhelmed by this book bazaar, which is arranged into seven color-coded rooms, with 122 sections and 4,000 subsections, alphabetized by author. The end result is what manager Miriam Sontz refers to as Powell's "funk factor."

It's not surprising that Powell's employees kiddingly refer to the store's entrance as "the duh zone." That pretty much capsulizes the stunned reaction of some of Powell's 3,000 daily visitors, who walk in, look around, come to a complete halt, read the overhead signage, and then immediately head to the information desk, where a helpful employee is there to answer virtually any question, as well as offer a full-color, color-coded store map, which unfolds to 17 by 22 inches. And if you need additional help, there are a couple of hundred staffers to answer your questions. One doesn't browse so much as explore the store's endless rooms and recesses, its cubbyholes and corners.

Blackboards announce the latest choices in Oprah's Book Club and the winners of the Caldecott, Newbery, and National Book awards. Staff favorites are recommended near the Green entrance. Calendars list frequent readings, author visits, and book clubs.

One of the most interesting new features in Powell's year 2000 expansion is a column called the "Pillar of Books," which anchors the store's remodeled northwest entrance. The pillar is composed of eight of the world's great books, carved from Tenino sandstone, stacked one on top of another to form a 9-foot column. Each title weighs about 500 pounds and is carved in the language script in which it was originally printed: *War and Peace* in Russian, *The Mahabarata* in Sanskrit, *One Thousand and One Nights* in Arabic, *Hamlet* in English, *Tao de Ching* in Chinese, *Psalms* in Hebrew, *The Odyssey* in Greek, and *The Whale (Moby Dick)* in English. In addition to its literary significance, *The Whale* was chosen because, early in his career, Michael Powell found and purchased a set of leather-bound Melville titles at an auction house in Chicago. One of these titles was *The Whale*. This symbolizes and drives home the point that essential to the experience of visiting the City of Books is the joy of locating that special used or rare book.

Powell's carries about 1.5 million used and new books, which are inimitably organized and shelved together—new and used copies of the same book can be found stacked right next to each other. (A tiny poster in the fiction section urges: "Save a tree! Buy a used book!") Biographies are stacked according to subject, rather than in their own separate section. Powell's is wheelchair accessible. To pluck books from a high shelf, customers need only ask an employee for assistance.

"To me, the best customer service in this industry is having more titles," opined Michael Powell. "We want to offer the broadest breadth of titles, new and used. The used offers a price-point attractiveness that the new doesn't. So, you can shop us and have the best hope of finding the book new or used. We started out as a used bookstore and we added new books as an add-on feature. We are still unique in mixing the two products. Typically, the two cultures didn't coexist."

City of Books is open 365 days a year, from 9 A.M. to 11 P.M., and often hosts author appearances. As Julie Mancini, executive director of Portland Arts & Lectures, has said, "If there's a new edition of the Bible, people expect God to be at Powell's to sign books."

Powell's also has book stores specializing in travel, health and nutrition, cooking, children's books, technical topics, and a store at the Portland International Airport. But Michael Powell has no interest in opening any more.

"We've spent a lot of money either remodeling or expanding most of our stores to take on additional inventory, but you have to do that anyhow to keep your walk-in customers feeling that you are keeping the stores neat and clean and current," said Powell. "People have asked: 'With the risky environment, with Borders and B&N as competition, why would you remodel and expand?' I believe it helps our walk-in business and it makes room for more books that we can access. But if we don't get that walk-in customer, the space is also there for the Internet customer. So, it gave two rationales for expanding the stores. In a sense, the Internet provided a safety net for the expansion of the retail. Retail stores are not the optimum environment from which to serve the Internet customer. Books tend to migrate; customers pick them up and move them. It's a strategy of more legs under the table to support those stores."

After initially pulling off the sales floor all the books ordered online, Powell's slightly altered its approach when it added a warehouse. "I became aware that we could buy more books than we could easily get on the sales floor, and that there were categories of books that we could sell on the Internet more successfully than on the sales floor," recalled Powell. The company pulls books from both the sales floor and a nearby four-story warehouse, which employees call "the catacombs." The warehouse has a capacity of 400,000 volumes, which complements the 1.5 million volumes in the main store, and 350,000 off site, which are all available online.

When electronic orders are received, "runners" are designated to pull the books, many of which are already on the shelves in Powell's seven brick-and-mortar stores in the Portland area. An order is transmitted directly to the store that has the book. If the customer orders six books from six Powell's locations, those orders go straight to the six locations. After the books are pulled by the runners, they are transmitted by truck to a central processing and shipping space near the flagship store City of Books.

One memory of Powell's that I will always remember: I was visiting Powell's modest Internet operation, which is basically run by five people, in a small office in a building across the street from the main store. While I was there, one young lady was typing in a book order that had just come through. Ten minutes later, I was walking around the book store, and noticed the same young lady pulling the ordered book off a shelf. That was a graphic example of multichannel customer service.

Nordstrom Plays Your Song

A horse of a different color is Nordstrom, which has always made its physical stores a reflection of its customer service because Nordstrom has long realized that customer service is not just about a smiling, helpful, and knowledgeable salesperson. It's also about making the customer feel good and look forward to visiting the store.

A typical 180,000-square-foot Nordstrom store is designed with a residential sensitivity, simple layout, soft lighting and wide aisles. An open feeling and an emphasis on convenience combine to create a place where it is easy for customers to get around and shop. Deeply upholstered chairs and sofas provide the perfect respite for customers as they are serenaded by a real live piano player. A concierge is stationed at one of the entrances to provide any kind of service, from validating parking to holding purchases to calling a cab. The customer service department in each store provides check-cashing privileges for Nordstrom cardholders, immediate posting of payments to Nordstrom accounts, answers to inquiries regarding those accounts, monthly statements and credit line increases, complimentary gift wrapping, and purchase of gift certificates.

Larger Nordstrom stores offer customers a choice of refreshments—from a simple latte stand to a cloth-table-and-napkin restaurant, The Grill—as well as beauty salons that provide facials, massage, and other beauty treatments. At SPA Nordstrom clients can choose natural aromatherapy, herbal body wrap, massage therapy, natural sport manicures, and aromatic facials. Inexpensive shoe shines are available in the men's area. The whole idea is to do whatever it takes to make the customer happy.

Branch Dressing

Only recently have some banks taken a similar Nordstrom-like approach. While many banks once made a big deal about pushing customers out of the branches and into the cold arms of automated teller machines and Web sites, smart banks, such as Wells Fargo, have never discouraged customers from paying them a visit, because those visits are opportunities to sell more products and services. While they have been perfecting their online operations, Wells Fargo has also been finding ways to capitalize on their 5,400 branches by converting them to one-stop financial centers where customers can do everything they need, from small business loans to home mortgages to stock-trading.

Wells has been experimenting with branches that offer the complete customer-service experience, but with a warmer, friendly feel. Some branches offer Starbucks coffee—a latte with your loan, you might say. In a store in the affluent San Diego suburb of La Jolla, customers are greeted at the entrance by a concierge stationed at a sleek wood and stainless steel service desk. The concierge guides customers to the branch's features, including Internet kiosks or a series of private, glass-enclosed offices where they can meet with a broker or a loan officer. Customers can view the latest financial market news on video monitors.

"In some people's minds branch banking is dead," said Robert Chlebowski, Wells's executive vice president of distribution strategies. "What's dead are branches limited to banking transactions."

Wells Fargo has even found ways to develop check-cashing machines for people who don't have checking accounts (an estimated 13 percent of all U.S. households). In 1999, Wells Fargo teamed up with Cash America International, Inc. to install more than 1,300 machines in grocery and convenience stores. The gadgets require the customer to provide personal information before being able to scan a check. To minimize security risks, the machines keep track of customers through high-tech biometric photos that store images of the customers' facial bone structure. The photos are also used to prevent pilfered checks or to flag a person who has previously bounced a check.

Washington Mutual Inc., the Seattle-based largest thrift institution in the U.S., is another financial institution that is aggressively working on innovative, inviting branches. Washington Mutual's research found (not surprisingly) that customers don't like standing in lines or waiting to talk to bankers behind desks. They want transactions to be easy to complete.

Based on that feedback, Washington Mutual successfully tested a new branch design called "Occasio" (Latin for "favorable opportunity"), where teller windows have been replaced by "teller towers" that enable customers to stand next to bank employees and view their account information on computer monitors. Desks have been swapped for "customer consultation areas" and, in the bank's words, "a special area where financial consultants can sit

down with customers and discuss investment opportunities."
That's not all. WaMu (as it is popularly known) branches have
concierges dressed in khaki; computerized touchscreens; Internet
services; a children's play area called "WaMu Kids"; and a retail
sales space stocked with software, books, and magazines. Washington Mutual has taken a page from Nordstrom's playbook. At
Nordstrom, if a customer can't get a table at one of the store's
restaurants, a Nordstrom employee will take her reservation and
give her a beeper so that she can continue to shop throughout the
store until she is beeped to let her know that her table is ready. At
Washington Mutual, if a customer has to wait for a particular service, the concierge gives her a beeper so that she is free to visit a
nearby restaurant or store.

The Tesco Model: Pick, Pack & Deliver

A visit to a Tesco store in the affluent Kensington section of
London reflects how upscale the chain can be. The 45,000-
square-foot store, with 37,000 square feet of wide-aisled selling
space, is bright and airy—floor-to-ceiling windows let in the sun-
light that is reflected off the painted white walls. Mirroring the
cosmopolitan nature of its clientele, the front of the store features
a deli with a wide variety of multiethnic convenience take-out
food, and a Starbucks-like coffee shop with 10 computer stations
wired for access to the Internet. (Some 300 Tesco stores offer
Internet shopping.)

There are several signs reminding customers that they can shop
for anything they desire on the Tesco Web site. At check out
stands, customers can take home the latest Tesco paper catalogs
for women's apparel or children's products. At a station near the
front of the store, customers can use telephones connected

directly to Tesco operations where they can sign up for instant access features such as credit cards or pet insurance.

In 2000, tesco.com was the first e-tailer in the U.K. to extend Sunday trading hours for home delivery from 10 A.M. to 3 P.M. to 10 A.M. to 10 P.M. to meet a big increase in demand.

Unlike the ill-fated Webvan, which spent hundreds of millions of dollars building automated warehouses, which were supported by costly and elaborate automated distribution systems to pick, pack, and ship groceries, Tesco turned to a more economical strategy of gathering groceries from its existing stores, which reach 90 percent of the British population. When Webvan was in operation, semi tractors in its mammoth warehouses transported customer orders to intermediate substations, and then delivered the orders in small refrigerated vans. In addition to investing about $1 billion in constructing and setting up its elaborate system, Webvan had difficulty scheduling delivery to customers to make sure they would be home. More important, Webvan failed at the much more difficult job of changing people's shopping behavior. That's tough to do in a business where the most successful grocers eke out about a 1 percent profit margin.

When Tesco launched its online operation in 1996, the company believed it would essentially be the next logical progression for home delivery—a cyberspace interpretation of "the kid on the bike with a bag of groceries from the corner store," recalled Carolyn Bradley, Tesco's director of e-commerce. To Tesco's surprise, the service piqued the interest of busy urban professionals, who were looking for any opportunity to save a little time. Early on, Tesco decided to fulfill online orders from its existing stores, which "are an asset, and we wanted to use that asset," added Bradley.

The grocery chain arrived at that decision after a long period of analysis. Tesco officials discovered that "it was very unlikely—if not impossible—to make money doing this out of a warehouse," said John Browett, CEO of tesco.com. After looking at the warehouse models of Webvan, HomeGrocer and Streamline, Tesco believed that following such a strategy would not work because of distribution costs that would be too high and initial volumes that would be too low. "We did the math. At current order volumes, you couldn't make warehouses work, because wherever you situate them, they are too far to reach your customers. What you may gain in efficiencies, you lose on delivery." For example, for its business model to work, Webvan had to be able to get enough business from 300 square miles. Delivery costs were prohibitively expensive because drives had to cover such huge distances. "The distances between their drops were so far, that they couldn't make it work economically—regardless of how efficient you are in the warehouse."

In addition, to get the necessary economies of scale, a retailer would have to fill up the warehouse with merchandise. To get tens of thousands of orders into a warehouse would require huge acquisition costs.

"We looked at doing it out of stores and looked at doing it out of warehouses," noted Browett. But Tesco officials immediately figured that the only way they could do home-shopping profitably and efficiently, especially at low volumes—which they knew they were initially going to have—was to do it within the stores. "We set a team together, and for 2 1/2 years, they carefully and painstakingly worked out how to get the picking economics right. We now have the lowest costs of picking in the world." By using "some very clever, elegant software, we've re-engineered the process by which you do the picking in store. The technology is not that complicated. It's just a matter of thinking about how we were going to make this work in practice."

Here's how the Tesco model works: An online customer logs on to tesco.com, shops the site, and places an order, which goes to the Tesco Direct server in Dundee, Scotland. The order is processed overnight and is sent the following morning to the server computer in the cluttered stockroom at the store nearest the customer's home, where it is assigned to one of Tesco's delivery vans. It is in this store that the orders are filled.

Online customers can buy as wide a range of goods as they could in a store. The order is transmitted to a "picking trolley," which is an oversized computerized shopping cart that operates "shelf identifier" software, which guides an employee, a "picker," on a route through the store where he can locate on the shelves each item on the shopper's list. No paperwork is involved. By scanning each item—a 2-liter bottle of Coca Cola; a chicken breast; etc.—the system prevents a picker from inadvertently selecting the wrong merchandise because the scanned results appear on the trolley's computer screen, just as it would on the terminal at the regular customer service checkout. The picker examines each item to make sure, for example, a can is not dented or the sell-by date has not expired. Or, if a listed item is out of stock, the picker must check to see if the customer will accept an alternative. Although some supermarket industry observers believe that picking from existing stores is too disruptive, Tesco has dealt with that issue by restricting the times that pickers work to when the stores are not busy, usually between 6 A.M. and 10 A.M., and from 11 A.M. to 3 P.M. An average order is about 60 items, with the most popular being fresh fruit and vegetables, rather than bulk items such as laundry detergent, which had been expected to form the basis of home delivery.

Tesco has worked out a system that makes picking orders most efficient for the staff. Each employee does picking for six orders at a time. By picking in different "zones" of the stores at different times, walk time between zones is reduced to an efficient minimum. "It's all about walk time," said Browett. A typical picker selects about 90 items an hour.

Tesco claims that it receives more than 70,000 orders per week. At a typical large Tesco store, the staff processes about 600 Internet orders per week, but Browett claimed that Tesco wouldn't have any problem raising that number to 2,000. Since a typical Tesco superstore draws about 40,000 customers a week, another 2,000 "is neither here nor there," said Browett, who pointed out that Internet sales are not scanned at the checkout area.

Online orders average $152 each, which is almost four times as much as the average in-store shopper spends on one visit. There is no minimum or maximum order. (One customer in Kensington ordered home delivery of a sandwich and a newspaper, according to assistant store manager Andy Cropper.) Regardless of the total bill, the charge for a Web delivery is the equivalent of about $7.00.

Once the order is filled in, a Tesco employee encloses the receipt along with some targeted promotional information. The goods on the picking trolley are loaded onto one of Tesco's 600 delivery vans, which are equipped with dry goods, frozen, and refrigerated sections.

Tesco has to dedicate a lot of thinking to the logistics for the vans. Before an order leaves a Tesco store, someone has to make sure that the right orders are loaded into the right vans at the right times. Then, they must select routes for drivers that are designed to coordinate deliveries in an efficient sequence. Because Tesco uses smaller vans to cover shorter distances, the grocer allows customers to arrange convenient delivery times. But, if you can't deliver an order because the customer wasn't home, you've got yourself another problem to work out.

The stores schedule the vans for two delivery time slots a day. Tesco breaks down the number of products that it can manage to deliver through its combination of people and delivery vans. For example, said Kensington assistant store manager Andy Cropper, "We have three delivery vehicles working flat out. The customer will choose what time they wish their shopping to be delivered. It's done on a first-come/first-serve basis. If you want a delivery by 12 noon and it's full, you would be offered the next slot or the next day for delivery by 12 noon."

Tesco determines the level of inventory in each store with what Browett described as "some of the most advanced replenishment systems in the world," based on a combination of historical sales and sophisticated algorithms. "Because we're picking for home delivery off the shelves in the store, that volume is automatically fed into that system. Therefore it anticipates what are the right things to put in the store."

Should U.S. grocery chains emulate the Tesco model? The jury is still out on that one. In early 2001, Albertson's, the Boise, Idaho–based supermarket chain, closed its Seattle distribution center, which was used to fill online orders in the Seattle area, and transferred that business to its five brick-and-mortar grocery stores, ending a two-year experiment. Even Tesco officials say that they might eventually build warehouses, if the demand exceeds its physical store capabilities. Tesco benefits from being an international brand name, which certainly helps when you're trying to build an Internet business. Another advantage is that Tesco stores are less than a 25-minute drive from 90 percent of the British population. The U.S. population is more dispersed, and no supermarket chains are truly national.

Tesco itself is breaking into the U.S. market in a partnership—agreed to in June 2001—with Safeway, Inc., a leading U.S. supermarket retailer, through GroceryWorks (Safeway's exclusive online grocery channel). GroceryWorks will emulate the Tesco online shopping model and will serve Safeway's 1,500 stores in the U.S.

With annual sales of $420 million out of a corporate total of $22.8 billion, online represents just 1.8 percent of Tesco's business. And although most customers would still rather shop in a store and squeeze the melons, tesco.com continues to attract new customers—who will shop both channels.

Business-to-Business Brick-and-Mortar

Business-to-business companies have a different relationship with their brick-and-mortar facilities, but the simple principle remains the same: make it easy, convenient, and, yes, even enjoyable for your customer to do business with you anytime, anywhere.

That's what FedEx is doing. In an effort to have, in the words of FedEx's senior vice president Laurie Tucker, "that seamless interface throughout all of our customer-facing units," FedEx has expanded its physical presence "where customers are doing business."

In early January of 2001, FedEx Corp. and the U.S. Postal Service entered into a milestone two-part agreement that allowed FedEx (1) to locate its purple-and-white express-delivery drop-off boxes at the approximately 10,000 retail postal outlets across the country and (2) to use its fleet of freighter aircraft to take care of the USPS's air priority and express mail transportation needs. Under that agreement, USPS is guaranteed space on FedEx's planes to haul Priority Mail and Express Mail between airports throughout the U.S. FedEx will fly the equivalent of about 30 wide-body DC-10 aircraft a day, which will be working during the daylight hours—when many FedEx planes, which would normally fly overnight, would be on the ground. Express

Mail shipments are promised to arrive no later than 3 P.M. the next day. The Postal Service is paying FedEx about $6.3 billion over seven years. Over the same period, according to USPS, FedEx will pay USPS between $126 and $232 million to install its boxes at post offices.

In the physical world, FedEx has about 70,000 different physical retail sites, including 35,000 drop boxes, 1,400 manned facilities, 8,200 FedEx Authorized Ship Sites, and 2,200 Kinko's locations, as well as pickup locations at Mailboxes, Etc., and now, the post office, where FedEx customers' packages can be dropped off as late as 8:30 P.M. and still have next-day delivery.

"We found that when we place a physical unit—a drop box—next to a competitor's drop box, our drop box is more productive, because of accessibility and ease of use," said Tucker. "It's customer convenience. It's helping that small business user. It's for the writer at home. We all know where the post office is. Seven million people go through post offices every day. Part of seamless service is being where the customer is. Our focus is on smaller businesses because they are more likely to benefit from the convenience of late drop-offs."

In early 2001, FedEx extended pickup and drop-off deadlines for next-day deliveries by as much as three hours, lengthening cutoff times in New York, for example, to 11:30 P.M. from the current deadline of 9:30 P.M. The service adds $15.00 to the price of a FedEx Priority-Overnight or International-Priority delivery.

"Seamless service is about accessibility," said Tucker. "We live in this fast-paced world. FedEx stops by at 4 or 5 or 6 o'clock. If I miss that stop what I am going to do? Our customers have asked for extended hours. The customers are working later. They want to be able to drop off their packages at a later hour. We obviously had to add to the operation in terms of flights and all. So, it does add physically to our operating hours and our ability to move aircraft out of those major markets at a later time. But, this, again, came out of customer research. It gave us something to do that is unique to the industry."

FedEx is rapidly expanding its Home Delivery network—the first small-package service dedicated exclusively to residential delivery—to cover the entire U.S., with hundreds of strategically located home-delivery centers. This service is aimed at mail-order and Internet retail shippers and their customers.

FedEx Ground picks up the package at the shipper's business and delivers it to time-constrained customers, who can select from a menu of options, including specific delivery date and time. Shippers apply a residential bar code label and transmit shipment information electronically for each home delivery package they ship. FedEx Ground picks up business and residential packages at the same time, then segregates them at the destination hub for delivery by either FedEx Ground or FedEx Home Delivery service.

To help ensure that the packages arrive on time, home delivery uses a proprietary Automated Delivery System (ADS), which simplifies delivery and assigns packages to each contractor's route. The system prints a detailed delivery manifest for the contractor, complete with the most efficient delivery route, directions, and delivery instructions. Deliveries can be made by appointment.

(FedEx has expanded Home Delivery because it was the weakest area of business compared to their chief rival, UPS, which is the leader in shipping parcels by ground. That's the fastest growth market in shipping, and UPS owns about 70 percent of it.)

The packages are delivered in smaller trucks "that are more neighborhood friendly," said Tucker. "Almost a third of our users on the Web are from their homes."

FedEx has worked with Ziba Design, a branding-consultancy and product-development firm in Portland, Oregon, to redesign all of its 1,400 World Service Centers to make them more customer friendly. FedEx has coordinated the look of all of its drop boxes, trucks, planes, courier carts, handheld scanners, and delivery people to present a consistent branding strategy and message to all customers all along the way. Ziba even tweaked the timbre of the drop box closing, to make it sound more reassuring.

FedEx felt that its World Service Centers "could communicate a lot more," said Gayle Christensen, director of global brand management. "We know why people drop things off—convenience." One-quarter of the 3.5 million packages FedEx Express delivers each day begin their transit through the FedEx system in a drop box or at one of the drop-off centers. FedEx has been promoting use of the drop-off because it's more cost effective for the company, "but only if it's a great experience for the customer."

The redesign is intended to promote an unhurried feeling of orderliness to reassure the customer that FedEx will get the job done. The interior is divided into three different zones. The Agent Wall includes an electronic menu board that explains the different levels of FedEx services, and has plenty of room for the agents to stack the boxes so that they don't get in the way of the customers. The curved Customer Wall is where the public locates brochures, software, packaging, and airbills. There's a drop-off window for packages that already have their paperwork filled out. The Brand Wall provides a soft presentation of the FedEx brand, with pleasant-looking visuals.

Take Me Out to the Ballgame— and Let's Take a Meeting

For premium customers desiring a different kind of place to hold a business meeting, the San Francisco Giants offer a business center within their Pacific Bell Park. Officially known as the Bank of America Business Center, it comprises two conference rooms that can be reserved for private meetings. One space holds 30 people; the other 12, and the two can be combined for larger groups. Located on the Suite Level, the Business Center provides elite clients a range of services, including faxing, copying, and modem connections. It is equipped with television monitors and projectors for laptop presentations, as well as a catering service and a spectacular view of downtown San Francisco thrown in for good measure. The facility also has another room that holds 80 to 100 people.

"A lot of customers who want an off-site meeting generally go to a hotel conference center," said Tom McDonald, senior vice president of consumer marketing. "We thought it would be great if people could have their meeting at the ballpark, and we could give them a tour while they were here." Many clients like to have a late-afternoon meeting in the business center, finish up business, and then repair to their luxury suite or box seats to take in an evening game, which usually starts at 7:05 P.M. Occasionally, a special treat at the meeting will be a visit by a current Giants player or one of the team's retired Hall of Fame players, such as Willie Mays (whose statue marks the main entrance to the stadium), Willie McCovey, or Orlando Cepeda. The Business Center is also popular in the off season. Companies can book the space for catered meetings during regular business hours throughout the year. The package also includes a tour of the stadium.

Physical Relationships and Commitments

The Enron Industrial Markets division buys physical assets—paper plants, for example—so that its divisions, such as Clickpaper, can assure customers that it will meet its commitments, including timely delivery. The plants provide Enron

Industrial Markets—through clickpaper.com—with liquidity and flexibility in the marketplace, while leased warehouses and transportation help make work the physical spot markets, where commodities are bought and sold for cash and delivered immediately. "Our ideas have to be consistent with how the product has been flowing in the real world," said Bob Crane, Enron Industrial Markets' vice president. "People will eventually stop what they've been doing for 40 years and change, but the idea needs to be free and consistent with how they do business,"

In 2000 and 2001, to help it to quickly convert its pulp and paper assets into cash and to create a spot market for trading, Clickpaper acquired two newsprint mills: Garden State Paper Company in Garfield, New Jersey (in 2000), and the Daishowa Forest Products facility (now called Papiers Stadacona) in Quebec City, Canada. Enron Industrial Markets made those purchases because, Crane explained, "We have found that, in newsprint, it is easier if we owned the asset to start with. We are feeding our spot market with the product that we own, to sort of prime the pump."

Besides the newsprint mills, Clickpaper also utilizes other physical sites—called trading hubs—to help move the commodities.

"The best thing you can have for a trading hub is a location where product leaves one vehicle and gets on another one. Ports are wonderful for that. But, if you add another transportation link into the logistical flow of the product, your idea will fail," said Crane. "Our solution is to define our hubs as Delivery Points." For example, if in the next six months Clickpaper wants to move 5,000 tons a month out of the Garden State mill, a clickpaper.com trader will list on the Web site the amount and the price of the commodity for delivery in, say, a 15-county area in the Northeast. If the trader chooses, he can divide those 5,000 tons into ten 500-ton increments, so that one customer doesn't have to take it all.

"The trader can then adjust the sales price, depending on the interest in the product."

Crane cited another possible scenario: "Let's say [the trader] has no physical newsprint, but he's making an offer to sell newsprint in some other location. His thinking is, 'I don't own it right now. But if I sell a load of newsprint in Chicago, I'll pick it up from someone else later.' That's what a market maker does. Let's say he makes a six-month sale of newsprint in Chicago, and he starts getting close to the delivery point, and he's not able to pick it up where and when he needs it. He knows he can always go pick it up, if he has to, and truck it to its destination. But that's not an ideal situation because, when you are a market maker, you are in the business of making sure you can support what you're doing. So, if he sells newsprint on Clickpaper in some other location, and he finds that he can't get it some other way, he will still have access to that product at his 'buy' price. He may also call another trader in the market and say: 'If you deliver into my contract into Chicago, I'll deliver into your contract in New Jersey.'"

The company's physical commodities are bought and sold at hubs throughout North America and overseas. Clickpaper.com lists prices for pulp in Vancouver, Rotterdam, Wisconsin, Maine, and Oregon; newsprint in every major market in the U.S.; and lumber and structural panels in Chicago, Atlanta, Dallas, and Houston, where Enron also has a pickup and delivery site and a rented outdoor inventory-storage facility.

Drug-and-Data Dispenser

Oncology Therapeutics Network considers that part of its reason for being is its ability to help respond to the challenges facing oncology practices.

In that spirit, OTN developed Lynx2OTN, which is an integrated, point-of-care drug dispensing and tracking system that manages inventory, enhances revenue, and provides powerful information management tools. Lynx2OTN, which is installed in the offices of oncology practices, is a tool for managing the practices' relationships between customers, suppliers, employees, and partners. It helps capture, share, and leverage customer information across marketing, sales, service, and support functions. The system also provides vital information on new products, industry alerts, safety data sheets from manufacturers, industry issues that will potentially have an impact on their businesses, and advice on securing financial reimbursement for the drugs they buy.

The Lynx System acts like a combination of an ATM and a candy vending machine. A simple touch screen and self-help menus guide the user through a sequence of user-friendly steps. Behind the scenes, a sophisticated, fully-integrated data system links ordering, dispensing, tracking, billing, and reporting. The goal is to cut time- and labor-intensive inventory procedures.

The Kiosk Connection

Lynx Systems are a part of the emerging popularity of kiosk-type facilities through all corridors of business. The kiosk—once dismissed as merely a cost-saving customer service desk—is now enjoying a new-found respect as a tool for generating new business. In-store, web-enabled kiosks are an innovative marriage of the physical and the digital, helping companies make their technology-challenged customers feel comfortable using the Internet. One analyst has likened them to "training wheels for neophytes." Not surprisingly, the number of Web-connected kiosks is rising rapidly, with at least 60,000 in stores all over the country at the end of 2001, according to Summit Research Associates, Inc., a retail-technology consulting firm.

Banks such as Wells Fargo are using kiosks and Web-access ATM networks as marketing tools. Wells Fargo's in-branch video kiosks offer customers online services in branches. Customers who desire to open accounts or make transactions can speak simultaneously via phone and Internet collaboration with experts in online banking and other services. The bank's Diebold ATMs, with Pentium III microprocessors, act like personal computers, but faster.

"You don't want to offer in the store [bank branch] the same self-service experience via the Internet that you have at your PC at home," said Wells Fargo executive vice president Gailyn Johnson. "The value of being in that store is not to get to the existing wellsfargo.com, but to have another type of interactive experience. Web-enabled ATMs also have a different interface than wellsfargo.com or the kiosks."

Wells Fargo's Video Banking Centers use Web collaboration technology, along with video. They allow the people in the branch to not only service the customers but to also let the customers know about products and services, such as insurance or brokerage. These branch employees can refer the customers to go online to find out other products and services. For example, the centers include services such as BillPay, for automatic payments of recurring bills of the same amounts (such as mortgage or cable TV) or simple payments for different amounts at different times (such as the phone or utility bill), and allow the customer to send money to any individual in the U.S. "The kiosk allows the customer in the branch to work with a real person live on the screen to help him set up his first BillPay," explained Johnson. "Web collaboration software allows us to push additional information to the customers based upon their needs."

Added Wendy Grover, senior vice president of corporate communications and director of public relations for the Internet Services Group: "Our goal is to provide services to customers through as many channels as possible, whether it be in a store, via phone, online, or through a wireless device."

In addition to reaching customers with kiosks and Web-access ATMs, Wells Fargo also uses a 45-foot-long, 26-ton wells fargo.com bus with three servers and 15 miles of wiring. The bus serves as an education center for both existing and potential Wells Fargo customers nationwide, including small-business and commercial customers. "In the early days of Wells Fargo, the stagecoach was the most efficient way to move money from one point to another," said Clyde Ostler, group executive vice president of the Internet Services Group. "In our era, the wellsfargo.com bus is a state-of-the-art means for bringing the next stage of financial services to all Wells Fargo customers and communities."

The bus has two outside terminals and 16 inside Internet terminals to bring customers secure, high-speed Internet access to wellsfargo.com. Customers can easily enroll for Internet access to personal accounts, pay bills, trade stocks or mutual funds online, and apply for a wide variety of other online products and services.

"The wellsfargo.com bus is another step in this evolution of customer accessibility," Grover told me. "By bringing the technology directly to the customers in their hometowns, we can eliminate the mystery surrounding online banking and demonstrate the best services available for individual needs."

The financial services company Fidelity Investments has kiosks in its self-described "investor centers," where customers can open new accounts, make trades, deposit money, and consult advisers. Different kiosks are assigned to give information on specific tasks, such as check deposits. There are safety and security features as well: Because customers are wary of making transactions in public, Fidelity's kiosks automatically log off when the customer walks away.

Retailers have found that when customers leave a store without buying something, the primary (and simple) explanation is that they couldn't find what they were looking for. That's why many retailers are installing Web-enabled kiosks, which make available every stock-keeping unit in the retailer's entire inventory. An average Borders Books & Music store stocks only about 200,000 titles. So, in all 340 of its retail stores, Borders has brought in kiosks that have an in-house search application called "TitleSleuth," which enables customers to explore 3 million items—including current and out-of-stock titles—on a slightly altered version of the Borders Web site. Once the customer locates the title she's looking for, she is given instructions to walk to the information desk to special order it. Borders's kiosks are powered by a software application from Netkey Inc., whose CEO and founder Alex Richardson told the *Wall Street Journal* that an Internet kiosk generates significant cost savings because it "runs 365 days a year without a coffee break."

Steve Chaffin, who heads the Internet kiosk program for Kmart, has said that, "Everyone talks about how they want their Web sites to be sticky. Well, with [kiosks], it's just the opposite. We're trying to make them slippery, so the customer can get in and out quickly." In-store kiosks access—and generate traffic to— Kmart's Web site, bluelight.com. In an initial test, Kmart found that 20 percent of bluelight.com customers came from operating kiosks inside Kmart stores.

Recreational Equipment, Inc. is considered one of the leaders in using in-store kiosks to generate greater sales across all channels. In 1997, REI was the first major retailer to install Internet-enabled kiosks, which enabled shoppers to find detailed information on every product in the REI system—not just what was available in the stores. REI continues to upgrade the kiosks' line speeds to improve and quicken the Web-based data transmissions. (The kiosks provide access to all of REI's e-commerce sites.) Since 1999, all of REI's cash registers have been Internet-enabled as well, so that cashiers can look up items online or place orders for goods from their registers. Today, every REI store has a minimum of two kiosks, which are generally located in departments, such as footwear and hardgoods, that require a lot of information. Being able to show the breadth of its merchandise is one of the primary advantages of in-store kiosks because few REI stores have the space to carry all of the consumer cooperative's more than 78,000 different items, nor all of the sizes of apparel and footwear.

REI considers kiosks a major enhancement to its customer service. Before their installation, if a customer found out that an item he was looking for was out of stock in the REI store, he would have to stand in line while a customer service representative would look up the item. With the kiosks, the customer can look up any item without the help of a salesperson, view product shots and information, and order it online. The kiosks offer more information than the paper Product Information Guides that used to be found in the stores. Because product information and assortments are constantly changing, the fluidness of the Web site allows REI "to be fresher and current, in an effort to get to more real time," said Brian Unmacht, vice president of retail. "You don't have to go back and reprint everything. You have it right there electronically."

Although REI's employees are renowned for their expertise, none of them has the encyclopedic knowledge of rei.com, which provides specific information on every item and every variation on that item. If a customer is curious about the relative thermal characteristics of 30 sleeping bags, the salesperson *or* the customer can find a chart on rei.com that compares the degree ratings (and a number of other criteria such as price and weight) of all sleeping bags that REI carries. Armed with that information, the salesperson is in a better position to make the sale—not only on the item the customer was looking for but also on other products that the customer might need. The initial sale paves the way for suggestions for multiple sales.

With all these value-added features, kiosks help to keep the customer in the store a little bit longer and explore other REI services, such as the REI Adventures travel agency. Customers can produce a full-color, high-resolution, topographic map of virtually every wilderness area in the U.S., and print it out. A digital in-store technology called Maps On Demand enables an REI customer to zoom in on a section of the map and print that out in the store on high-quality paper that is water-resistant and tear-resistant. This feature enables REI to reduce its wide-ranging inventory of hiking maps from Green Trails and the United States Geological Service, thereby saving space for other items. Saving space is especially critical in smaller REI stores that can't offer the full product assortment.

With all these options, it's no wonder that the average REI store visit lasts nearly *two hours*—an impressive figure for any retailer.

Although many REI retail employees were initially resistant to the kiosks, they ultimately discovered that the kiosks complement what they do. Nowadays, according to Brian Unmacht, the number one request among store managers is for additional kiosks, which have become "more a part of the store itself. It's another fixture; another way we do business."

Before the kiosks, REI was very labor intensive in its inventory control. "We had customer-service counters at all locations. If we didn't have what you wanted, we would send you up to customer service to find it, and they would do all the work," pointed out Unmacht. "We are now de-emphasizing our customer service counters in our new stores because customers have that information available to them."

With each kiosk generating sales comparable to those of an average 25,000-square-foot retail store, these in-store customer-service aids are a money maker for REI. They are essential to REI's multichannel strategy because they help acquaint shoppers with the Web experience. Data shows that retail customers who then shop online with REI spent 22 percent more in the retail stores than they had the year before, according to Joan Broughton, REI's vice president of direct and online sales.

REI is starting to roll out smaller 10,000-square-foot stores that carry its best products. Those stores will have seven kiosks. "We can serve a contingency of our customer base with best products because that's what most of them are shopping for. It also allows them easy and fast access to the broader superset of products," said Unmacht.

✿   ✿   ✿

The San Francisco Giants have been using guest services kiosks ever since Pacific Bell Park opened at the beginning of the 2000 baseball season. Fans can use the kiosks, which are stationed all around the stadium, for a variety of services, including wheelchair requests, lost and found, information on public transportation, game schedules, and finding lost children.

In developing Pacific Bell Park, the Giants have been in the forefront of using innovative technologies to enhance the overall ballpark and game experience. In June of 2001, the Giants teamed up with Palm, Inc. to bring Pacific Bell Park fans even closer to the action by installing three "beaming station" kiosks in the stadium that enable handheld computer users to keep score and track the game more closely. Developed by WideRay Corporation of San Francisco, the stations contain three small servers that deliver broadband, custom information to handheld devices via high-speed infrared beams. Any fan can walk up to any of the three stations, hold up a Palm OS–based handheld device from Palm, Handspring, Sony, IBM, Kyocera, or Symbol, and receive a "beam" of a score-keeping application from TurboStats, as well as the latest information, such as the statistics, lineups, pitching match-ups, biographies, and rosters for the Giants and the visiting team for easy reference during the game. The stations are updated before each home series, enabling fans to receive the latest statistical information on the team. In addition, a scoreboard video runs during select Giants home games to help educate fans about how to use the beaming stations and how to keep score.

Not every company has found kiosks to be the magic bullet. They are costly: Maintenance, training, and networking equipment can run between $3,000 and $25,000 each, according to the Yankee Group. Several retailers including The Gap removed them from their stores for lack of use. The problem with The Gap's experiment was that the kiosks didn't do anything special— in contrast to REI's, which perform specific functions to help generate sales.

FedEx, in the early 1990s, tested shipping kiosks in shopping malls, truck stops, and airports. The idea was that customers could push icons on a screen, enter their information and credit card number, and receive a shipping label. At the time, "it just was a real foreign concept to people. They played with them more than they used them," admitted vice president Laurie Tucker. "So, we abandoned that. We believed that maybe when the Web and ATM technology became more familiar to people, we would come back to it someday." FedEx plans to test kiosks again, but it will take advantage of new technology and learning as well as focus on making it easier for customers to get their packages. Today's consumers are more mobile than ever; they need more control over their time.

Provide Person-to-Person
Customer Service

Essential to the brick-and-mortar channel are nice, motivated, well-trained people to take care of the customer. You can have all the high-tech bells, whistles, and gee-gaws that you want, but if you don't have the high touch of human contact, everything else is a waste of time and money.

Remember those Tesco delivery vans that were heading out to customers' homes? To make sure that the men and women who drive those vans give the best possible service, tesco.com owns and operates all the vans—rather than subcontracting them—and trains the drivers to give great service. The reason for that, explained John Browett, is that, "It is our only point of [personal] contact with the customer. Online, you don't have any other contact." To drive this point home, Tesco's online operations created a program called Delivering Excellent Service "to ensure that our van drivers give good service on the doorstep. They have turned out to be our heroes in the eyes of the customers. They are fantastic."

These drivers have been asked by customers to do a wide variety of peculiar jobs and favors including: holding a ladder, changing a tire, putting things away in the cupboard for an elderly customer, changing the clock on a videocassette recorder, choosing wallpaper, changing a lightbulb, mailing a letter, returning library books, unblocking a sink, and answering the phone and telling the caller that the party they were calling for was not at home. Some of my favorites include: feeding a pet while the owners were on holiday, joining a customer for a candlelit dinner after she was stood up on Valentine's Day, and driving a pregnant customer to the hospital. (Turns out, it was a false alarm.)

"At Tesco we pride ourselves on looking after our customers but there are limits," admitted Carolyn Bradley, chief operations officer. "We are advising our drivers to be as helpful as they can, but we have to strike a balance without inconveniencing other customers by being late [for deliveries]."

Then there are the customers who don't want to be seen buying from tesco.com.

The supermarket chain has had to make accommodations for wealthy customers who were embarrassed to be seen buying from what some snobbish Londoners still view as a down-market retailer. Ever eager to please, Tesco, when delivering to certain neighborhoods, sends out unmarked green four-wheel-drive Range Rovers—with tinted windows—driven by a man in a suit and tie. This is in sharp contrast to the typical large white Tesco van driven by a man in a supermarket uniform. The move was in response to a major upturn in orders from wealthy city people who were buying food for their country cottages. As Dave Clements, the marketing direction for tesco.com, told *The Times* of London, "Many [customers] are switching from places like Harrods and Fortnums, but often they don't want the neighbors to know, so discretion is important."

Hey, that's customer service, too.

Rock, Roll, and RAM

At The Geek Squad, part of the reason that customers keep calling the Minneapolis-based computer-repair firm is that they've made an everyday service into something fun. They arrive on the scene in one of the Geekmobiles—a new VW Beetle or maybe a 1963 Renault Dauphine or a 1953 Morris Minor—dressed in white shirt, black clip-on tie, black slacks, white socks, and black shoes. They are in character and they like what they do. They are there to fix your problems, which could be as simple as setting up a computer for a home user or installing a network for small businesses. They will debug your infected machines and find your lost files. And they will do it quickly, because The Geek Squad charges by the project rather than by the hour.

Because they do their job with élan, expertise, and a sense of humor, The Geek Squad technicians have become the computer-repair service of choice for a wide variety of movie production companies and traveling rock bands.

In 1995, when the movie *Mall Rats* was being shot in the Minneapolis area, The Geek Squad president and founder Robert Stephens was called to the set to fix a computer for one of the crew. He was soon asked to fix the director's computer and then two of the actors' PCs as well. "Next thing you know, we're like the computer people for the movie industry in the Twin Cities," Stephens recalled. The Geek Squad has also worked on *Grumpy Old Men* and *D3: The Mighty Ducks*. With movie people overnighting their laptops to The Geek Squad, Stephens saw an opening to expand to Hollywood.

"Movie crews, like rock stars, are telecommuters," said Stephens. "They go from town to town and they rely on their laptop for everything. I thought, 'If I can have anybody as a client, why not have celebrities as clients? Why not be Computer Repairer to the Stars?' All the rock stars said I should come to L.A. I always wanted to, but I knew I couldn't until the company was ready. Everything came together in January 2001. I needed a Web-based system because I needed to keep my overhead low. The margins in this business are 6 to 7 percent; it's profitable, but you've got to watch yourself."

Stephens shipped a couple of Geekmobiles to Tinseltown and was in business. He didn't even need to set up a physical office because all Geek Squad work is done on-site. When someone in the Los Angeles area needs The Geek Squad services, she'll go to geeksquad.com and type in a request, which goes to the The Geek

Squad server in Minneapolis and is then transmitted to a Geek Squad technician in Los Angeles. "L.A. is a rough town for people who are in the business of rejection," Stephens noted. "We just take care of your computers. When we walk on a movie set, we are not a threat to anybody. We're not trying to muscle in and take somebody's job. Everybody loves us. I love being the only guy at a Hollywood cocktail party who's not in the industry. I don't have a movie script hanging out of the back of my pocket. Everybody wants to talk to me because they never get to talk to any normal people. I'm the most fascinating person in the room."

The Geek Squad technicians are similarly treated by traveling rockers such as the Rolling Stones, Prince, Smashing Pumpkins, Ozzy Osborne, and Kiss. Stephens described rock stars as "the most finicky, demanding people. They're great practice for us." The Rolling Stones and their 40-person traveling entourage began using the services of The Geek Squad in 1997, for their "Bridges to Babylon" Tour. The Geek Squad offered overnight delivery support and telephone support for laptops or printers anywhere in the world that band was playing.

With its reputation for great customer service with a sense of humor, The Geek Squad members "get the best concert tickets," said Stephens. "We get the best seats in every restaurant in town because we do everybody's computers."

That's Me All Over

At FedEx, "Our couriers know our customers because they visit them every day," said Senior Vice President Laurie Tucker. "The former mayor of Shelby County, Tennessee, Bill Morrissey, told me once, 'My courier has been coming to my house for several years. I just love her. She always brings a treat for my two dogs.' I love that story."

In order to further extend that interpersonal relationship, FedEx has equipped its sales professionals with a portable laptop called Salesforce Automation Manager (SAM), which they can use to access a very rich database about their client list. SAM allows them to download personal information about customers and to upload additional information on customers' needs back to head-quarters to provide a seamless view of the customers. For exam-ple, the salesperson will learn from the customer the best time of the day to make a pickup. "That kind of information in a file allows us to give customers much more personalized service," said Tucker. "The overriding idea behind this technology is to better understand and know our customers. Salespeple have linkage to all of our intranet sites that have more information than the cus-tomer will ever need to know about FedEx products and serv-ices."

When working with large shippers at the shippers' sites, FedEx uses its technology "to do everything we can to eliminate work on the customer's behalf" and to "capture the data so that we can make the experience rich for the customer," said Tucker.

The Nordstrom of Baseball

"Our goal is to become the 'Nordstrom of Baseball,'" proclaimed Russ Stanley, vice president of ticket services and client relations for the San Francisco Giants. "To get there, the client needs a per-sonal contact so he can say, 'I have a friend at the Giants.'"

That 'friend' is one of six client relations executives (CREs), who are responsible for about 2,000 customers who account for about 5,000 stadium seats. Every piece of mail the client receives from the Giants comes directly from that CRE. Each CRE is responsible for one of the six different seating categories in the stadium. During a game, a CRE will work the assigned area for three or four innings to develop relationships with clients. That's important because most of the one-on-one interaction with the clients takes place at Pacific Bell Ballpark.

Before the stadium opened for the 2000 season, the Giants put on a couple of events so that customers would have a chance to sit in their seats before actually watching a game. If there were any problems with the seats, they could be rectified before the first pitch. "We were able to take care of 50 percent of our problems at those events," Stanley recalled. "At the [pre-season] exhibition games, we designated a clients relations area on the promenade level—which was staffed with 10 people—where people could go if they had a problem. We learned that there was an area in the upper deck that obstructed the view. So, we moved those fans to alternate locations while we took care of the problem."

For the high-end customer—typically a CEO of a major corporation—who owns a luxury box or suite, the Giants are bringing in "Ritz-Carlton-level service," said Stanley. The luxury-seat director and her assistant make sure their 63 accounts "are well taken care of. They meet with the clients during every game without being obtrusive. We are always looking to add new features, such as shoe shines, haircuts, and massage."

Tom McDonald, senior vice president of consumer marketing, said the Giants "consider ourselves to be in the entertainment business. People have higher and higher expectations for how they spend their entertainment dollars and what kind of value they get for their money. So, from our point of view, service means providing a top-notch entertainment experience every time they come to the ballpark. It encompasses not only the process of acquiring season tickets or individual tickets from the Giants, but also everything that happens to you when you attend a game— from your experience in the parking lot, to your experience with the person who takes your ticket, to the guest services person who shows you to your seat or answers a question for you, to the game experience: the music, the public address system, the video board, the promotions. It's all the different things—in addition to the baseball—that make a game entertaining. We are very clear that baseball is the prime motivator. But we also know that with a sold-out ballpark, we have a lot of casual fans, and we must make their experience a positive one."

When McDonald talks about starting the Giants experience in the parking lot, he is not exaggerating. The team has a partnership with a San Francisco parking company that sends their employees who work Giants games to a compulsory customized eight-session training program conducted by the team's vice president of guest services. The training is for all day-of-game staff, including guest services, maintenance, and retail workers in the stadium's souvenir shop.

"Our hope is that when fans first pull their cars into the parking lot, the first person they deal with—to either guide them to where they are going or to take their money—makes eye contact, smiles, and greets them with 'Thanks for coming to the Giants game today. How may I help you?' The next person who they come in contact with is the greeter at the front gate. Since we have electronic turnstiles that read barcodes on the ticket, greeters don't have to look down, check the date on the ticket, tear it, etc., which makes it difficult to have interaction with the customer. The greeters are simply there to make eye contact, smile, thank them for attending the game, and ask, 'Is there anything I can help you with?'"

The next contact a fan will have is with either a food/beverage worker or a guest services representative who is working that particular section of the ballpark. "We stress that whenever someone comes in contact with a member of our staff, that representative of the Giants should be helpful and show their appreciation that the fan has attended today's game," said McDonald.

In-person seamless service is "a constant challenge and an evolving process," McDonald added. "It's more challenging at the points of contact during the 3 ½ hours you are at the ballpark. We are spreading the service ethic of the company across a lot of different employees—full-time, game day, security, and outside organizations that have a little different culture than us, but who happen to be partners of ours. Our in-stadium partners—Volume Services America, which does the general concessions, and Bon Appétit, which does the food and beverage for the premium Club Level and Luxury Suites—both have their own training program in addition to coming to ours. You have to persistently communicate on a regular basis to all the people who come in contact with the fans that customer service is what's important to this company. It's important to us that they attend the training and that they understand what our core principles are. After that, it becomes a process of repetition of the core principles."

Of course, even with all that attention to detail, somebody, sometime, somewhere in the stadium is going to have a bad customer service experience. Consequently, there is are places in the ballpark where fans can fill out customer service forms. In addition, all Giants staff people working the stadium carry copies of those forms. If a customer informs them of an unpleasant experience, it is duly noted by time, place, section, and circumstances. "A guest services person compiles those and we make sure that the customer gets a personal phone call from one of our managers, and a response in writing regarding what has transpired. It's important that we do both," said McDonald. "We also use our Web site. There is a place on sfgiants.com where customers can give us immediate e-mail feedback, and then we respond."

✾   ✾   ✾

Takeaways

Whether your company is involved in business-to-consumer or business-to-business, the brick-and-mortar channel is essential because it is the only channel where you will have physical contact with your customer. At a time when the pundits were predicting the demise of brick-and-mortar stores, canny retailers were finding ways to enrich the in-person shopping experience. And B-to-B firms such as FedEx are finding that the physical touchpoint can make the difference between a disgruntled customer and a happy one.

- Offer customers an engaging, inviting space.
- Make your physical channel a manifestation of your customer service philosophy.
- Provide interesting value-added amenities, i.e., a Starbucks in a Wells Fargo bank branch; Web-enabled computer terminals in a Tesco supermarket.
- Seamless service is about accessibility, such as FedEx's 35,000 physical locations around the U.S.
- Use kiosks as a channel that connects the physical with the digital.
- Provide person-to-person customer service.
- Constantly reinforce your core principles that customer service is essential to the future of your organization.

Seamless Customer Service

A big corporation is more or less blamed for being big, but it is only big because it gives service. If it doesn't give service, it gets small faster than it grew big.

—WILLIAM S. KNUDSEN,
A VICE PRESIDENT OF GENERAL MOTORS, IN THE 1930S

Now that we've discussed the importance of each channel, it should be clear that the primary challenge facing any business is to coordinate all these channels to deliver seamless customer service. Meeting this formidable task requires five key elements:

Commitment: Pledge to make customer service not a strategy but a way of life.

Preparation: Train your people to give great service.

Knowledge: Understand your customers intimately across all channels.

Communication: Communicate both internally with your colleagues and externally with your customers.

Foresight: Be proactive; anticipate your customers' needs.

If all these measures sound basic, it's because they *are* basic—they are common sense. But then again, as one wit once said, "Common sense is not that common."

Today's common sense is that a significant percentage of your customers want to do business with you across all channels, depending on time and circumstances. The decision should be theirs, not yours. As Avid Modjtabai, executive vice president of Wells Fargo's Consumer Internet Services, put it, "The majority of our online customers make fewer phone calls, but they still make phone calls. They make fewer branch visits, but they still make plenty of branch visits."

So, Wells Fargo offers "Anytime, Anywhere" banking.

"Ultimately, every company will have to provide the expected customer service to each channel," said Gary K. Landry, president of fredericks.com. "If a store customer expects to be greeted at the door, you must do that. If an Internet customer expects to be able to follow the status of her order and to track her package online, you must provide that."

Matt Hyde, senior vice president at Recreational Equipment, Inc., aptly sums up the reasons why seamless customer service is crucial to a multichannel strategy: "If somebody walks into our Seattle store and they get bad service, or they buy a product that falls apart, there is no possible way we're going to get them to shop with REI online. That's why customer service is a company mission. We have to take care of customers across the board. That's the barrier for entry. If you're not playing at that, you're not even in the game."

Commitment:
Make Customer Service a Way of Life

I once heard a college football star, who played the game with great desire, described by a TV announcer as a young man with a lot of "want-to." Companies who consistently give great customer service have to have a lot of "want-to." They want to give customer service. They are committed to it because you can't have customer service without commitment. What kind of relationship could survive without it?

This is where the hard work comes in. A culture of customer service must be constantly nourished, supported, and reinforced. Nordstrom is constantly encouraging the importance of customer service among its employees. One of the ways the company does this is through corporate storytelling—passing down and around the culture great examples of doing what it takes to satisfy customers. In the Nordstrom culture, these stories are called "heroics," and they are essential to the corporate culture and folklore because they serve as ready reminders of the level of service that all employees should aspire to. They are, simply, the ideal way to pass on a company's cultural values. Employees who witness a colleague giving great service are encouraged to write up a heroic, which describes what happened. The heroic is then given to the store manager, who might read it over the PA system before the store opens. It might be written up in the local employee newsletter or the national employee newsletter. One example is the story of the customer who had accidentally left her airline ticket at the counter in a women's clothing department in the Nordstrom flagship store in downtown Seattle. The Nordstrom saleswoman discovered the ticket, called a clerk at the airline, and asked if she would write the customer another ticket at the airport. Have you ever lost an airplane ticket? The airline representative, of course, said she couldn't possibly do that. So, the Nordstrom saleswoman got some money out of petty cash, hailed a cab, went to the Seattle-Tacoma International Airport (a 30-minute drive), paged the customer, and handed her the ticket. This saleswoman, who is paid primarily on commission, took at least an hour and a half off the sales floor to help out a customer.

But these gestures don't have to be so grand. They can be small. A woman I know who worked at Nordstrom in the late 1970s told me of a day when Bruce Nordstrom, the chairman of the company, walked through the women's sportswear department where she was working. Someone had left an empty can of soda on a counter in the department. Bruce noticed the can, put it in the waste basket, and continued on his way. "Bruce didn't say a word. He didn't ask why the soda can was there. He didn't tell someone else to put it away. He just took care of it himself. That happened more than twenty years ago, and I remember it like it was yesterday. It was a great lesson of leading by example," recalled the woman, who now runs a successful business.

FedEx also makes "heroic" corporate storytelling a key element of its customer service initiatives. Ever since FedEx was founded in 1971, the company's philosophy has been People, Service, Profit, and it is one of the first things every employee learns.

"Each employee learns that you have to treat your customers and each other right," said Laurie Tucker. "Service will ultimately lead us to profit, which allows us to reinvest in the customer experience. We stress that we help the economy move by keeping businesses moving. This company cares about its people and cares about its customers. That's a long-term relationship that you can feel good about in terms of working for a company. We always talk about bleeding purple (the primary FedEx color)."

From the beginning, founder Fred Smith, a U.S. Navy veteran, initiated programs to instantly recognize someone who has performed well above expectations for the company. The primary recognition program is something called "Bravo Zulu," a Navy term from the Allied Signals Book that means "well done." The program began when managers notified executives that they wanted to reward outstanding effort without having to go through a formal process. Managers have the freedom to, on the spot, hand out rewards such as theater tickers, dinner certificates, and cash (up to $100). Special Bravo Zulu events honor outstanding customer service. "Any management person can initiate it. This is done to encourage and instill 'go-beyond' behavior in our work ethic. It's important to retell the stories so that new people understand where we came from," explained Tucker.

One example is the story of Yvette Wright, a delivery person in Columbia, South Carolina. When her van broke down one morning at 9 A.M., after her first delivery, she notified dispatch, then started running—literally. She loaded as many shipments as possible onto her hand truck and carried them on foot to their destinations. She returned to the van, reloaded, and repeated the process throughout the five-block route. By 10:27—within minutes of the 10:30 schedule delivery commitment—she had dropped off 122 packages at 27 stops. "I didn't think anything of it," Wright said. "I always think about service."

✿   ✿   ✿

Wells Fargo took its commitment to service a step farther than most companies when it created a group called "Doing It Right for the Customer," which is headed by senior vice president Concetta F. Conkling, who in almost three decades of service has worked in almost every area of the bank. Conkling and her colleagues have championed Wells Fargo's customer service initiative around four actions that are necessary, she said, "to exhibit to the customer in every interaction: Commit, Assurance, Responsiveness, Empathy." The program is known by its acronym: CARE.

"The unit has a corporate-customer advocacy role for all channels across the company," explained Conkling. "Our role is to partner with everyone. We work with our online operations and our stores. We look at the overall experience. What does it mean to the customer when Wells Fargo touches them?"

The group was started in 2000 after Wells Fargo had acquired First Interstate Bank in a high-profile merger. Wells Fargo discovered during the merger conversion period that it was faced with some customers that were "unhappy and alienated. In some instances, we made too many changes way too fast. We discovered we had some learning to do," recalled Conkling.

Wells Fargo responded by looking at what it needed to do "to reestablish credibility in the minds of both our employees and our customers," said Conkling. "That's when we came up with our mission of 'Doing It Right for the Customer.' We needed to understand how our customers viewed their interactions with Wells Fargo." After a few months of looking at the situation, senior management came up with the idea of creating an ongoing group of five people who would oversee customer service initiatives. Although these people were not directly involved in the day-to-day operations of the company, they were in a position to make sure "that we never lose sight of the customer." Conkling described herself and her colleagues as "that part of Wells Fargo's conscience that asks ourselves, 'Is this the best that we can do for our customer?'"

The group's concerns include things as mundane as font types on bank brochures and as sensitive as the paperwork for a customer's account.

"We went through 'goof-proofing,'" continued Conkling. For example, "If I had to send a piece of paper to you, and then you did something with that piece of paper, I'd ask, 'Why would I send that piece of paper to you? Why couldn't I just fill that out myself?' When there isn't a legal requirement, why do I need the customer's signature on a piece of paper? Wherever you have multiple steps in a process, you have multiple opportunities for failure. If you can eliminate a step, it's usually a win for the company and a win for the customer because it's generally less expensive once you eliminate that opportunity for error." Conkling and her group want customers to have a consistent, positive experience, so that "one way or another, the customer will be able to get her inquiry answered and the information that she wants."

Resolve Issues Quickly

Powell's Books is strongly committed to in-house resolution of customer service issues by people who know books—Powell's employees.

"First, you try to answer as many questions as you can from customers in an upfront way," said Michael Powell. "For example, electronic books (e-books) is a new technology that frequently has customer service issues. If something goes wrong with the download, you have garbage on your screen. We have people in our Internet office who know the issues on e-books and can handle the queries on a one-call basis. The person who took your call could literally say to someone across the room: 'We have an incoming call on an e-book problem,' and it's soon taken care of. We are heavily committed to it. That may be easy for me to say because we don't have scale challenges that a Barnes & Noble or an Amazon has. But I still think you have to be committed to that. Otherwise, you begin to get the reputation of someone who can't solve problems and customer service issues."

He takes the surprisingly contrary position that, "Sometimes, the answer to good customer service is just saying, 'I'm sorry. I wish I could solve that for you. I can't.' For example, we have only one copy of a lot of books because they are used or out of print. (We are still working on having a real-time database that lets us know our inventory.) So, a certain number of customers are going to be disappointed because we sold a book before that order came in. You have to deal with that disappointment.

"We can't make everybody happy 100 percent of the time. If you give people a sincere and honest apology and an explanation that makes sense, you're going to satisfy 95 percent of customers. You have to find that balance. You can solve 90 percent of the problems. The question is: How many resources do you put into solving the remaining 10 percent? A lot of companies want to go to 99.9 percent. I can tell you that, in retail, if you go to 99.9 percent, you're out of business. The sooner you realize that, and figure out a way to handle that difference [between 90 and 99.9 percent] in a way that doesn't offend a majority of people, you will have gone a long way toward meeting your customer service goal."

Promote Corporate Values

Tesco's commitment to customer service is wrapped up in a set of corporate values. "These values are not just for the customers. They are also for the 200,000 employees at Tesco," said John Browett, CEO of tesco.com. These values include:

- No one tries harder for the customers.
- Treat people how you like to be treated.
- Trust and respect each other.
- Strive to do your very best.
- Give support to each other.
- Praise more than criticize.
- Ask more than tell.
- Share knowledge so that it can be used.
- Enjoy work.
- Celebrate success.
- Learn from experience.
- There is only one team: the Tesco team.

"These values are taken seriously at Tesco. They are not just empty words. By creating that kind of environment, our people can do things very straightforwardly for customers," Browett continued. "We want to understand customers better than anyone. We want our people to be energetic and innovative, and be first for customers. We want to use our strengths to deliver unbeatable value to our customers. At the same time, we want to look after our people so that they can look after our customers."

Browett cited as an example of hassle-free customer service an experience his own mother had shopping in a Tesco store. "I don't know how it happened, but when she got home, she discovered she had been charged three times for the same item," he recounted. "She was in a panic. She asked herself: 'How can I prove this?' She took her receipt back to the store and the first person she spoke to said, 'No problem. We'll sort it out straight away.' And they did. If you have to give something back to the customer, make sure there is not some huge palaver about it. Our core purpose is to create value for customers to earn their lifetime loyalty."

Browett said Tesco has simplified its standards for good customer service so that every employee in the grocery chain understands what that means. "For example, in the produce department we have a simple test: 'Would I buy it?' That means, if you see a rotten apple on the shop floor, remove it. There's no point in having other people pick through it. That's just bad service."

Andy Cropper, assistant manager of the Tesco store in Kensington, told me that store management spends a lot of time talking to the people who are working with the customers, to make sure that they are giving the best possible service. "We train our people to explain what we want and we get them to buy into it. They learn that if they don't give good customer service, everything falls apart. As a management team, we vet all our new recruits. We don't leave that as a personnel function. We like to bring in people who already have an understanding before they start. Once they are in, it's up to us, as managers, to help them and to devote time to train them. Otherwise, it's completely pointless." Cropper described the ongoing training and coaching as a two-way process: "We do ask for some feedback. We try to get the message across that once these employees have become a part of their departments, we really rely upon them to carry forth that message. We are not just paying lip service to some training, but to actually do it with some meaning and thought, and to show by example."

(In fact, in the afternoon that I spent in the Kensington store with Cropper, I witnessed him "show by example." At one point, our interview was briefly interrupted when a customer asked Cropper where he could find some horseradish. Rather than point him to the aisle, Cropper walked the customer over to the horseradish display and handed him a bottle. A few minutes later, a gray-bearded customer, who claimed to be a retired management consultant, bent Cropper's ear for about 10 minutes, suggesting improvements in the layout of the store, while Cropper listened patiently.)

Browett stressed the importance of leading by example because, "Quite often in organizations, the head office becomes divorced from the customers. At Christmas and Easter, we all go to work in the stores. I go in and stack shelves. While we're there, we talk to the people who are working in the stores about what's going on. People come back with lists of things that have to get sorted out. You don't want the store staff to be frustrated because things don't work. We have a saying in the business: 'Better, Simpler, Cheaper.' Better for customers, simpler for staff, and cheaper for Tesco."

Promote Employee Empowerment

If there's a bigger cliché than "customer service," surely it must be "empowerment." I remember visiting Powell's Books in the mid-

1990s, and the buyer of business books told me that the store stocked an entire subsection of books just on "empowerment." It's not all that complicated. You empower people by empowering them. It's just that obvious. If you boil the Nordstrom system, for example, down to its essence, it's that Nordstrom gives the people on the floor—or the call center or the Web site—the freedom to make decisions. Everything else flows from that premise. Most important, management backs up the decisions of those frontline people.

Jack Covert of 800-CEO-READ, the Milwaukee-based business bookseller, agreed that empowerment was a cliché, but that didn't make it less important. He related a pivotal story about the early development of his business that hinged on the empowerment of one motivated employee. Back in 1992, that employee, Kris Carmichael, gave such spectacular above-and-beyond-the-call-of-duty customer service that she helped 800-CEO-READ snare its first Fortune 100 client.

A representative of that Fortune 100 company came across a copy of 800-CEO-READ's *Business Book Gazette* newsletter, and was moved to buy a couple of books via the mail. Some time later, that company's representative sent out a request for a very obscure title to six booksellers/jobbers (including 800-CEO-READ) to see who could fill the order. The enterprising Kris Carmichael quickly got on the phone and kept making calls until she tracked down the book. Eventually, Carmichael used the then-nascent Internet technology to locate the book in Holland. She bought it and shipped it to the Fortune 100 company, where it arrived one full week before the first of the five other booksellers called the client. The purpose of the call was to say that the book could not be located because it was out of print.

"After that, we started to get serious orders from that company," recalled Covert (who chose not to identify the name of the firm). "By the mid-1990s, they changed their purchasing policy and wanted a single source for all their business purchases." That single source became 800-CEO-READ, which supplies that company—and many others—with a wide variety of products, including books, CNN transcripts, treatises, CD-ROM products, videos, and audios.

"Kris Carmichael felt empowered enough to call Holland. The customer wanted the book, and Kris just did it. Everyone on staff has that message instilled in them. Our company is run with the customer in mind," said Covert, whose customer-service philosophy was inspired by the book *Moments of Truth*, written by Jan Carlzon, who once headed SAS Airlines of Sweden. "That book really moved me," he recalled. "Carlzon's premise was that your frontline person is the one with whom your client should have a positive service experience, because that person represents your company to the customer. We've tried to implement that here. We allow people to do what it takes to get it right."

❧   ❧   ❧

At Wells Fargo, "Empowerment comes through the tools that we give people," said Senior Vice President Concetta Conkling. "It's one thing to tell me that I am empowered, but what does that mean? What's changed after you tell store managers or bank officers that they should feel empowered? They look the same and feel the same."

One tool that Wells Fargo uses is a clearly deliniated escalation-contact list of managers that employees can get in touch with to help resolve problems. That list goes up as high as a group head. "We've published the names and phone numbers of three key executives in every single functional area—with their blessing."

Establishing standards of response is crucial to the empowerment equation.

"People should expect to hear back from you within a certain amount of time," said Conkling. "They have basic guidelines. You don't necessarily have to escalate through your chain of command. You can just pick up the phone, and if you go through the normal channels and that doesn't work, here are three more contacts that you can use, when you're trying to resolve a customer issue.

"We tell them that they own that experience with the customer. 'You touch it, you own it.' We have found that instruction to be very helpful. We provide you with the tools to know where to go to solve the problem, but you still need to stay in touch with that customer. You're the ambassador; you're the contact for the customer. Very rarely do we encourage a handoff. If you do have to hand off, then you should follow up with that customer within a reasonable time, and ask: 'Did it work? Did you get your question answered?' A lot of this is common sense. The number of calls people make is less important to me than the fact that they know where help is available. We get the feedback on whether it works, and when it didn't work. For example, did somebody on the contact list disconnect their phone number and not tell anybody? That's really a no-no."

Wells Fargo believes in local autonomy. "If you have to talk to five people to get something done, you're not empowered," Conkling emphasized. "We tell our people that anybody in the store can make the customer whole—up to a specific dollar amount. Over this dollar amount, you need approval. It's basically a no-questions-asked policy. *You* make the judgment. If the customer got a parking ticket because they waited too long in our store, and they complain, pay them for the ticket. If a check bounced and Safeway charged them 25 dollars, pay them for it. You could send the customer a box of candy. We track it to make sure that something funny is not going on."

Conkling, who has worked in virtually every area of Wells Fargo since she joined the bank in 1975, compares Wells Fargo's relationship with the customer to a rubber band. "Our goal is to keep real lax, because lax means tolerance. Every single interaction is going to have an impact on that rubber band. If every interaction pulls and pulls and pulls, you are never going to know when that rubber band is going to break, because very rarely do customers leave your company over one incident. So, we need to make every interaction positive. We can't afford to take the risk that this is going to be the one that we're not going to recover from."

Preparation: Train Your People to Give Customer Service

In a poll by Jupiter Media Metrix of New York, 1,900 American shoppers listed among their primary complaints about shopping online having to deal with customer-service representatives who had sparse knowledge about the products and services that their Web site was offering. Those same respondents complained about long response times in answering e-mails, and the inability of the company's in-store staff to be able to view their online account information while they were in the store.

Clearly, training is—and will always be—a key issue in giving service to customers. When do customers usually need help? When they are either unhappy with something or require an answer to a question. Handling unhappy customers in particular requires a deft touch by people who are empathetic, don't get flustered easily, and know their product line. For some customers the most important thing a rep can do is answer the most commonly asked question: *"Whismo?"*—the customer-service acronym for "Where is my order?"

At REI, salespeople are extremely knowledgeable, because they use the gear they sell. "We are trying to be more holistic in what we provide our customers," said Brian Unmacht, vice president of retail. "Our service goal is to help people enjoy the outdoors. We are looking for salespeople with passion. REI employees enjoy and respect the outdoors. It's what makes us different. If you look at any of our channels, what comes through is our passion and sincerity to help our customers enjoy the outdoor experience."

At FedEx, "one of the attributes that we test in our customer research surveys is our employees' knowledge of our services," said Senior Vice President Laurie Tucker. To give them greater understanding of the services and to offer on-the-spot training, FedEx uses FX-TV, a closed-circuit television network that the company uses for global broadcasts—both live and Webcast—to virtually all its physical locations. FedEx has used FX-TV for a variety of purposes, including imparting information about new pricing systems or new automation that is about to be rolled out. "We use it as a face-to-face training technique, rather than trying to bring in 3,000 people at one time."

At Powell's Books, which specializes in used and rare books, the success of the operation depends on the store's 30 used-book buyers, who train for a minimum of two years. These buyers take turns positioned at a long counter near the front door of the City of Books, where they pass judgment on the worth and value of the tomes brought in by optimistic sellers. While Powell's turns down many of these books, the buyers still acquire some 5,000 every day. (Sellers receive one-third of Powell's sale price in cash, or 20 percent more in store credit.) Although the buyers are equipped for quick research with a computer as well as price guides for used and rare books, for the best buyers, the information they store in their head is their foremost reference.

Hire People with the
Right Attitude

The Geek Squad has an interesting take on the qualifications of its technicians. None of The Geek Squad's members is certified. Although thousands of certified technicians (even people with degrees in computer science and information technology) in the Twin Cities send resumes to the company, president Robert Stephens is not easily impressed with those official credentials. The Geek Squad's Web site even tells prospective applicants: "We believe your accomplishments are more important than your resume, and we'll get back to you right away." Stephens prefers people with "the right attitude and a passion to pick up the knowledge they need," as well as persuasive verbal communication and networking skills and a strong knowledge of DOS/Windows and/or Macintosh hardware and software. He described his ideal candidate as some who is "a maverick and who loves technology."

The Geek Squad provides customers with in-home, one-on-one training. "You can get classroom training anywhere, but you can't call someone and say, 'Will you come to my home and show me how to use a Palm Pilot?'" said Stephens. "We have customers who are doctors and lawyers, who have a lot of anxiety about technology, and don't have the time to learn."

The Geek Squad is committed to customer service with the cheeky Geek Squad attitude.

"Why should you use me instead of someone else?" Stephens asked rhetorically. His immodest answer: "Because I'm better and faster than my competitors. My prices are flat-rated and I guarantee my work. I've been around for 10 years, and while many companies have come and gone in that time, we're still here. Why? Because we love this work. You're not just paying us to take care of your computers, you're paying us to back up the work, to make sure that we install a good quality part. You want us to be around if you have a question afterwards. And while we're at your home or office, you probably want to get some value-add out of the visit. We might show you something extra. Why would we do that? Because my employees are happy. When they're happy, they have a good time. When they're having a good time, they will offer to help you with other things while they are with you. I've got a business model that allows me to give the guys freedom enough to spend enough time. If my guys [who are paid on a base salary plus a 35 percent commission on every job they perform] want to give you a discount, they are taking a discount off their own salary. So, I don't have a nickel-and-dime atmosphere.

"What prevents them from doing shoddy work?" Stephens again asked rhetorically. His answer: *recalls*. "If a customer calls back within 90 days, we go to their house for free and take care of it. No questions asked. But," he added, "if it sounds like it's their fault, we tell them in advance that we will charge them."

A couple of years ago, The Geek Squad began offering even more assistance to their customers when Stephens coauthored a book called *The Geek Squad Guide to Solving Any Computer Glitch*," a resource of Mac and PC tips for "when the help desk doesn't help." An entertaining read, the *Guide* begins with how to purchase a computer, walks the reader through the computer-owner experience, and answers the most basic frequently asked questions that The Geek Squad techs have compiled from customers over a decade of business, such as: "How do I deal with a dead battery?" "What do I do if my floppy disk gets stuck in a floppy drive?" "Can I donate my old computer to charity and get a tax deduction?"

"What you're buying from The Geek Squad is our knowledge," said Stephens. "Before the book, we delivered that same information either through phone support or house calls. That is right in line with what we do—providing something that's really not available. There was *DOS for Dummies* and *Windows for Dummies*, but there hadn't been a book written in clear language to explain users' relationships with their computers." The book also has text support at geeksquad.com because "we stand by the purchase and our brand, so if a reader doesn't find what they need, they can call us at 1–800-Geeksquad or go to our Web site."

Teach Special Skills for Conducting Business Online

Lands' End employs about 2,500 customer service representatives during the course of the year, with a peak number of about 3,500 at Christmas. There is a very low staff turnover during the year, and each holiday season the company welcomes back many returning part-timers. On an average day, Lands' End's customer-service representatives—who work on 300 telephone lines—handle between 40,000 and 50,000 calls. In the weeks prior to Christmas, over 1,100 phone lines field more than 100,000 calls a day. Those numbers add up to some 15 million calls every year, as well as over 200,000 e-mail messages—each of which receives a personal response.

Many of those e-mails are directed to Lands' End's specialty shoppers, who are trained to give personalized wardrobe advice. Even though Lands' End considered its operations fast—the company provides answers to customers' questions within two hours of receiving an e-mail—it understood that the best option was *immediate* feedback, which would enable Internet customer-service reps to furnish even more personalized service.

In 1999, Lands' End explored a new initiative that would provide that immediate feedback: Lands' End Live. To implement

Lands' End Live (which is discussed in detail in Chapter 4), the company assembled a team of 20 employees, who were drawn from practically every department, including customer service, telecommunications, the Web site, and information services. Over 100 new positions were open for the new service, with more than three times as many applying to fill those spots, which would require four additional 6-to-8-hour training sessions beyond the minimum of 80 hours of product, customer service, and computer training that new hires receive "before they are turned loose on the telephones," said Bill Bass, senior vice president of lands-end.com. They receive an additional 24 hours of training for every year after they are first hired.

Those 100 new positions were more challenging than catalog orders, "which are fairly simple for the most part," said Bass. "Unless a customer is having a problem, the typical conversation is: 'I need your name, address, credit card number, and the items you'd like to order.' When shopping on the Web, all of the answers have already been handled before the customer contacts a Lands' End Live personal shopper."

By contrast, when customers require additional help on the Web, Bass continued, "you're getting the harder questions, like, 'Can you recommend a tie that will match this suit?' or 'I bought this pair of pants last year, and I'm trying to buy something that will go with them this year. Can you tell me what goes with the canyon heather pants?' Then you need customer service reps that not only know the product from last year but can also go over and pull out the merchandise [which is available for them to look at], get it, and match it with other stuff to see if it looks good. It's a more complicated interaction."

Lands' End instituted a number of qualifying factors for all cus-tomer-service reps who were going to communicate with cus-tomers on Lands' End Live, including basic experience on computers in general and the Internet specifically. They were tested on their grammar, spelling, writing, and typing skills, because a person with excellent telephone-conversation skills won't necessarily be as adept at quickly typing responses to customer questions.

The 100 people selected to be Lands' End Live personal shoppers brought to their jobs an average of nine years' experience assisting Lands' End customers, and an average of nearly 500 hours of training. The additional customized training covered basic PC and Internet skills, followed by another four-hour class on the unique features of Lands' End Live. The training was a shared responsibility for Lands' End staff and support personnel from Cisco Systems, whose Customer Interaction Suite was the tool that Lands' End used to synthesize Internet commerce, customer support, and telephony infrastructure. Over a five-day span, Cisco trainers tested Lands' End people on the features of the software, while Lands' End trainers conducted "what-if" sessions—likely customer-service scenarios—and set the rules and code of behavior for the online service.

Ann Olson, vice president of customer services, told *IQ Magazine*: "Good customer service is essentially the same at a high level, regardless of how you're doing it or what technology you're using. This is our ongoing Internet strategy to provide the best and most consistent online customer service in the marketplace."

❖   ❖   ❖

At nordstrom.com, online customer-service reps are taught the importance of voice inflection in communicating and providing information, such as how well one piece will go with a piece that the customer has already selected. (Nordstrom.com customer-service reps, like those at landsend.com, have easy access to the merchandise they are selling.) The company doesn't use recommended phrases, because it doesn't want those people to be something that they are not. "You must come across as genuine," said Dan Nordstrom. "It's the individual personal shopper's personality that makes the difference. Many of our personal shoppers have actual store experience. They can carry that knowledge and experience through those conversations. In the catalog business, service is not that different from the store. You've got people involved and they need to know about the product. You are working only with your voice. About 30 percent of Web transactions end up having some sort of human involvement through our contact center whether it's e-mail or live chat or phone."

Nordstrom launched its online beauty store in the summer of 2001. It was the logical Web extension of its 1-800 number channel, which had been offering advice from cosmetics experts and the ability to order beauty products since 1992. The telephone business receives about 15,000 calls a month, or 180,000 calls a year. Those same consultants are also advising online customers in a live chat room, where they talk about the best fragrances to be worn at night, cosmetics for sensitive skin, and the best shades to wear with a person's skin tone and hair color.

✿   ✿   ✿

"Just because you do the phones very well doesn't mean you do e-mail well," said Gailyn Johnson, executive vice president at Wells Fargo. "Those are different talents. You can't just assume that anybody can answer e-mail. We do evaluations and quality reviews of people who are good at e-mail. We know exactly who does what well. We give those people free rein to answer e-mail."

Wells Fargo is using the information tools available to help their customer service people, "who can't know everything—nor do they need to," said Johnson, who recalled that in 2000, "We had an awakening. We realized that the mind share is just too great. The amount of time it would take for customer-service reps to know everything about every bank product and technology is great. The position doesn't necessarily warrant that."

Wells Fargo's traditional training period had been six weeks of intense, full-time instruction before people were allowed to interact with customers. In early 2001, Wells Fargo revamped its online customer-service training and moved toward more specialized queues. There is one "nesting queue," where new agents focus on opening online accounts, including authenticating customers, linking existing accounts, and providing access for customers to self-select their passwords and IDs, and handle transactions for the BillPay service, which, among other things, sets up automatic payments for recurring bills of the same amounts (such as mortgage or cable TV). This new approach allows them to specialize in one major functional area prior to learning the more complex products such as BillPay, Quicken, or Money.

"They train for three weeks, where they get phone skills and enrollment skills and learn how to authenticate transactions," Johnson told me. "Then they are put into additional classes where they work for another three weeks, and get comfortable with doing those services. If we have a big marketing campaign or some other program, we can extend that training class. The beauty of their being in the nesting queue with their trainer is, if they are having difficulty, they are led off the phones and put back into training. It's given us greater flexibility, plus some back-up support on days that we really need it. It's a daily shuffle."

An important feature to Wells Fargo's ongoing instruction is interactive web-based training, which is available to customer-service people on an ongoing basis. "Even when they are talking to customers, if they have a quick question that they need to look up, they then can go into the computer-based training and find it," said Johnson.

Wells Fargo also offers an escalated queue called "Gold Mine," which typically answers questions on the Money and Quicken financial programs, and is also available for banking questions that can't be answered by either the first or second levels of customer service.

Early on, Wells Fargo encouraged its employees to sign up for free online service, "because it's hard to talk about something you've never used," said Concetta Conkling. "We found that using the service is a huge lift for their comfort level. They can say to customers, 'I've tried it; it's neat.' When I worked in the stores, I loved it when the customer would ask me, 'Well, what do you think?' They look to you to be their advisor. So, if you say you've never used it, then the natural reaction of the customer is 'What are you trying to sell it to me for?' We installed computers in our stores so that our people can do demos for customers. We also did incentives. If you sign up a customer and refer them to wells-fargo.com, you get points. It's win-win."

Knowledge: Know Your Customer Across All Channels

How often have we dealt with companies where the right hand doesn't know what the left hand is doing?

I have a cellular telephone account with AT&T Wireless (at least as of this writing). One day, I got a flyer in the mail, asking me if I'd like to be a customer of AT&T Wireless. Then I got a telephone call from somebody—obviously part of a boiler-room operation—asking me if I would like to sign up with AT&T Wireless. I know that somewhere in the catacombs of AT&T Wireless they must know that I'm a customer because they send me a bill every month. All this begs the question, why can't *every-*

body at AT&T Wireless know I'm a customer? I'm still trying to find out.

I think Dennis Madsen, chief executive officer of Recreational Equipment, Inc., hit the nail on the head when he said, "This business isn't about technology. It's about understanding the customer and translating that understanding into strategies and tactics that will take care of his needs and expectations."

At FedEx, "The account executive who goes out to visit the customer needs to know if that customer had a conversation with someone in the call center," said Cynthia Henson, vice president of customer service. "Otherwise, they will be surprised to know that you have a claim issue or a tracking issue, etc. My reps need to know if Sales just went to see the customer and committed to do something. Sales needs to know if there are some open issues with the customer. As the person in the back office does the research and gets the answer, our system automatically flags the rep to tell her to make that outbound call. Or, if the customer doesn't get an answer prior to the time that we had committed to calling him back, another flag will remind me to do what's necessary to get the answer and meet my commitment to the customer."

Today's customers expect the companies with which they do regular business to know about them regardless of the channel.

"If I interacted on your Web site and I call your call center, I want you to know what I just did," said Henson. "Don't make me redo what I've already done. If I called you with claims information, and then you send me a form to fill out, make sure the information that I just gave you at least shows up on the form that you send me back again. Don't make me fill this out again.

"These are where the touchpoints [customer contacts] come together: You can drop a package off at a drop box or FedEx facility. You can call the 800 number to schedule a delivery. You can call us on the phone and get information on the FedEx location nearest you. The system will automatically tell you, based on where you are calling from [zip code], the five closest locations to you. You can print that list off the Web site. That question can be answered a lot faster on the Web than if you called the rep. But our team is here to promptly assist you on any of the issues or problems," said Henson.

By dealing with the customer across all channels, companies like FedEx are building up powerful customer profiles.

"These profiles tell you a little about the customer, about their average daily revenue, and that type of information, which helps us make new decisions on process," said Tucker. "We found that a customer's average daily *volume* means something. If you ship a hundred packages a day, that means something only if we identify that you have potential for growth. That's where our Sales department comes in to let us know that there is potential. The customer profile will also let us drill down and be able to see that a customer has called 30 times in the last month with a daily pick-up. Maybe we need to talk to the customer about a regular stop at a regular time, so she doesn't have to call in."

As FedEx adds new features to its Web site, "we give our agents on the phone detailed information and explanations of what these features represent, the benefit to the customer, and how to direct the customer to those features," said Karen Rogers, marketing vice president. "The real challenge is the human interface."

Sheila Harrell, vice president of customer service, strategic planning & analysis, noted that, "We're only as good as the information in that terminal. We don't want the Web to be a crutch. We want the Web to be built out rich, so that's where customers go first."

Look at Customers As Human Beings, Not Account Numbers

"Historically, banks have looked at customers as accounts," said Wells Fargo executive vice president Gailyn Johnson. "When we look at them as human beings, we ask: 'What are their relationships? What are their accounts?' [Customers could have both a consumer account and a business account.] Then you can see the expanded relationship. The CRM (customer relationship management) software that we are developing will allow us to start doing that."

When it comes to the small business side of banking, too often, large financial institutions "first see you as an individual customer and then as a business owner," said Johnson. "You can't force them together; they don't mix. You must take the approach that the customer is a human being and you have a particular type of relationship with that customer. At Wells Fargo, we have the ability to prospect that customer. We can combine relationships. I may be a [bank] user, but also a controller of a company. Wells Fargo has the ability to look at me, the customer, as one person. You know how I have a relationship with one company. I might have it with ten companies because I might be a bookkeeper that works for ten different companies. And I also have my personal account."

In other words, it's up to the bank to know you and see all of your relationships and figure out how to best service you.

All this coordination is part of seamless service at Wells Fargo, where "no matter whether you are at the store, or the ATM or online, you are gaining the same information," Johnson continued. "What's more, we know who you are, and we make sure you are treated the same, wherever you do a transaction. If you communicate with us through another channel, that other channel should know that in real time. If you do a transaction on wells-fargo.com, we should see that when you visit a store [branch]. If you go to a store to cash a check, when you go home and get online, you will see the same information. There are still people out there who want to see a live person before they hand over their money. We realize that won't change any time soon. But that's the power of anytime, anywhere, the multiple channels—you get treated the same. The customer can find you and know you, and we will know the customer."

This knowledge is important because it will determine the best channel of dealing with the customer. Gomez Advisors has studied people who bank on the Web and has classified them into distinct personality profiles. The most typical Web banker is an "Internet transactor"; the least typical is a "saver." The former uses the Web for the accessibility it offers in managing checking and credit card accounts and for paying bills. A saver, on the other hand, logs on to a bank Web site to maximize rates received on deposit products.

To share information with its reps and its customers, Wells Fargo put in place a customer relationship management project called eCIC—E-Commerce Customer Interaction Center. "It includes Web-based tools—such as collaboration—that our agents use to be able to do their work. It also includes our Intranet site, which is a sort of portal that provides easy access to perform transactions and allows them see the customer's history and information in their entirety. No matter where you are, you will be able to see the same view as the customers see," said Johnson.

Build a Customer Profile

Enron Energy Services defines "knowing the customer" as comprehending and appreciating their business and their energy uses.

Marty Sunde, vice chairman of EES, described his division as being in "the systems integration business. We exist to serve clients who want complex problems to be solved by a group of experts." Enron doesn't lack for "experts." The division's researchers include an army of engineers and physicists who analyze a customer's office or factory to identify the best cost-saving measures, such as installing energy-efficient lightbulbs or slowing down the pumps on an air-conditioning system. EES's Internet-based system enables its engineers to monitor and control customers' equipment from its Houston headquarters.

Sunde said that his division realized, early on, that as an energy management company, "we have to run this place in an integrated way, totally process-driven, all functions knowing what the others are doing. We became absolute process maniacs because we think that seamless service means absolute commitment to processes and systems."

Enron starts at the prospecting level of building a customer profile. In its databases, the company collects information that relates not just to the basic facts of the contract but also to the financial health of its clients and the topography of where their buildings or plants are located. Enron keeps building on that information as a potential deal matures. To get to know the customers and their needs, Enron account people "ask a lot of questions, and try, real time, using the power of technology to keep our knowledge of the client up to date," Sunde explained. "We try to earn the clients' trust and respect by demonstrating how much we are committed to knowing their environment. That gives us access to more insight-based information. And if I can get true insight into what the client is focused on, then I am totally comfortable with bringing that insight and concern back here to Enron, and throw it into the middle of the table, and let very bright, innovative Enron people chew on it for a while. I guarantee you that we will come back with three or four ideas, and at least one of them will be interesting to pursue. That's a neat part of our culture."

Enron extends its research about a client or potential client by talking to the analysts who follow the client's particular industry.

"Senior executives of a company want to hear what the analysts are saying about them. We add value to the conversation no matter what. It's our attempt to prove that we've gone the extra mile, and that the other guys haven't," said Sunde.

As an example of Enron's thorough research, Sunde suggested: "Let's say you are a business person who is interested in knowing more about where your leverage is. Our big, sophisticated databases tell us where value is. If you say, 'I have a 15,000-square-foot restaurant in Terra Haute, Indiana. My energy bill is this much per month,' one of our people can click a pulldown screen on his computer that will come back with a little diagnosis that says, 'You score out pretty well. Statistics show that your leverage might be in the following three areas. Would you like to learn more?'"

Relying on the skills and energy of the managers it appoints to oversee contracts and contacts with customers, Enron, Sunde explained, "creates a 'partner-in-charge' mentality among its managers, whose job it is to know as much as they can about Enron and its innovations, and how to apply those innovations to the needs of each of our clients." Enron encourages these managers to take the time twice a year to write a memo to the client that reviews the status of Enron's efforts, and offers several new ideas worth considering based on new services and capabilities that the ever-evolving Enron can offer them.

"With an innovative culture like ours, there is so much new going on in the company. We presume that there is going to be some new thing in the whole portfolio of new things that will have application across our client base, and will be new and provocative for the client," said Sunde. "We put metrics in place, and reward people for being driven to add value to the client. When clients know and sense that, they are always happy to have a conversation with you.

"For example, I witnessed that myself at a dinner we had with some clients. Our very best account manager grew up in an engineering and manufacturing environment, and is known in the industry for her skill. She manages our relationship with a *Fortune* 500 manufacturer. Do we have an arrangement with every single plant that manufacturer has worldwide? No. But over a period of a year and a half, she visited every single one of those plants worldwide, to understand exactly how those plant managers think and operate. She is keenly aware that just because an agreement is signed at headquarters doesn't mean it will be accepted with open arms at the plant level. So, she has a personal relationship with every single one of those plant managers. And when she speaks to senior managers at headquarters, she can speak with authority about what's going on in those sites."

Create a Single Source of Customer Information

Oncology Therapeutics Network is taking a similar approach. OTN is working on providing a single source of customer information across all of its delivery channels.

"We are compiling a tremendous amount of information for analysis," chief information officer Sue Dubman told me. "We are putting together a consolidated picture of everything a customer does with us. So, if a customer calls to a call center or the Web center or comes in through the Lynx machine [located in clients' offices], all that information will be in a central database. We will know not only what they did but what they *didn't* do, which may be just as important. If they click on a price [for a particular medication] and leave our Web site, we will know that."

OTN's knowledge of a customer's needs can sometimes be a matter of life and death. Peggy Lehmann, manager of marketing communications, cited the example of a patient receiving treatment with a particular drug that must be administered through a special type of tubing. A client might have bought the drug, but forgot to check its supplies to see if it has the tubing. Using CRM software from Blue Martini (discussed previously), "we can remind them with a message dynamically presented on their computer screen, that while they have the drug, they don't have the ability to administer it. These patients are on very strict schedules, and they need to follow a particular administration plan for the protocol work."

The Blue Martini CRM messaging is user driven. If a medication causes nausea, the customer's Web site will suggest antinausea medication. This feature provides obvious opportunities for cross-selling of additional products. If a customer bought five of a particular product, they are told automatically that they'd get a better discount if they bought six. The software determines what the customer sees on the Web site—as well as what the customer-service rep sees.

At OTN, servicing physicians is the essential element of its commitment to customer service.

"Our customers have two primary issues," said Sue Dubman. "(1) How do I better manage my practice? That gets translated into the whole issue of reimbursement: How do I get paid better? and (2) How do I improve patient care?"

For its individual clients, OTN provides a variety of value-added services, including consulting on reimbursement for the costs of cancer medication, claims processing, recruiting subjects for clinical trials, and management of those clinical trials. OTN provides a monthly inventory management report—a rolling, twelve-month snapshot of a practice's purchasing trends and costs.

OTN gives clients assistance with Web-based programs that provide funding for indigent patients. (With the older population of people with cancer, there are many patients who lack health insurance or who require some financial assistance.) Clients use OTN as a resource when they have patients who need a particular treatment but can't afford it. For people who need help, OTN provides them with a hotline number to designated contacts at OTN's parent company Bristol-Meyers Squibb and other pharmaceutical manufacturers that have their own programs for indigent patients. Additional assistance might come in a more informal way from an OTN sales rep, who might know the pharmaceutical company sales rep that's responsible for that product in the same zip code where the client resides.

Seamless customer service takes on many hues at OTN, as Peggy Lehmann, manager of marketing communications, explained: "Physicians go to medical school to learn how to successfully treat patients. When they actually establish their own practice, they find that behind the treatment of that patient is a huge, complex system that the physicians have to follow up on, in order to stay in business and to continue to be able to treat their patients. When you open a practice, you have to have contracts with manufacturers to even be eligible to purchase drugs. There are many things that happen on the back end of their operations that they may not be fully aware of. So, OTN stepped forward and said, 'There is a need here. What can we do to allow this physician to continue treating patients? How can we make the rest of it seamless for the physician?' Not everything that we are talking about is necessarily a service or a program that OTN manages, but we make sure our accounts are aware of that service or program. So, we give them a course in Business 101. A small single-doctor practice in oncology could be a million-dollar-a-year business, with drugs and staff, but that doctor usually has little business acumen. We are providing a source for that business information so that doctor can deal with the business end of the practice and still treat the patients in a timely manner."

Be Available to Hold
the Customer's Hand

This kind of service requires a lot of attention and hand-holding. To show clients how to order drugs from Lynx2otn.com, OTN sales specialists will take the client's office manager online and walk her step by step through the process. They show the office manager how to select payment terms. They make sure the people listed as part of their practice are still part of the practice. They check to see if any information needs to be updated.

"That attention brings about a higher acceptance rate for this service," said Lehmann. "By walking them through the process, we make life easier for them and we get a cost savings for OTN. We are always going to be available to our customers with live people online, providing that person-to-person contact. At OTN, we are 'people people.'"

"Sometimes we offer services we don't even know we offer," said Mary Seguine, customer service manager. "When a nurse leaves a practice, the doctor will ask if we have someone trained on our system that we can recommend. We never walk away from a sale. We never walk away from the client. There is a lot of turnover, so we are there to train the new people."

OTN's philosophy "is to continue to support the client in an ever-changing environment," said Dubman. "There isn't an environment that's changed more drastically in the last five years than health care, specifically oncology. Seamless service means keeping up with those changes while continuing to provide a recognizable brand. Ten years ago, we started by delivering to the first practice in the trunk of a car. Then, over the years, we began supporting the oncologist with information on drugs and with connections to certain reimbursement programs. We handle the administration of the most complicated manufacturing programs—not only for the oncologist but also for the manufacturer. The day-to-day lives of oncologists have become so complicated and their environment is changing so fast, they need someone to connect the dots for them. If we are successful in connecting every dot, we are providing a one-stop shop for them."

On the technology side, seamless service means "making it easy for them to order drugs, getting the drugs delivered to the customer, helping them with their reimbursement problems, helping them understand how these drugs are used and what the effect of those drugs are in terms of their patient care," added Dubman. "So, the more integrated we can be with their systems, and the more integrated we are at OTN (in terms of our delivery to the customer), the more seamless it's going to be."

Feedback: Metrics

Most smart companies elicit feedback from their customers.

OTN periodically brings together advisory boards of medical professionals to discuss their current issues and to see where their businesses are going. These meetings give participants an opportunity to bounce ideas off each other, and help OTN staffers understand the state of mind of its clients and to generate ideas and options for the future. OTN's Web chat collaboration feature affords office managers in different parts of the country a medium to talk to each other, providing the backbone for the community.

REI researches customer service metrics in a number of ways. "We do primary research through surveys of every single customer who checks out with us online," said Senior Vice President

Matt Hyde. "So, if you shop with us online, you are asked if you want to take a customer service survey. We aggregate that information and we look at it every month. Secondarily, we do a bi-yearly mail-in survey of customer service. We watch particular metrics. Periodically, if we want some particular information, we'll do focus groups or usability groups. We'll bring people in and actually ask them some questions. The most important tool for us is the ongoing monthly service that we do with shoppers on rei.com."

At Tesco, the company frequently conducts panels with customers who are invited to a store or to a hotel. While the panels are hosted by a professional moderator, also in attendance are in-store staff, the store manager and, on occasion, members of the tesco.com board. "We give the customers something to eat or drink, and then we get to ask them a series of questions of how they are finding things; what's on their mind. 'What's good? What's bad? How do we improve things for you?'" said John Browett.

Communication: Speak to Your Customers with a Single Voice

Communication—whether internal or external—is the Achilles' heel of most companies. Because internal and external communication often intersect, it is essential that all divisions of a company talk with each other all the time. If you can't communicate among yourselves, how can you possibly hope to communicate with your customers?

OTN went through a restructuring of its customer service operations after it saw that the various parts of its organization—drug-dispensing technology group, call center, Web operations, etc.—had developed into independent "silos," with separate customer databases all over the U.S. To create an integrated multichannel delivery system with CRM features, OTN enlisted Blue Martini Software to devise an issues-management system that enables the customer to call for service and be connected to the person or department who can help her, without being transferred all over the organization. That system is supported by the feet on the street—the people out there talking to the customers every day.

FedEx, with its many different divisions and services, was also faced with the rise of dozens of silos. But the package-delivery company recognized that it had to speak to the customer with a single voice and has been taking steps to reorganize the company to achieve that end. To provide more seamless service, FedEx has been integrating its teams of marketing, sales, and customer service, which had been separated for two years until the company brought them together in 2000. At that time, FedEx redesigned its infrastructure, bringing in a new integrated desktop system that consolidated all the customer service information from every channel, new Local Access Networks, and new servers on its computers, which were able to display all the available information on each customer.

"There's been a revolution going on here," senior vice president Laurie Tucker told me. "We've reorganized ourselves as a company, so that we could talk to the customer with a single voice." In June 2000, FedEx created a new corporation called FedEx Corporate Services, which brought together the marketing, sales, and information technology operations from all FedEx companies and created one entity under one CEO, "so that we could face the customer as one. Our operating companies still operate independently, but our customer sees a single face so that we can present the full solution. FedEx wants to be able to say 'yes' to all of our customers' various shipping needs."

Several years ago, when FedEx began acquiring other package-delivery companies, "there was a lot of debate about whether we could make our other companies match the service expectation of the FedEx brand," Tucker recalled. "We soon realized that these companies would need to meet that FedEx gold standard within their service area. Our ground business has got to be the gold standard for ground service. Reaching that understanding was a breakthrough for us. In the future, as we continue to acquire or develop new services that build up our portfolio—both on the information side and the physical-transportation side—the constant challenge facing us is to provide the seamless experience across all areas of FedEx. When you contact us, we will answer your questions about any of these various transportation services or information services."

In January 2000, FedEx gave all its companies the FedEx name. Prior to that, the company was operating under several designations: FedEx, RPS, and Viking. The premise behind the renaming was to reorganize everything under the powerful FedEx brand and present that single face to the customer. "We've been working toward this goal of having the customer go only to one place, to receive only one bill, to go to only one Web site, to talk to only one person, or be sold to by only one person," said Tucker.

Along with its customer-relationship-management software, FedEx has a plan to implement a customer compliment and complaint system, through which it will direct both bouquets and brickbats to the appropriate department. When a customer submits a complaint, it will be routed to a staff person who is charged with solving it. If that person doesn't solve it within a certain time, it gets flagged to the next level of management, all the way up to the CEO, who will be able to see on-screen the customer's complete interaction history (telephone calls and e-mail), whom he spoke to and/or e-mailed (the information includes the ID number of the employees who dealt with the customer), and how the problem was (or was not) dealt with. These details will be shared in a database at FedEx's Information Super Hub. "We would then give instantaneous information to all channels (including the Web) to the customer to view the status, to the account executive who may call on the customer, or to the customer representative or courier who may have contact with the customer," said Sheila Harrell, vice president of customer service, strategic planning, and analysis. "Our strategic direction is to provide a seamless point of access to all channels, to integrate our systems, and to automate solutions for all transactions so that we make it easier for our customers to do business with us. We want as much of our operations integrated as possible to enable any employee who has contact with the customer to provide the best possible service."

Cynthia Henson pointed out, "You need everybody to be looking at the same information *and* it has to be *not* in FedEx jargon but in terms that are understandable to the customer, and presented in an easy fashion, so that the customer automatically thinks of going to the Web or the Interactive Voice Response system to get the simple things done, such as scheduling a pickup without having to talk to a rep."

Can Canned Responses

Concetta Conkling's Wells Fargo group works as an internal consultant entity within the bank. "We don't really own anything," she conceded, which is why her group succeeds by striking the right internal political balance.

"We try to work with the groups within the company," she said. "Sometimes, that means bringing other groups to the table, and getting visibility to the issues. All sorts of things pass through my desk. People love to find someone they can pass things off to; that's human nature. I usually help by connecting the dots. I take their hand and put it in somebody else's hand and say, 'work it together. If you need me, I'll come in and help.' A lot of times, I'm prompted to look at something based on my experience as a Wells Fargo customer. I look for inconsistencies in the experience. If I find that a customer can do X at two of the three channels but when they try it on the third channel, they can't, I'll find out why. What would it take to do it on the other channel? Is it important for the customer to be able to do it on the other channel? It's a matter of looking at costs versus benefits."

Wells Fargo reinforces to its team members the bank's customer-service standards—the promises it makes to its customers. "We tell them what the customers should expect," said Conkling. "If you don't tell employees what they should tell customers, the employees will make it up. If you tell them, and try to make it easy, you've got a better chance of them telling the right thing. Otherwise, you've got service failure before you start."

Wells Fargo, like many companies dealing with customer service issues, has gone back and forth between canned responses based on frequently asked questions and fuller responses depending on the situation.

At first, "We would write paragraphs that suggested an answer for an e-mail to a customer," explained Gailyn Johnson. "We then did full e-mail responses that would conclude, 'Thank you for your inquiry to Wells Fargo.' We learned that only 50 percent of the e-mails that come in ask just one question. They always ask two or more questions. None of those e-mail responses really addressed the question. Even though you may ask what appears to be the same question four times, the answer is usually different."

Consequently, Wells Fargo is moving away from the canned, automated e-mail responses because "the customer would come back and say, 'You didn't even answer my question,'" Johnson noted. "But they didn't know that some human really did read it, and really picked from 250 suggested responses. We decided, if we've gone to all that trouble, why not make it a human touch e-mail? How do you turn stodgy e-mail responses into a personal communication?"

Wells has been looking at ways to make the online experience as personal as the branch experience. Johnson admitted that, "Some canned responses go out with my name on them. Sometimes I wish they didn't. If a customer e-mails us that we made a mistake, I will e-mail or call them myself. They get blown away that there really is a Gailyn Johnson and that I've actually called them. Many believe it's a ficticious name." Johnson enjoys making those calls because, "The most valuable feedback you can have is talking to the customer. People talk to our agents by name, and the agents develop a relationship with them. What makes electronic financial services really powerful is that when you are doing a chat, you're chatting with 'Dave from Wells Fargo.' When someone asks an off-the-wall question—not one with a simple answer—and you get it answered by Dave, that's great service. A real person knows the answer."

Increasing functionality on the site is another way to better lever-age the customer service staff. Through the use of technology-based programs, Wells Fargo is able to give better customer serv-ice, because its customer-service representatives have greater access to information through technology. The bank continues to make a lot of self-service functions available on the Web, such as automating the process that reminds customers of their passwords.

Communicate to Enrich the Relationship

The San Francisco Giants' Client Service Group is composed of personal account managers who are considered by season tick-etholders as their personal representatives with the Giants. These account managers are there for their clients—from answering the most mundane questions to making sure that the tickets are sent out in plenty of time.

Every November, after the conclusion of the baseball season, Client Services sends to all season ticketholders a "proof of performance" brochure—a four-color annual report that recaps the season's highlights. After the first of the year, the Giants follow that up by sending out a special highlight video. Some client representatives even send birthday cards to Giants fans who don't find that kind of attention to be intrusive. These gestures are part of a series of interactions, such as in-person meetings, mailings and correspondence, that are intended for clients "to see their Giant relationship as something more than the bill they get to renew next year's season ticket," explained Tom McDonald, senior vice president of consumer marketing.

Russ Stanley, vice president of ticket services/client relations, believes that all these channels tie together with how well customers are treated when they order their tickets, when they receive the tickets, and when they are invoiced for tickets.

"We decided a few years ago that the operational side and the customer-service side should be married together, because we look at every step along the way as a customer-service opportunity, as a way to impress our customers," said Stanley. "Ten years ago, we would send customers an invoice, which was nothing more than an NCR form in triplicate. It looked like a bill you would get after you just had your house painted. Over the past five years, we have upgraded the presentation of the way the tickets are delivered, the way we invoice people—i.e., the way we interact with our customers."

The Giants have even improved the quality of the look and feel of the tickets themselves. "It used to be a paper ticket with a game number on it. Now, the ticket is four colors, and typically has a photo that commemorates something special from Giants' history," said Stanley. "In 2001, we used highlights from the 2000 season, with the opening of the new ballpark and the team's winning the National League West championship. As we focus in on service, we ask ourselves how we can ease the process of collecting money; sending tickets; delivering a good-quality ticket. For example, we make sure they have their tickets on time before the first game. We don't send an envelope. We send our white vinyl boxes that say 'Giants Season Tickets' that arrive inside a FedEx envelope."

Know and Respect
Existing Client Relationships

Enron Energy Services' issue-management system is driven by a specially designed software program. Anyone in the company who is working on any issue that deals with servicing the client—a billing question, for example—can log and date the issue in the issues-management system. An Enron employee will be assigned to resolve it. If the issue is still unsettled after the deadline date has passed, "I get a little love note on my PC, as does my chief operating officer and friend Dan Leff. Everybody knows that the e-mail goes to me if something is delinquent," said Marty Sunde.

EES ranks issues from "very high in impact to a client to low impact on the client, but an irritant internally," explained Sunde, who focuses on the issues with the highest impact on the client. "For example, a client receives a phone call from the local utility that is providing the service, and the utility tells the client that they are going to cut off service. Uh-oh. What have we done? In that case, the screen burns red right away. People are deployed to go fix that."

Because EES faces those kinds of time- and cost-sensitive decisions, "That's why we are so committed to the whole process, which requires that anybody who's going to interact with a client must first check the database to see if that client is not already somebody else's client. It doesn't restrict you from interacting with a client, but it does require you to show the respect of an existing relationship," said Sunde.

"Our philosophy is that even big companies are aggregations of lots of different kinds of buyers," he added. "We don't constrain ourselves to believe that everything has to be checked at one door into the client, because that might put us at a disadvantage. But everything does have to be checked against a database, which we require to be constantly updated from multiple channels. With the biggest relationships, where there is somebody assigned to manage all the complexity, we require that there be some kind of interaction—either electronically or voice-to-voice—to let them know what you are doing. If you want to have interaction with Customer X, you must take note of who the account manager is. You are required to send that account manager an e-mail, which shows up as a little alert on her screen that says, 'New interaction notification.' That gives the account manager the opportunity to decide what to do next. The work flow of the software allows us to have those triggers. We know that on any given day, a different Enron person might interact with that client. They can, at least, have an edge in being able to interact with the client by referring to the data when they pull up that client's record."

Internal Communication
Improves Service

Internal communication can be just as challenging in a 50-person company as it is in a 5,000- or 250,000-person company. The Geek

Squad uses Nextel two-way radios, with text messaging, so technicians can call back the client right away. Every tech can access The Geek Squad's customer database to find the last time a client was serviced. "It helps having the extra information," said Robert Stephens. "There might be a note that says, 'This client is very adamant about being on time.' Or 'they like you to sit down for 10 minutes each time.' It's like when you check into a hotel that already knows your likes and dislikes."

The entire internal billing system is available on the Web site for the company's technicians, who are able to book a job from home. Rather than come into the office, techs can get up in the morning, log on to the internal, secure The Geek Squad Web site, print out their schedule, and go straight to their first job. Motivated by being paid by salary plus commission, the techs can use the extra time to squeeze in one extra job per day. They can also download driving directions from their home address to the customer site through Yahoo Maps. At the same time, The Geek Squad's in-house staff can track exactly where any of the Squad's remote technicians are. When the technicians connect to the site for their day's schedule, they are given updated traffic reports and the approximate time it will take to finish the job.

Foresight: Be Proactive in Anticipating Customers' Needs

According to Cynthia Henson, vice president of customer service at FedEx: "We decided to change the way we approach service. Service is what's going to make or break us. It's not going to be price because we've got that in line. It's going to be the relationship we have with the customer and how that customer feels about his interactions with FedEx."

Based on research, FedEx learned that its customers wanted more from FedEx than they were getting. They wanted the company to be more proactive when it came to problem solving. The one thing customers wanted most was for FedEx to call them "when we think they're having a problem," said Henson. FedEx had been doing some of that, but not as a matter of course on every shipment. "We want to know about the problem before the customer does, and be able to solve it."

FedEx has discovered the importance to customers of being proactive in the notification of the status of their shipments.

"A lot of things can happen when a package crosses borders," said Laurie Tucker. "If a customer has issues with documentation, or the customs agent in a particular country just decides he wants to hold the shipment for a day and inspect it, that's very frustrating. Let's say the customer is Intel, which is shipping chips to Dell Computer, whose strategy is built around carrying no inventory. If that shipment were held in customs in Anchorage, and Dell and/or Intel are not notified of that, the chips could sit there in customs with no proactive action going on."

It took FedEx several years to develop a system to address this situation.

"Customers subscribe to a service called Insight on fedex.com," Tucker told me. "They would tell us which shipping/account numbers they wanted us to track. Then, we proactively notify that customer—or anyone else the customer designates—of the status of that particular shipping number. So, when that shipment starts to leave the country of origin, we immediately begin to give the client access to the information on that shipment that was scanned into the system. They can log in to fedex.com, they enter their Insight number and they go straight into a Web-browser-based screen that shows them the status of that shipment all the way. If it were to hit a problem in customs, we've set up alerts that will then notify that customer in their preferred way—fax, page, or e-mail—and inform them of the problem. We give them the necessary document or form to fill out or finish. They send it back to us, and we will get the shipment out of customs. That is radically new in our industry. No one had been able to provide the customer with that level of control over their International shipments. Before, we would tell them what was wrong and then work to get that shipment out of customs."

Sheila Harrell noted that when FedEx talks to a customer, and looks at their issues and concerns over recent weeks, "you can see where the patterns are and you can work to solve those issues in a much more proactive manner. I don't mean just calling the customer and telling him that there will be a delay in the delivery of his package. But rather, you identify a problem and find a way to resolve that problem in advance, so that the customer never has to call you back to tell you about the problem. Our proactive philosophy is 'anticipate their needs and they will buy more.'"

As an example, Harrell cited the mundane—but important—task of ordering supplies, such as FedEx boxes and envelopes and airbills. "If a customer calls to order preprinted airbills, you can say to them, 'Do you know you can shop via the Internet at fedex.com?' At that moment, our customer service people are educating the customers. They can tell customers that they can print their airbill from fedex.com with their own printer. They can set it up to get automatic notification and proof of delivery when the package is shipped. We can send notification out to the recipient, etc. But, if the customer wants to trace a package that's been lost, we are not going to mention the Web to them; that's not the answer for them. Instead, we're going to take the information and commit to doing the research ourselves."

Her colleague, Henson, agreed: "You don't want the reps to have the information before it's posted on the Web, because then the customer will think that they can't rely on the Web, and need to go to the rep."

OTN is also working on being more proactive with its clients. The ideal vehicle for that is the Lynx System, the integrated, point-of-care drug dispensing and tracking system that OTN installs in the offices of oncology practices. Lynx System acts like a combination of an ATM and a candy vending machine. A simple touch screen and self-help menus guide the user through a sequence of user-friendly steps. OTN develops interfaces between the practice-management systems and the Lynx machines, which benefits the customers because it reduces the amount of manual labor they have in their office. The benefit for OTN is cleaner data. If the Lynx system sees that a client's inventory levels are dropping, Lynx automatically puts in replenishment orders.

Louis Chinn, OTN's director of quality leadership, explained: "We want to be proactive in anticipating our clients' needs and letting our clients know how we think the environment will change. For example, when we introduced Lynx technology, nobody in this country had done this in oncology practice. We saw that doctors needed more time with patients and needed quality information to be able to treat patients. They need to anticipate what their costs are, their clinical aspects, etc."

So, part of OTN's issues-management is product planning. For example, "We call their office and tell them that we are ready to install the interface for the Lynx system, and we ask them if they've installed the phone line that they will be needing to use for the system," said Robin Sippel, vice president of customer service. "We continue to follow up with them and remind them when we will be in to install the system."

Simple gestures like that are the essence of great customer service—anytime, anywhere.

✼   ✼   ✼

Takeaways

Without the "high touch" of customer service, all the bells and whistles of the Web, the customer-relationship-management software, the fancy new stores and the Web-enabled kiosks don't mean a thing. The primary challenge is being able to coordinate all these channels to deliver seamless customer service. The five key elements are:

Commitment:

Make customer service not a strategy but a way of life. All the top companies are constantly reinforcing the importance of customer service among their employees. They find ways to single out and reward those people so that the ethic of customer service becomes an integral part of the corporate culture. Management should lead by example. At the same time, recognize that total customer satisfaction is an impossibility. Michael Powell said: "A lot of companies want to go to 99.9 percent. I can tell you that, in retail, if you go to 99.9 percent, you're out of business."

- ♦ Resolve issues quickly.
- ♦ Promote corporate values.
- ♦ Encourage employee empowerment.

Preparation:

Train your people to give great service. Once you hire good people, constantly find ways to educate them on the products and services you sell. When appropriate, encourage them to use those products and services so they are equipped to talk about them. Good customer service is essentially the same, regardless of how you're doing it or what technology you're using.

- Hire people with the right attitude.
- Teach special skills for conducting business online.

Knowledge:

Intimately know your customers across all channels. One of the advantages of technology is our ability to gather massive amounts of data on our customers. Customers are willing to give up this information if, in return, companies will use it to provide better customer service. This knowledge of customers is especially important because it will determine the best channel of dealing with the customer.

- Look at customers as human beings, not account numbers.
- Build a strong customer profile.
- Create a single source of customer information.
- Be there to hold the customer's hand.

Communication:

Communicate internally within your organization, and externally with your customers, suppliers and partners. Poor communication—whether internal or external—is the Achilles' heel of most companies. Because internal and external communication often intersect, it is essential that all divisions of a company talk with each other. If you can't communicate among yourselves, how can you possibly hope to communicate with your customers?

- Speak with a single voice.
- Can canned responses.
- Communicate to enrich the relationship.
- Be aware of and respect existing client relationships.
- Improve service with internal communication.

Foresight:

Be proactive in anticipating your customers' needs. Customers want you to be able to take the information that you have on them and use it to deliver great service. Cynthia Henson of FedEx noted: "The one thing customers wanted most was for FedEx to call them when we think they're having a problem." If you are able to forecast what your client needs before the client knows it, you may just have gotten yourself a customer for life—anytime, anywhere.

Source Notes

The bulk of the material for this book came from my independent research and exclusive interviews with key executives of the featured companies, which took place between January and April, 2001. Secondary material came from the following sources:

Chapter 1

"I enjoyed the treasure hunt," he recalled. *The Oregonian,* August 15, 1999.

Although Tesco possessed one of Britain's most powerful brands, "you could have raised a laugh in the City [of London] by suggesting Tesco of all companies was destined to be Britain's prime contender for membership of an elite of international retailers." *Financial Times,* Mar 24, 2001.

"If we were worried about cannibalization, we would never have moved from small High Street stores to supermarkets to superstores to hypermarkets. For us, grocery home shopping is just another format that delivers for a particular set of customer needs." *Time International,* October 30, 2000.

"Many businesses have been like deer frozen in the headlights because of their channel conflicts," opined Matt Hyde. *Context Magazine,* September 1999.

Chapter 2

"When customers think of REI, they don't think of us as a dot-com business or a catalog business or a brick-and-mortar business. They think of our brand as encompassing all of those channels of distribution. And the expectations they have of us are identical no matter how they shop from us." *Darwin* magazine, February 1, 2001.

"Cannibalization is Good." *Forbes,* July 24, 2000.

Dan Nordstrom: "You just sell more." *Wall Street Journal*, July 17, 2000.

"If a customer is in possession of a good they're dissatisfied with, it doesn't do you any good to have them keep it," Dan Nordstrom reasoned. "Every time they look at it, it gives them a weird, negative connotation that filters back to where they got it. We'd rather get it out of your closet and give you something you feel good about." *Wall Street Journal*, July 17, 2000.

"Customers are not all that interested in our channel operations," said Dan Nordstrom. "They are interested in a relationship with a retailer." *BusinessWeek*, November 11, 2000.

Clyde Ostler, group executive vice president of Wells Fargo's Internet Service Group, has noted that the bank may eliminate bank officers having to answer mundane questions, such as the status of wire transfers or interest rates, so they can focus on more value-added tasks. "We hope that with the Internet, we can do in one step what now takes two or three." *Fast Company*, page 145, © September 2000.

Chapter 3

Dan Nordstrom envisions the day when people will have access at home to fast, broadband Internet connections because "That's the point at which we expect fashion products to really take off. With most people now using 56K modems, you have to have a pretty spare presentation on the Web site. The things that are going to increase business online are more speed, better search tools, and an environment that's merchandised in a way that makes sense." *Women's Wear Daily*, April 9, 2001.

"When you come into a store, you need a soft landing where you can take a breath and orient yourself, as opposed to getting assaulted by a barrage of offers all at once. We wanted to create that soft landing online," explained Maryam Mohit, vice president of site design for Amazon, who told the *New York Times* that her design team was influenced by the book *Why We Buy: The Science of Shopping*, by Paco Underhill, founder of Envirosell, a marketing research firm that studies shopping behavior. According to Underhill's book, "In the world of cyberspace, everywhere is an exit. You have the capacity to bail out at any point, and an enormous number of people do." *New York Times*, October 30, 2000.

But when you have 60,000 images, at a price of $300 to $500 each, you get costs that are "out of control," said Dan Nordstrom. *Ecompany*, April 2001.

"In a physical store, we're confined by a box," explained Hyde. "The Internet allows us to grow and expand business." *InformationWeek*, May 1, 2000.

According to a survey by Jupiter Research, 90 percent of online customers prefer some form of human interaction during an e-commerce transaction. *Lands' End Press Release*, September 15, 2000.

Chapter 4

Yet, less than 20 percent of retailers have access to a customer's online and offline purchasing history, according to a poll by Jupiter Media Metrix. *Wall Street Journal*, October 23, 2000.

E-mail's greatest virtue is that its effect can be easily tracked and readily quantifiable. William Park, the chief executive of Digital Impact, once told the *New York Times* that e-mail was "the most measurable marketing vehicle of all time. You know exactly who you are sending e-mails to, you know how they are responding—did they click, did they buy? People respond to their e-mails in a matter of days or they won't respond at all. So marketers can determine if their campaign was a success in 48 hours versus the four-to-six weeks it might take for a direct mail campaign." *New York Times*, December 13, 2000.

"We long ago quit worrying about safeguarding every piece of information about ourselves," Bob Wientzen, president and CEO of the

Direct Marketing Association, told *Business 2.0* magazine. *Business 2.0*, January 21, 2001.

According to the Pew Internet & American Life Project, 64 percent of Internet users have shared, or are willing to share, personal information such as an e-mail address or name in order to use a Web site. *Business 2.0,* January 21, 2001.

Chapter 5

"We will never make Amazon.com fun and engaging in the same way as the great physical bookstores are," Bezos has admitted. "You'll never be able to hear the bindings creak and smell the books and have tasty lattes and soft sofas at Amazon.com." *New York Times,* February 27, 1999.

As Julie Mancini, executive director of Portland Arts & Lectures, has said, "If there's a new edition of the Bible, people expect God to be at Powell's to sign books." *Seattle Post-Intelligencer,* December 29, 1998.

"In some people's minds branch banking is dead," said Robert Chlebowski, Wells's executive vice president of distribution strategies. "What's dead are branches limited to banking transactions."*Forbes*, October 30, 2000.

FedEx felt that its World Service Centers "could communicate a lot more," said Gayle Christensen, director of global brand management. "We know why people drop things off—convenience." *Ecompany,* April 2001.

Steve Chaffin, who heads the Internet kiosk program for Kmart, has said that, "Everyone talks about how they want their Web sites to be sticky. Well, with [kiosks], it's just the opposite. We're trying to make them slippery, so the customer can get in and out quickly." *New York Times*, February 19, 2001.

"At Tesco we pride ourselves on looking after our customers but there are limits," said Carolyn Bradley, Chief Operation Officer. "We are advising our drivers to be as helpful as they can, but we have to strike a balance without inconveniencing other customers by being late [for deliveries]." *Times of London*, July 9, 2000.

Chapter 6

In a poll by Jupiter Media Metrix of New York, 1,900 American shoppers listed among their primary complaints about shopping online having to deal with customer-service representatives who had sparse knowledge about the products and services that their Web site was offering. *New York Times*, March 25, 2001.

Ann Olson, vice president of customer services, told *IQ Magazine*: "Good customer service is essentially the same at a high level, regardless of how you're doing it or what technology you're using. This is our ongoing Internet strategy to provide the best and most consistent online customer service in the marketplace." *IQ Magazine*, April 2000.

I think Dennis Madsen, chief executive officer of Recreational Equipment, Inc., hit the nail on the head when he said, "This business isn't about technology. It's about understanding the customer and translating that understanding into strategies and tactics that will take care of his needs and expectations." *Darwin* magazine, February 1, 2001.

Index

Absolutely Amanda column,
108–109, 151
Accel Partners, 46
Affinity programs, 150–155
Aggregation, 132
Airplane Read, The, 63
Akamai Technologies, Inc., 92
Albertson's, 177
Alliances, 114–117
Amazon.com, 33, 88, 89,
125–126, 165, 255, 256
Andreessen, Mark, 26
Anytime, anywhere banking, 25,
27, 28, 204
ATM networks, 186
Automated Delivery System
(ADS), 180

Banking business. *See*
Washington Mutual Bank;
Wells Fargo & Co.
Bank of America Business Center,
181–182
Barnes & Noble, 46, 47

Bass, Bill
on employee training, 221
on multichannel
synchronization, 50, 51, 54
on My Virtual Model feature,
143, 145
on online sales, 7, 8
on privacy policy, 156–157
on Web site design, 83, 91–92,
102–103
Better Business Bureau, 156
Bezos, Jeffrey, 165, 256
Blue Martini Software, 238
Bon Appétit, 200
Book business. *See* Amazon.com;
Barnes & Noble; Borders
Books & Music; 800-CEO-
READ; Powell's Books
Borders Books & Music, 188
Boston Consulting Group, 86–87
Bradley, Carolyn, 173, 193–194,
257
Bravo Zulu, 206–207
Brick-and-mortar channel, 163–201

business-to-business, 178–181
Enron Industrial Markets
    paper plants, 182–184
FedEx, 178–181
Nordstrom, Inc., 169–170,
    172
Oncology Therapeutics
    Network (OTN) oncology
    practices, 184–185
Powell's Books, 165–169
Recreational Equipment, Inc.
    (REI), 163–165
San Francisco Giants Business
    Center, 181–182
Tesco PLC, 172–178
Wells Fargo & Co. branch
    banking, 170–171
See also kiosks
Bridgett, Helen, 154
Bristol-Myers Squibb Company,
    28, 136, 234
Broughton, Joan, 60, 61, 82, 88,
    90, 96, 128, 191
Browett, John
    on Clubcard customer-loyalty
        program, 151, 153–154
    on corporate values, 210–211
    on customer service, 212
    on e-mail, 146
    on multichannel
        synchronization, 47, 55–56
    on online sales, 30–33
    on personalization, 134–135
    on store inventory, 177

on warehouse models, 174
on Web site design, 84
Business 2.0, 155, 256
Business Book Gazette (catalog),
    62
Business Book Gazette
    newsletter, 213
BusinessLink, 10
BusinessWeek, 254

CancerEducation.com, 116–117
Candlestick Park, 34–35
Cannibalization, 46, 48, 50,
    55–56, 59, 79, 253, 254
CARE (Commit, Assurance,
    Responsiveness, Empathy),
    207–208
Carlzon, Jan, 214
Carmichael, Kris, 213–214
Cash America International, Inc.,
    171
Catalog Age, 6
Catalog(s)
    channel, 62–63
    Frederick's of Hollywood, 13,
        51, 57
    Lands' End, 6, 50, 57, 63
    Nordstrom, Inc., 37, 38, 57
    Recreational Equipment, Inc.
        (REI), 42, 53–54
    retailers, 3
    Tesco PLC, 153
Chaffin, Steve, 188, 256
Chinn, Louis, 249

Chlebowski, Robert, 171, 256
Christensen, Gayle, 181
Clements, Dave, 194
Clickpaper.com, 15, 16–17
    customer feedback and, 101
    design of, 83–84, 95
    Enron Industrial Markets
        paper plants and, 182–184
    personalization and, 138–141
    speed of, 89
Client Relations Executives
    (CREs), 197–198
Clubcard customer-loyalty
    program, 151–154
Cohen, Jack, 30
Comer, Gary C., 6
Commitment, 203, 204–216, 250
    to corporate values, 210–212
    to customer service as way of
        life, 204–209
    to employee empowerment,
        212–216
    to resolving customer issues,
        209–210
Communication, 203, 237–246,
    251
    avoiding canned responses,
        240–242
    for customer relationship
        enrichment,
        242–244
    with existing clients, 244–245
    internal, 245–246
    with single voice, 237–240

Community, 106–107
Computer-repair business. *See*
    The Geek Squad
Conkling, Concetta F., 207–208,
    214–216, 225, 240–241
Context Magazine, 253
Cookies, 159
Cooperative, consumer. *See*
    Recreational Equipment,
    Inc. (REI)
Corporate values, 210–212
COSMOS, 9, 10
Covert, Jack, 62–63, 65, 142–143,
    213–214
Crane, Bob, 139–140, 183, 184
Cropper, Andy, 176–177, 211–212
Cross-marketing, 52–56
Customer Compliment and
    Complaint system, 239–240
Customer resource management
    (CRM), 125
Customer service, seamless,
    203–252
    corporate values and, 210–212
    feedback and, 236–237
    foresight and, 246–249
    issues resolution, 209–210
    takeaways, 250–252
    See also Commitment;
        Communication; Knowledge;
        Preparation
Customization vs. personalization,
    125–128. *See also*
    Personalization

Daishowa Forest Products, 183
Darwin, 254, 257
Datamonitor PLC, 7
Dickens Books Limited, 40
"Doing It Right For The
    Customer" group, 207–208
Double play exchange window,
    103–106
Drobny, Jerry, 35, 36, 148–149
Dubman, Sue, 29, 94, 117, 232,
    233, 235–236
Dyer, David, 50–51

eCIC-E-Commerce Customer
    Interaction Center, 229
eCommerce Builder, 110
eCompany, 13–14, 255, 256
Eddie Bauer, 53, 62
800-CEO-READ, 6, 39–40,
    62–63, 65, 68, 141–143,
    213–214
E-mail
    Frederick's of Hollywood and,
        51, 150–151, 158
    Lands' End and, 7, 64, 157,
        220
    loyalty and, 146–150
    Nordstrom, Inc. and, 37
    Park on, 255–256
    Powell's Books and, 72, 158
    Recreational Equipment, Inc.
        (REI) and, 156
    Wells Fargo & Co. and, 223,
        241–242

Employees, 205–207, 209,
    210–217
Energy business. *See* Enron
    Corp.
Enron Corp., 6, 13–17, 140
Enron Energy Services (EES),
    15–16, 77, 229–232, 244–245
Enron Industrial Markets, 17,
    182–184
EnronOnline, 15, 89
Envirosell, 89
Ernst & Young, 96

Fargo, William G., 24
Fast Company, 254
Federal Express Corporation. *See*
    FedEx
FedEx, 4, 6, 8–12
    commitment to customer
        service, 206–207
    communication with customers,
        238–240
    kiosks, 192
    knowledge about customers at,
        226–227
    on moving customers across
        channels, 77–78
    Oncology Therapeutics
        Network (OTN) and, 131
    partnerships, 114–115
    personalization and, 128–131,
        196–197
    preparation for customer
        service, 217

proactive customer service, 246–249

returns and, 58–59

stores, 178–181

telephones and, 66–68

World Service Centers, 256

See also FedEx Web site

FedEx Corporate Services, 238

FedEx Custom Critical, 9

FedEx Express, 9

FedEx Freight, 9

FedEx Ground, 9

FedEx Overnight Letter, The, 9

FedEx Trade Networks, 9

FedEx Web site

alliances on, 115

design, 83

ease of use, 93

feedback from customers on, 99

international business on, 113–114

moving customers to, 78

personalization on, 129

small businesses and, 109–111

speed, 86–87

start up, 10–11

training employees for, 227

Feedback, customer, 98–101, 236–237, 242

Fidelity Investments, 187–188

Financial Times, 30, 253

Flowers, 108–109

Food retailers. *See* Tesco PLC

Forbes, 254, 256

Forbes's Best of the Web, 20, 43

Foreign Exchange Online, 53

Foresight, 203, 246–249, 252

Forest products, 16–17

Forrester Group, 39

Forrester Research, 147

Fortune, 14

Frank, Amanda, 108–109, 151

Frederick's of Hollywood, 6, 12–13, 73–74

e-mail and, 147, 150–151, 158

multichannel synchronization, 51–52

returns and, 57, 58

Star Club affinity program, 150–151

Frederick's of Hollywood Web site

Absolutely Amanda column, 108–109

channel synchronization and, 51

feedback from customers on, 98–99

international business on, 111, 112

moving customers to, 73–74

privacy/security, 158

shopping on, 13, 82

Star Club affinity program and, 150–151

FX-TV network, 217

Gap, The, 192
Garden State Paper Company,
    183
Gartner Financial Services, 75
*Geek Squad Guide to Solving Any
    Computer Glitch, The*
    (Stephens), 219–220
Geek Squad, The. *See* The Geek
    Squad
Global Reach, Inc., 111
Global Trade Manager, 110
Goldstein, Mark H., 123
Gomez Advisors, 76, 229
Gomez.com, 156
Grocery retailers. *See* Tesco PLC
GroceryWorks, 177–178
Grover, Wendy, 47, 99, 187
GUARANTEED.PERIOD, 7

Haba, Toto, 136
Harrell, Sheila, 66, 227, 240, 248
Healthcare services. *See*
    Oncology Therapeutics
    Network (OTN)
Henson, Cynthia, 4, 77, 226, 227,
    240, 246–249
Home Delivery Network, 180
HomeGrocer.com, 33
Home Shopping Network, 52
Hyde, Matt
    on channel conflicts, 42, 253
    on customer feedback, 237
    on the Internet, 255
    on multichannel

synchronization, 3–4, 48, 49,
    54–55, 59–60
    on seamless customer service,
    204
    on Web site, 42–43, 91, 97–98,
    100–101

ImageTwin Personal Body
    Scanning, 143–144
InformationWeek, 255
Institutional Investor, 27
International business, 111–114
International Resource Center,
    110–111
Internet
    banking service, 26
    Enron Corp. and, 14–15
    FedEx and, 10, 12
    Lands' End and, 8
    Major League Baseball (MLB)
        and, 36–37
    Nordstrom, Inc. and, 37–39
    Powell's Books and, 19–20, 168
    privacy, 155–160
    San Francisco Giants and, 35
    security, 25–26, 155–160
    Tesco PLC and, 30–33
    Wells Fargo & Co. and, 25–28,
        68
    See also E-mail; Web site(s)
Internet Bulletin Board system,
    19
Internet Security Server Digital
    ID, 159

Internet Services Group (ISG), 27, 47, 75, 99, 187, 254

IQ Magazine, 222, 257

iVillage,Inc., 107

Jack Covert Selects, 63

Johnson, Gailyn A.
  on customer knowledge, 228–229
  on e-mail, 81, 241–242
  on employee training, 223–224
  on kiosks, 186
  on multichannels, 52
  on online banking, 25, 26, 27
  on Web-access ATMs, 186
  on Web site design, 94

Jupiter Media Metrix, 45, 123, 216, 255, 257

Jupiter Research, 56, 101, 255

Keane, Sheila, 69, 70, 71, 126–127, 149

Keen Thinker, The, 63

Kinko's, 114–115, 179

Kiosks, 185–192
  Borders Books & Music, 188
  FedEx and, 192
  Fidelity Investments, 187–188
  The Gap and, 192
  Kmart Stores, 188, 256
  Recreational Equipment, Inc. (REI), 49, 188–191
  San Francisco Giants, 191–192

Web-enabled, 188

Wells Fargo & Co., 186–187

Kmart Stores, 46, 123, 188, 256

Knowledge, about customers, 59–62, 123–124, 203, 225–236, 251

Kovacevich, Richard, 27, 28

Landry, Gary K.
  on customers, 13
  on e-mail, 147
  on international business, 111, 112
  on multichannel synchronization, 51–52, 58
  on privacy policy, 158
  on seamless customer service, 204
  on Star Club, 151
  on Web site, 73–74, 82, 98–99, 108–109

Lands' End, 5, 6–8
  catalogs, 6, 50, 53–54, 57, 63, 64
  e-mail and, 64, 157
  multichannel synchronization, 50–51
  personalization and, 143–146
  returns and, 57
  telephone channel, 64

Lands' End Web site
  design, 83
  international business on, 111–112

Live Chat, 101–103, 220–222
multichannel synchronization
    and, 53–54
navigation, 91–92
personalization and, 143–146
as PowerRankings winner, 39
privacy/security, 156–158
selling on, 6–8
training employees for,
    220–222
Lay, Ken, 14
Lehmann, Peggy, 233–234, 235
Live Chat, 101–103, 220–222
Locations, physical. *See* Brick-
    and-mortar channel
Loyalty, 146–155
affinity programs and, 150–155
e-mail and, 146–150
Ludlam, Tom, 116
Lurie, Bob, 34
Lynx2OTN, 136, 185
Lynx System, 185, 249

Madsen, Dennis, 42, 48, 226, 257
Magowan, Peter, 34
Mailboxes, Etc., 179
Major League Baseball Advanced
    Media, 36–37
Major League Baseball (MLB),
    36–37
Mancini, Julie, 167, 256
Mason, Tim, 134, 152
McDonald, Tom, 36, 85–86,
    104–106, 182, 198–200, 243

Mellinger, Frederick, 12, 13
Modjtabai, Avid, 68, 75, 76, 77,
    132–133, 204
Mohit, Maryam, 88–89, 255
Moments of Truth (Carlson), 214
Morrissey, Bill, 196–197
Multichannel synchronization.
    See Synchronizing channels
My FedEx, 129
My Personal Shopper (MPS), 143
My Virtual Model, 143–144, 156
My Virtual Model, Inc., 143
My Web software program, 135

Neiman Marcus, 89
Netkey Inc., 188
NetReturn, 58
Newsprint, 17, 183
New York Times, 147, 255, 256,
    257
Nielson Net Ratings, 103
Nixon, Richard M., 34
Nordstrom, Bruce, 206
Nordstrom, Dan
on knowing customers across
    channels, 62
on returns policy, 57, 58
on Web site, 38–39, 83, 86, 91,
    223, 254, 255
Nordstrom Direct Sales, 37
Nordstrom, Inc., 5, 37–39
commitment to customer
    service, 205–206
e-mail and, 146

employee empowerment, 213
multichannel synchronization,
    61–62
personalization and, 123–124
returns and, 57–58
stores, 169–170, 172
telephones and, 64–65
Nordstrom, Inc. Web site
    beauty store, 223
    design, 83
    navigation, 91
    photos for, 92–93
    returns policy, 57–58
    selling on, 61–62
    start up, 38–39
    training employees for,
        222–223
Nordstrom, John W., 37
Nordstrom Way, The (Spector),
    123

"Ocean-to-Ocean" service, 24–25
Olson, Ann, 222, 257
Oncology Therapeutics Network
    (OTN), 6, 28–29
    customer communication, 236,
        237–238
    FedEx and, 131
    on helping customers, 235–236
    knowledge about customers at,
        232–235
    oncology practices and,
        184–185
    partnerships, 116–117

personalization and, 135–138
proactive customer service, 249
Web site, 29, 94, 135–138
One Body, 117
One-stop shopping, 141–143
Online Customer Service
    operations, 27
Ordering, 96–98, 141–143
Oregonian, The, 253
Ostler, Clyde, 27, 75, 187, 254

Pacific Bell Giants Rewards Club,
    155
Pacific Bell Park, 35, 103,
    181–182, 191
Papiers Stadacona, 183
Park, William, 147, 255–256
Partnerships, 114–117
Personalization, 121–161
    affinity programs, 150–155
    Amazon.com and, 125–126
    business-to-business, 135–138
    Clickpaper.com and, 138–141
    customization vs., 125–128
    800-CEO-READ and, 141–143
    e-mail and, 146–150
    FedEx and, 128–131, 196–197
    Kmart Stores and, 124
    Lands' End and, 143–146
    Nordstrom, Inc. and, 123–124
    Oncology Therapeutics
        Network (OTN) and,
        135–138
    one-stop shopping, 141–143

Powell's Books and, 126–128
privacy and, 155–160
Recreational Equipment, Inc.
 (REI) and, 128, 133–134
security and, 155–160
takeaways, 160–161
Tesco PLC and, 134–135
Wells Fargo & Co. and,
 131–133
Pew Internet & American Life
 Project, 155, 256
Photography, 92–93
Pile It High and Sell It Cheap
 (Cohen), 30
"Pillar of Books," 166–167
Piper, Greg, 17, 83–84, 89, 141
Portfolio Tracker, 53
Powell, Michael
 background of, 18
 on customer service, 209–210
 on e-mail, 149–150
 on international business,
  112–113
 on multichannel
  synchronization, 70
 on personalization, 127–128
 on privacy policy, 158–159
 on stores, 167, 168
 on Web site, 19–20, 55,
  72–73
Powell's Books, 6, 17–20
 commitment to customer
  service, 209–210
 e-mail and, 149–150, 158

employee empowerment,
 212–213
personalization and, 126–128
preparation for customer
 service, 217
stores, 165–169
telephones and, 65
Powell's Books Web site
 ease of use, 94–95
 international business on,
  112–113
 moving customers to, 68–73
 navigation, 90–91
 privacy/security, 158–159
 selling on, 19–20
Powell, Walter, 18
PowerRankings, 39
PowerShip, 10
Preparation, 203, 216–225,
 250–251
 with employee training,
  216–218
 with hiring practices, 218–220
 for online business, 220–225
Privacy, 155–160

Recreational Equipment, Inc.
 (REI), 3–4, 5, 40–43
 commitment to customer
  service, 204
 customer feedback, 236–237
 kiosks, 188–191
 knowledge about customers at,
  226

multichannel synchronization,
    48–50, 54–55, 59–61,
    254–255
personalization and, 128,
    133–134
preparation for customer
    service, 217
returns and, 59
stores, 163–165
Recreational Equipment, Inc.
    (REI) Web site
abandonment and, 96
community and, 106–107
design, 82
e-mail and, 156
feedback and, 100–101
multichannel synchronization
    and, 48–50, 54–55,
    59–60
navigation, 91
ordering on, 97–98
personalization on, 133
privacy/security, 156
selling on, 41
speed, 88, 89–90
start up, 42–43
REI. See Recreational
    Equipment, Inc. (REI)
REI Adventures, 41
Resource Center for Small
    Business Owners, 53
Returns, 56–59
Reuters Health News, 117
Richardson, Alex, 188

Rogers, Karen, 67, 83, 93, 99,
    115, 129, 227
Royal Bank of Scotland Group
    PLC, 32
Rubin, Harriet, 63

Safeway, Inc., 177–178
Salesforce Automation Manager
    (SAM), 197
San Francisco Giants, 6, 33–37
client relations, 197–200
communication with customers,
    242–244
e-mail and, 148–149
kiosks, 191–192
Pacific Bell Giants Rewards
    Club, 155
partnerships, 115–116
Web site, 35–37, 85–86,
    103–106, 107, 200
Schwartz Business Books, 39–40
Schwartz, David, 39
Schwartz, Harry W., 39
Search engine, 91
Seattle Post-Intelligencer, 256
Secure Sockets Layer, 159
Security, 155–160
Seguine, Mary, 131, 135–136, 235
Sennett, Darin, 71–72, 73, 94–95,
    159
ShareBuilder IRA, 53
Shop With a Friend, 145–146
Single Sign-On service, 131
Sippel, Robin, 249

Small Business Center Link, 109

Smith, Fred, 206–207

Smith, Frederick W., 8

Sontz, Miriam, 166

Stanley, Russ, 86, 149, 197–198, 243–244

Star Club affinity program, 150–151, 158

Stephens, Robert, 21–24, 65–66, 85, 195, 196, 218–220, 245–246

Stock-keeping units (SKUs), 61

Stoneham, Horace, 33–34

Stores. *See* Brick-and-mortar channel

Summit Research Associates Inc., 186

Sunde, Marty, 16, 77, 230–232, 244–245

Synchronizing channels, 45–79
  catalog channel and, 62–63
  cross-marketing and, 52–56
  knowing customers and, 59–62
  returns policies and, 56–59
  takeaways, 78–79
  technology and, 75–78
  telephone channel and, 63–68
  Web sites and, 68–74

Takeaways
  brick-and-mortar channel, 201
  channel synchronization, 78–79

multichannel, 44

personalization/customization, 160–161

seamless customer service, 250–252

Web site, 117–119

Task Tracker, 53

Tax and Portfolio Trackers, 27–28

Telephones, 55, 63–68, 220, 223

Teradata Warehouse, 128

Tesco PLC, 2, 5, 29–33, 253
  Clubcard customer-loyalty program, 151–154
  commitment to customer service, 210–212
  customer feedback, 237
  delivery vans, 193–194, 257
  e-mail and, 146
  multichannel synchronization, 47–48, 55–56
  personalization and, 134–135
  returns and, 56, 57
  stores, 172–178

Tesco PLC Web site
  Clubcard customer-loyalty program and, 151–154
  community and, 107
  design, 84
  multichannel synchronization and, 47, 55–56
  personalization on, 123, 134–135

start up, 30–32
stores and, 172–178
The Geek Squad, 6, 21–24,
    194–196
internal communication,
    245–246
preparation for customer
    service, 218–220
telephones and, 65–66
Web site, 195, 246
Time, 43
Time International, 253
Times of London, 257
Times, The, 194
Travel service, 41
TrueSpectra, 93
Tucker, Laurie, 9–10, 11, 12, 67,
    77–78
  on accessibility, 179–180
  on customer communication,
    238, 239
  on customer profiles, 227
  on customer service, 247
  on drop boxes, 179
  on employees and customer
    service, 206–207, 217
  on home delivery, 180
  on international business,
    113–114
  on kiosks, 192
  on partnering, 114
  on personalization, 130, 196–197
  on Web site, 83, 86–87,
    99–100, 109–110, 111

Underhill, Paco, 89, 255
Unmacht, Brian, 49–50, 59, 107,
    189, 190, 191, 217
UPS (United Parcel Service), 180
U.S. Postal Service, 178–179

VeriSign Inc., 159
Volume Services America, 200

Wallin, Carl, 37
Wall Street Journal, 188, 254, 255
Wal-Mart, 46, 61
Walsh, Patrick, 138
Washington Mutual Bank,
    171–172
Webcam, 36
Web site(s), 81–119
  abandonment on, 95–96
  alliances/partnerships and,
    114–117
  Barnes & Noble, 47
  CancerEducation.com,
    116–117
  customer feedback, 98–101
  customization/personalization
    on, importance of, 122
  design, 82–86
  ease of use, 93–96
  Eddie Bauer, 53
  800-CEO-READ, 40, 68
  Enron Corp., 16–17
  Enron Energy Services (EES),
    77
  EnronOnline, 89

features, 101–106, 108–109

The Geek Squad, 85

Gomez.com, 156

home pages, 87, 89–90, 123, 124

Home Shopping Network, 52

international business on, 111–114

iVillage,Inc., 107

Kinko's, 115

Kmart Stores, 46, 123, 124, 188

Live Chat, 101–103

Major League Baseball (MLB), 36–37

moving customers to, 68–73

navigation, 90–93

Neiman Marcus, 89

Oncology Therapeutics Network (OTN), 29, 94

ordering on, 96–98

photography, 92–93

for QVC television shopping channel, 90

retailers and, 45–46

San Francisco Giants, 35–37, 85–86, 103–106, 107

sense of community on, 106–107

shipping costs on, 96, 97–98

speed, 86–90

takeaways, 117–119

Wal-Mart, 46, 61

See also Amazon.com; Clickpaper.com; E-mail;

FedEx Web site; Frederick's of Hollywood Web site; Internet; Lands' End Web site; Nordstrom, Inc. Web site; Powell's Books Web site; Recreational Equipment, Inc. (REI) Web site; Tesco PLC Web site; Wells Fargo & Co. Web site

Webvan, 1, 31, 33, 173, 174

WellsChoice, 27

Wells Fargo & Co., 6, 24–28

branch banking, 170–171

commitment to customer service, 207–209

communication with customers, 240–242

customers as individuals at, 228–229

employee empowerment, 214–216

kiosks, 186–187

multichannel availability, 75–77

multichannel synchronization, 47, 52–53

personalization and, 131–133

telephones and, 68

Video Banking Centers, 186

See also Internet Services Group (ISG)

Wells Fargo & Co. Web site

Bus, 187

customer feedback and, 99

ease of use, 93–94

e-mail and, 81
multichannel synchronization, 52–53, 76
privacy/security, 159–160
start up, 26–28
training employees for, 223–225
Web-access ATMs, 187
Wells, Henry, 24
Whittaker, Jim, 41
Why We Buy: The Science of Shopping (Underhill), 89, 255

WideRay Corporation, 191–192
Wientzen, Bob, 155, 256
Wilshire Capital LLC, 13
Women's Wear Daily, 254
World Service Centers, 180–181, 256
Worth, 27
Wright, Yvette, 206–207

Yahoo! Internet Life, 20
Yankee Group, 96, 192

Ziba Design, 180–181